INVISIBLE LIVES

Books by Martha Barron Barrett

MAGGIE'S WAY

GOD'S COUNTRY

INVISIBLE LIVES

INVISIBLE LIVES

The Truth About Millions
of Women-Loving Women

MARTHA
BARRON BARRETT

WILLIAM MORROW AND COMPANY, INC.   NEW YORK

Grateful acknowledgment is made to the following people:
Margie Adam for permission to use lyrics from "Beautiful Soul," Labyris Music,
used by permission;
Robert A. Bernstein for permission to quote from *The New York Times*;
Sissela Bok for excerpts from *Secrets*;
John Calvi for permission to use lyrics from "The Ones Who Aren't There";
Meg Christian for use of lyrics from "Loveable Lady";
Elizabeth Jolley for permission to quote from *Palomino*, copyright © 1980 by
Elizabeth Jolley, used by permission of Persea Books, Inc.;
Holly Near for permission to use lyrics from "The Rock Will Wear Away," music
and lyrics by Holly Near, copyright © 1977 by Hereford Music, used by permission;
Joan Nestle for permission to use excerpts from *A Restricted Country*, Firebrand
Books, 141 The Commons, Ithaca, New York 14650.

Library of Congress Cataloging-in-Publication Data

Barrett, Martha Barron.
    Invisible lives : the truth about millions of women-loving women /
Martha Barron Barrett.
        p.   cm.
    ISBN 0-688-07730-7
    1. Lesbians—United States.   I. Title.
HQ75.6.U5B37   1989
306.76'63'0973—dc20   89-32167
                                                              CIP

Printed in the United States of America

2 3 4 5 6 7 8 9 10

BOOK DESIGN BY JAYE ZIMET

TO SANDY

ACKNOWLEDGMENTS

Heartfelt thanks to my friend Susan Major Jennings for her skillful editorial adjustments and to my daughter, Elizabeth, for her fine-tuning. And to the dozens of women who listened, made suggestions, and answered questionnaires.

The accolade "without whom" belongs to those women-loving women, both named and anonymous, who reached deep and found the trust and courage to tell the stories of their invisible lives.

CONTENTS

9

CONTENTS

CONTENTS

CONTENTS

12

Where after all, do universal human rights begin? In small places, close to home—so close and so small that they cannot be seen on any maps of the world. Yet they *are* the world of the individual persons; the neighborhood he lives in; the school or college he attends; the factory, farm or office where he works. Such are the places where every man, woman and child seeks equal justice, equal opportunity, equal dignity without discrimination. Unless these rights have meaning there, they have little meaning anywhere.

—ELEANOR ROOSEVELT (1958)

PROLOGUE

─────────

INVISIBLE Lives is the stories of women who early or late discovered their capacity to enjoy erotic relations with another woman. Challenging the belief that sexual lives are static entities to be labeled and filed, these stories reveal a sexuality more akin to music in its response to variations of theme, to songs in a different key. Compartmentalizing creates leaden stereotypes that mislead more than they inform. Life stories are complex and lead to understanding; they also raise questions. What does it mean when a lesbian says, "My closet has a revolving door"? How does a woman adjust to a double persona? *Invisible Lives* also probes and analyzes.

This book was written to appeal to and inform a wide audience: heterosexuals—parents, counselors, children, friends, male and female—who know a lesbian but do not understand her; women struggling to define themselves; lesbians who are isolated physically and/or psychologically or who simply wish to validate their lives; those who believe that in order to live fully in families, communities, nations that include diversity it is necessary to examine those diversities. It is a book written to bring corners forward and to eliminate cobwebs. To alleviate pain.

For forty years my brain absorbed both subtle and overtly negative impressions about lesbians. This information remained stored in an unexamined lump until the feminist challenges of the seventies dislodged simplistic fragments:

Homosexual women are huge and terrifying. They inhabit inner cities and drink to hide their sadness and the shame they have brought to their families. Their Greenwich Village bars are sideshows of perversion. At the first sign of lesbianism good parents send their children to a psychiatrist to be cured. Adolescent crushes on and physical explorations with the same sex must be overcome in order to reach maturity. Because adult lesbian couplings are against the natural order of things, they cannot last. Women who associate with homosexuals are latent ones themselves. Latency must be guarded against in anyone who associates with children or young people, because those tendencies consciously or unconsciously corrupt youth's budding sexuality. Homosexuals are a danger to national security in the military and the government. No normal unmarried woman (like Cousin V——) is a lesbian; they are women disappointed in love or overburdened with caring for siblings in their youth or who had to care for Mother. In short, if a person is sick with the disease of homosexuality, she is miserable because she cannot marry and have children; she drinks too much, is a possible seducer of the normal, attempts suicide, and if incurable, ends up in a mental institution.

I did not confront this stereotypical "them" until 1983, when I wrote a feature article for *Portsmouth Magazine* (Portsmouth, New Hampshire). Iris, the town's new women's club, was reputed to draw five hundred to six hundred women on Friday and Saturday nights, and I set out to inform readers about the life-style of local lesbians.

All that winter I listened to teachers, day care workers, executives, and women who owned their own businesses—twenty-five in all. I heard the stories of divorced women, women with children, women who have "always" been gay; women who are closeted, who are out; women who are apolitical or celibate or serially monogamous or bisexual; who are tall, short, beautiful, round, ambitious, boyish, shy. Who are, indeed, invisible lesbians—everyone's co-workers, neighbors, and friends.

I was chagrined at my previous ignorance. But more lasting was my amazement and anger. Here were women so ingrained with secrecy that they had never exchanged information even with other lesbians, whose stereotypes were as unexamined as mine had been. Here were women just as "nice" as straight women who were forced to hide in double lives, unable to share their hopes, joys, and disappointments because of hostility, prejudice, and ignorance. I was staggered by the realization that women-loving women were everywhere, that I had probably unknowingly brushed elbows with hundreds of them. I gaped when I recognized the jolly, pink-cheeked checker at the supermarket as one of the women who had danced with such abandon at Iris the night before. The article was printed; polite public silence followed.

I arrived at a deeper level of comprehension of the lesbian life more slowly. Gradually, and with sometimes painful self-examination, I came to understand that even the benign attitude of "live and let live" is in fact discriminatory. That toleration, even acceptance, is a far cry from genuine empathy; that pride and joy are for the lesbian virtually nonexistent.

As a writer I wanted to re-create for others my own experience—that intellectual and visceral understanding that comes from sitting in the homes of lesbians and hearing their stories. For four years my mind and sometimes my pen devised forms and strategies for accomplishing this. The scope, I decided, should be broad: nationwide, varied as to age, education, and economic level, encompassing a range of experiences vis-à-vis our heterocentric culture. I did not want it to be a book dominated by famous writers, nor bar women, nor leaders of gay-pride parades, nor gay men, nor a particular circle of like-minded women. I did not want it to be a rehashing of psychological theories or images portrayed in literature. To accomplish this goal, I had to find—all across the country—ordinary, garden-variety women presently involved in a sexual way with others of their gender who were willing to share their private lives.

How each of the 125 interviewees was located and the story of their struggles in determining whether to trust their intimate secrets to a stranger might be a book in itself. Success was a random affair. A friend in Baltimore called a friend of hers who had lived in Detroit. I reached her contact who was leaving on vacation, and she passed me on to a friend of hers, who invited me for the weekend. During that weekend I had seven long interviews with her acquaintances and women involved with the Michigan Organization for Human Rights (MOHR). In Spokane a heterosexual friend called her one lesbian friend, and a six-hour evening with four women resulted. In a San Francisco crafts store two women from Atlanta overheard my conversation about the book and invited me to stay with them and talk to lesbians they knew. Another name came from a straight woman whose friend has a gay daughter. Each actual individual interview took about two hours, each extra person added an hour. Most were taped, but in noisy conditions I resorted to furious note taking. They all took place in 1987.

I also wrote to lesbian newsletters chosen from a nationwide listing; one in Wisconsin and one in Oklahoma in addition to sending me printed material wrote that they knew women willing to talk to me. In Santa Fe a call to a feminist organization resulted in an invitation to a party where, from six to midnight, I sat interviewing women as laughter and burritos swirled around me.

Other contacts came through questionnaires that I mailed out to one hundred names gathered through friends of friends and that were copied and passed on to their friends. Because of the difficulty of locating women in out-of-the-way places, I ran an ad in *Lesbian Connection*, a national newsletter, and material from two southern women is included in the book.

I traveled eight thousand miles across the country and back, then took another trip down the east coast from Maine to Maryland. These random odysseys placed me in contact with a wide range of women. Roughly three-quarters of those interviewed had a four-year college education or more, about 10 percent were women of color—although I did not obtain any interviews within all-black groups—and well over half the women were in their thirties and forties. Occupations ran the gamut from doctors and lawyers to skilled technical workers. Obvious gaps I filled by attending meetings and conferences and selecting certain women to interview from my now full address book. The immediate viewpoints of those who "are not ready to talk about *that* yet" or who hold the opinion of one newsletter "that hets [heterosexuals] should not know our secrets" are not represented, but those interviewed did tell about their own days of ambivalence, or alcoholism, or choking anger, or relationships that had no name.

Very few women revealed their intimate lives casually, bravado was almost unknown. Most were passionate about conveying truths that had heretofore been denied an audience.

As a check on my own possible blind spots I compared my findings with the forty anonymous questionnaires that had been returned. I read newsletters from various parts of the country, I read fiction, nonfiction, and psychological studies. I went back over the material I had gathered in 1983. I spent hundreds of hours informally probing certain topics with both straight and lesbian friends, checking and rechecking my own impressions and ideas against theirs.

It is difficult to write on this topic without perpetuating stereotypes, because words and numbers in and of themselves categorize in misleading ways. Take, for example, the apparently simple question, How many lesbians are there in America? Ten million—one out of every ten, which is the historically accepted figure for gay men? But gay women have not been studied, and, even more confounding, the numbers would vary with the definition.

What is the definition? The word *homosexual* was invented by the medical profession in the late 1800s. A few years later *heterosexual* was added so that there could be "scientific" compartments for sexual behavior—one "normal," one "deviant." The word *gay*

18

came out of the closet in the late 1960s. *Lesbian*, a name taken from the island of Lesbos where Sappho, the great women-loving poet of 600 B.C. lived, is now the word in fashion. But who is a lesbian?

Are we counting women who have "always been gay" and led active sexual lives with women? Women who once had an affair with a woman? Married women with women lovers? Women who turn exclusively to women companions after their children are raised? College women who fill the lesbian bars after a sporting event? Women who take pride in not needing a man? Heterosexuals who support lesbianism as a political statement? Celibate women? Women who secretly long to embrace a woman but don't know where to begin? Women who have lived with a "special friend" all their lives?

But words, imprecise as they may be, must be used to convey ideas. The word *straight*, for example, was originally used by gays and meant "to enter the mainstream," "to go straight." *Sexual preference* is disliked by those who believe being lesbian is not a preference like choosing a kind of ice cream but rather an unalterable fact. *Life-style* trivializes, as though lesbianism is no deeper than a decision to buy a Jacuzzi. *Affectional preference* seems, by avoiding the word *sexual*, to imply the women are buddies. Indeed, any word that divides the sexes might be called sexist. But unfamiliar terms and spellings often confuse the very readers the writer is attempting to reach, hence the familiar—lesbian, gay, straight—in spite of their failings, are used.

Invisible Lives is a combination of analysis and women's stories. There are no composite women, no disguised women, every detail in each story is factual except where noted otherwise, such as the changing of a name. Unless clarity demanded a topical separation, such as with the therapist's contributions and "Julie's" baseline perspective as a lifelong lesbian, the stories remain intact so that the reader may understand each woman's statements within the context of her life. Because many lesbians cannot afford to be, or do not choose to be, identified as such in print, it was occasionally necessary to exclude some detail, such as where they live, in order to reveal other, more relevant points, such as occupation or connections to parents or lovers; in other stories place might be deemed more important. Those who did use their own names often did so after long soul-searching.

Lesbian invisibility is a double-edged sword. While it protects the woman herself from ridicule, indifference, ostracism, and sometimes rape and hatred, it also prevents others from changing their stereotypic misconceptions. Many people insist that they do not know any lesbians, when one is, in fact, occupying the next desk at work, living in the house across the street, sitting around their own Christmas table. Others will say, yes, I know Jane so and so, but will continue to be openly repelled by "them."

Why does this condition persist? Why are women-loving women still paying this unnecessary toll throughout their lives? Why don't they speak up? Why don't the ones they love say, "I know and it's okay"? Why is our culture so reluctant to celebrate human diversity? What are we afraid of? With whom does the shame truly lie?

Ten million women-loving women are not going to disappear. Neither are the questions. Communication gaps between the groups must be spanned. *Invisible Lives* provides a bridge.

PART 1

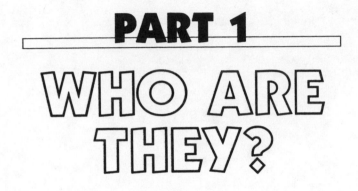

WHO ARE THEY?

1. YOU'RE LOOKING ME IN THE FACE

"IF I had been born lavender," a Spokane woman remarked, "my parents could have said, 'Oh, look, we got one of those.' Then they could have kept me or thrown me away."

A New Hampshire artist said, "I come out constantly, every day. And I'm tired of it. I wish we were lavender."

Lavender skin would save a Manhattan women-loving woman from wondering what it would be like "to speak without marbles in my mouth," save her from constantly "editing my life." An Akron, Ohio, woman would not have to silently plead, "Look at me. You are looking *me* in the face and you don't even know it."

One day of lavender lesbians would convince Americans that they are everywhere.

Patients would be shocked to see their doctor's face. Not cute little Lauren with the dark hair and soft, shy ways! If word got back to Erie, Pennsylvania, people would gasp, "How could it be —her parents have such a stable, loving marriage. You don't suppose they *know*!"

A secretary who once said to her supervisor, "I'd never be around those gay/lesbian people. They're sick!" would suddenly look up and see that the woman whom she has liked and respected for years is "one of them."

In Brooklyn a twenty-year-old, a competitor for the Miss USA title, would drop in to her mother's apartment. Her mother's skin would be lavender and so would that of her mother's "best friend."

A nurse walking into a hospital room would instantly know that her very ill patient and the woman who sat by her side were lovers.

At a town meeting on the Maine coast an older resident, a solitary woman, would rise to speak in a lavender accent.

Clients waiting to see their therapist in Atlanta, Georgia, would peer closely to catch the lavender tint to Marlene's black skin.

Baptist missionaries home from Asia would scream at their daughter, "What happened to you? Where did we fail?"

An audience applauding a well-known artist might hesitate, then fall silent in surprise.

In California a father who "would like to put all queers on an island and blow them up" would be confronted with not one, but two lavender daughters.

Parishioners in a Methodist church would see their minister's lavender hands holding the Bible.

On parents' night at a New Hampshire elementary school, mothers and fathers would be exposed to two women with a lilac hue, the mother and the "other mother" of three of their children's classmates.

Everywhere people confronted by women they knew would exclaim, "But they are such nice women," and, puzzled by previously conceived notions about lesbians, conclude, "Somebody must be lying."

A Mexican-American computer expert, a WASP producer of TV commercials, a University of New Hampshire student, a Cherokee poet, an Asian-American social worker, a high school gym teacher, a Detroit executive, an accountant in Frederick, Maryland, would all walk from their homes and onto the streets of their towns as lavender women. And in Ann Arbor, Michigan, Nancy and Sherry would place *their* child in his stroller.

Of these latter ten women, three have been married, three others have had serious relationships with men, and three have children. Seven live with women partners; their ages range from twenty-two to fifty.

Women-loving women are everywhere, and their lives are as varied as those of women whose erotic attention is focused on men. As a Washington State woman said, "The only thing true about all lesbians is they are all women."

2. LIVING TWO LIVES

TAYLOR, six feet tall with an athlete's body, a competent manner and a gentle voice, has lived in Spokane, Washington, all of her adult life. Short, dusty-blond hair curls around her face, glasses frame blue eyes. "What really tears me up inside is their ignorance. The straight world just doesn't understand. If I had the guts, I could help, but there's that part of me that doesn't want to shed my blood to be the sacrificial lamb for the women in the year 2040 to be out. I'm ashamed of that. But I have to live.

"The secretary that I had for eight years when I was teaching watched an ABC documentary and, as I came into the office, asked, 'Did you see that ABC News *Closeup* last night?' I said, 'Yeah, I did,' and I was about to say I thought parts of it were really good, when she said, 'I turned it right off. It made me nauseous. I wanted to throw up. I'd never be around those lesbian/gay people. They're sick.' And I was standing there. I almost said, 'Lou, I'm one of them.'

"She really likes me, and it would throw her into shock, but after she thought about it . . . I kept thinking, 'You're so ignorant. I'm right here. I'm in the flesh. You go out drinking with me. We've shared a room together during Special Olympics.' "

For the past twelve years Taylor, who is thirty-seven, has lived in an older suburban neighborhood of modest houses and has created a private backyard world by building a deck, an enclosure for a hot tub, and a high fence around the yard. On this July night her long, tan legs are stretched toward where Kate, her partner for three years, sits with her slender body carefully composed, her hazel eyes alert, her long black hair loose around her shoulders. Tara, delicate, bubbly, and Lisa, grave and watchful, a pixielike couple who have been together less than a year, share a lounge chair. Tara is twenty-five, Kate and Lisa twenty-nine; all are natives of Spokane. Their names, including Taylor's, are fictitious.

The women exchange stories about the raw edges where the lesbian and heterosexual worlds meet. A straight woman traveling with longtime lesbian friends hears the motel maid say she is sorry she forgot to put extra blankets for both beds in their room. With surprise and anger she realizes that her friends pretend to sleep in separate beds.

Taylor nods and adds, "When Kate and I were in Hawaii, we got up every morning and jumped around on the beds to make it look like they had both been slept in. You just do this constantly."

Tara leans forward. "It wasn't like that when I traveled with Lisa. She made all the reservations by phone, and I heard her say, 'No. Two women. One bed.' 'Lisa, what are you doing!' I yelled. She's determined. But we don't have any less service. I walk around like this"—Tara shields one side of her face with her hand—"but we're fine."

Lisa, who acknowledged her lesbian sexuality only eight months ago, is fighting not to lose self-respect, not to treat or be treated by the world any differently. "Every time you make reservations, you have to go through this, and it makes me mad. When we show up, it doesn't seem as though anyone stares at us strangely, but we look alike in a way, and maybe they think we're sisters." She describes the assumptions of heterosexuality that assault and invade her from store windows, billboards, and movies, then adds, "Tara will say, 'God, sometimes I just feel ripped off.' "

Kate was married for three and a half years, and Taylor is the first woman she has been with. Her entire family lives in Spokane. "Ever since Taylor and I have been together, there's been a distance between my mother and me. We used to be very, very close, and I'd talk to her about my relationships. I never pretend I'm interested in guys—that's just not happening. I can't lie to my mother, but I can't just go up and tell her. I'm too afraid to tell her. It would make it much easier if my mother would just come out and say, 'I'm okay with it.' "

The pretense of having separate bedrooms angers Kate, but "at this point it's something I need to do in order to stay in this relationship and to stay on the same terms that I want to with my family."

"Her mother's gotten to know me," Taylor says. "Not that that would help . . ." Everyone laughs. "But she used to call and just ask for Kate; now she talks to me for twenty, thirty minutes."

Kate explains that any sadness she feels about being lesbian "is because I feel separated from my parents. It feels like they don't really know who I am. There's a big part of me that's not connecting with them. I'd like them to see that part of me—to know that I'm healthy and everything is okay with me."

"The most important person in my world," Taylor says, "is Kate. And to not be able to share the most important thing in the world with your family hurts. I apologized once to my father, told him the only reason I was sad I wasn't married was because I couldn't give him a grandchild. 'You don't have to worry about that,' he said. 'But your mother and I are very happy, and our happiness in our life has been our marriage, and that's why we want you to be married.' I say, 'I am happy,' and he says, 'That's fine, then.' But there's this piece of them that is always waiting for me to call and say, 'Sit down, I've got something to tell you,' and tell them I'm going to get married."

Taylor speaks about her childhood: "My brother hates violence, hates the military, hates sports, hates TV, plays music, identifies flowers, and catches bees. He's a wonderful human being, but he's so different from your stereotypic macho male. And then here comes me, and I was in training for the Olympics. . . ." She pauses, then whispers, "It was my swim coach who raped me."

Lisa and Tara sit wide-eyed, biting their lips; Kate, whose pose all evening has been arms close to her sides, hands in her lap, reaches toward her lover. Taylor shifts in her chair and says, "So that ended my career. On my tenth birthday. It was my present from him. But we don't need to dwell on that.

"Anyway, I did everything that my brother should have done. My dad paid him to play Little League, and I cried tears because they wouldn't let girls play. And I was better than any of the guys on the team. I never, ever felt like I could please my dad. I broke my neck doing the things I heard him wanting my brother to do so that I would feel good."

Tara says, "Even in my circumstances, where people are so accepting of me, who like me and love me"—Tara has nine supportive siblings including two stepsisters who are gay, and a very understanding mother—"it was quite difficult to come out. Because of our society and how shameful it is. I am very happy with who I am, and yet I still go through those cycles of 'What is going on?' But they're getting shorter and shorter."

"The main reason I don't tell my parents," Taylor says, "is fear of rejection, which would be like saying, 'I just won't acknowledge your presence.' Like you're dead."

Lisa echoes, "Like you're dead," and Taylor continues. "An interesting thing that goes along with that is that every time I go home—except the last two times when Kate has gone with me—toward the end of my visit I lie in bed at night questioning, 'Why am I lesbian?' " A murmur of "Mm-hmms" accompanies her as she speaks. "Maybe I should . . . maybe if I was . . . maybe if I tried harder. . . . And I shake my head and I say, 'No, you don't have to try harder, you're fine.'

"Because at home I lose an identity, question myself, I go for short periods, never longer than seven days. But when I'm home —back here—there is no question in my mind that I'm happy. It always shakes me up because I am so at ease, so happy with who I am, but all I have to do is go home without another lesbian person around. Five days and I'm frantic."

Lisa assumed that she "would be like your average person, end up with a man, be as happy as anyone around me." He voice grows firm as she speaks of her work. "I've wanted to be a fiction writer since I was twelve, and here all of a sudden I was going to be a *gay* fiction writer, and that just scared the pants off me. So much of my identity is wrapped up in writing fiction. I'm working on a lesbian novel that I hope straight people can read and understand me and people like me. It doesn't begin with the trauma—right now I want to deal with the joy."

"We need writers," Tara says, "writing about women who are being women, not women who are being men-women, women who want to do everything better than anyone else as if the worst insult is just being a woman, being feminine."

Kate works, as Tara does, with mentally disturbed adolescents, but she is also an artist. "I know there was a time when I felt that feminist art—breaking away from what I had grown up to be—was a statement of me. But lesbian art that outwardly supports lesbianism—no, I've never done that." She speaks of a nude self-portrait. "The way I saw it was strength rather than—sexxxxx," and adds that she was married then and not consciously aware of her attraction to women.

Before Lisa realized her attraction, it was evident to others who read the manuscript of her first novel. "The first-person narrator had no conflict at all that she might be gay, but her descriptions of another woman were really, really erotic. I had no idea. It's like I was totally blind. When I finally came out to a writer friend who had read it, she said, 'Yeah. I saw it all over your book and I was wondering when you'd become aware of it.' I was so embarrassed. How come I didn't see it?" She speaks to Kate. "So perhaps with that painting you were becoming aware of your sexuality."

Kate, who has the high-cheekboned face of a model, frowns. "Maybe. I loved the guy I was married to and I was happy, but a part of me was dissatisfied. We mutually decided we were happier apart. It was after that that I began to talk to my counselor about my feelings for women. The idea of a relationship with a woman in this town just freaked me out, but I went to a dinner of professional women who were lesbians because I had heard about"— blushing, she motions toward Taylor—"her."

The two women tell their love story in day-by-day detail, agreeing that an approach/avoidance situation existed between them for a long time. They would go out and drive and talk until two or three in the morning, not wanting to say goodnight, yet not acknowledging their sexual attraction. Taylor admits, "In a lot of things I'm really assertive, but when it comes to women I'm not."

"Unless Kate's in the hot tub," someone suggests.

Taylor laughs. "That's a whole different thing."

Kate says that sexual attraction for her is based more on the person than on the gender. "And that's a hard thing for me, because my radical lesbian friends do not understand that."

Lisa agrees that it is person with her; Tara says gender, adding, "I have just never been attracted on a sexual level to men. I have intimate platonic relationships with them."

Taylor believes that for her a continuum expresses it best. "I think, given a certain time and space, it might be gender; given a certain time and space, it might be person. I personally feel more like Tara and I don't know why. I try not to ask myself the question, Had I never been raped, would I be with men? I don't know.

"I could beat myself silly trying to figure that out, and it's not going to make any difference. I'm just not attracted to men at all if you are talking sexually. I don't find any beauty in men's bodies. I'm madly in love with my boss—I'd do almost anything for him —but that's an emotional love and respect. And I have other men I really love, so it's not a hate thing. Yet I don't get turned on when I look at women either. I need to say that. I think they're beautiful, but—"

Kate interrupts. "When you first came out, didn't you do the little adolescent thing, you know, everybody is a possible—"

"Yes!" Tara shouts. "And I thought, 'No wonder men look at women like that!' And it just hit me, 'I'm a pervert, too!' "

Lisa murmurs, "Yeah. No wonder men like it. God . . ."

"Yeah. The lust—"

Taylor interrupts Kate. "But that's faded away for me. I *look* at the real beauties, the tens, but I'm *attracted* to women who are the threes and twos. But sexual doesn't happen for me until I know them." Taylor is, however, emphatically monogamous. "Kate could go away for ten years, and I wouldn't mess with anybody." She grabs Kate's hand. "But don't! I would have to end it with Kate before I could ever act on a sexual attraction for another woman. See, I'm real old-fashioned that way." Lisa and Tara have a verbal contract to preserve their openness with each other and the monogamy they both believe in.

Taylor recalls the deep excitement, the validation she experienced the first time she was with a group of lesbians and heard their coming-out stories. "The most support we have in Spokane is ourselves, sitting and talking. It's a rush for me to be around lesbians because I spend over half my life pretending not to be who I am. That is something that is sad to me. I have a heterosexual life and I have a lesbian life. When I'm at work, I talk hetero, and when I come home, I love to walk through that door, because then I can relax. I'm a pro at this double life."

She doesn't associate with her co-workers outside the office. Several years ago she told two people she was lesbian, and they responded by saying it was "okay with them," but Taylor hasn't seen them socially since.

Lisa tells of coming out to a straight friend at work who talked constantly about her boyfriend. "The woman looked blank and said, 'What do you want from me?' " Lisa lowers her voice, " 'I want your body.' " After the laughter subsides she continues. "No. I said, 'I want you to be as understanding of my relationship with Tara as I have been of yours.' And she got tears in her eyes. And what I imagined she was thinking was that she couldn't be. She realized that she did not have that capacity and she felt badly. So she doesn't talk about him anymore. So not much at all is left. It's sad."

"When the weekend comes," Taylor says, "I'm exhausted. I've spent a whole week being a hetero and I want to be able to sit and touch this person if I want to and not be playing that game. This separates lesbians, it makes us more a minority, but it is unifying for us."

"I don't realize," Lisa says, "how much I need validation until I get it. I don't go to bars and I'm not in any of these lesbian circles—these are my only two lesbian friends. But when I am at a lesbian party, there is something special and empowering about being able to express your love and your relationship in public. I feel myself beaming and I'm proud and I'm happy. I don't miss it until I have it, and then there I am in the middle and I want it all the time. That's what I wish the world understood."

Spokane, the women say, is a very conservative town—"The only place that you can wake up and believe Eisenhower is still president." The white-supremacy Aryan Nation headquarters are in Idaho, an hour's drive away; the gay Metropolitan Community Church has been invaded by disruptive fundamentalists and TV cameras; abortion centers are harassed. It is rumored that the local Presbyterian College conducted a witch-hunt and fired five lesbians. Taylor has seen windows of friends' cars, which were parked outside a gay bar, smashed and police who simply cruised past. People with whom she used to work would urge her to come to the bars on Fridays, their amusement being "to sit and watch the gays and lesbians come in."

Spokane has many college students, away from their homes, exuberant in discovering their sexuality. All four women believe the students do not realize that their loud openness in public jeopardizes the lesbians who live and work in Spokane. "They scare me," Kate says.

Kate describes what she feels is another threat. Her former boss—whose attitude toward her and two of her lesbian co-workers was, "Damnit, you have a right to be what you want to be!"—told a man who worked for the state child-protective services, "There're three lesbians out there and they're just doing a fine job."

Kate's back is very straight as she says, "One of the radical women saw nothing wrong with that, but I felt he had no right to reveal information about us that we did not give him permission to. We're talking about a state worker who can make decisions about people's jobs. My boss didn't see what living this life actually poses. What he saw was, 'Well, everybody out there ought to feel okay about it, and I'm going to see that they know that I feel okay about it.' I believe it's my personal life and it's up to me to tell people."

Taylor agrees. "It's more appropriate to talk about yourself. It's a lot easier to go spouting off about other people, showing how cool you are."

Kate declares, "We need to look out for ourselves. To see the realities of how society is going to take it."

Taylor, who acknowledges, "It's real difficult living two lives," firmly concludes, "I would choose this life and whatever you want to call it—oppression, living a double life—fifty times over trying to live a straight life. I would never get married to a man. I couldn't do it, just to do it. So my choices are to be single and not have a relationship with a woman and be okay to talk about anything I want to, or to live like this. I'd take this a million times versus going the other way—which is certainly easier in some ways.

"It's like what Lisa said and Tara said about things fitting. When I finally realized that I was gay, everything came together for me. I've certainly had my ups and downs since then, but I am terribly happy. I feel fulfilled. What was missing is there."

3. WHO CARES WHAT OLD MAIDS DO?

"I'VE just retired from thirty-four years of teaching." Alice—not her real name—is a stately woman and her accent is both Massachusetts and theater. She and her partner of twenty-four years live in a huge white house with black shutters that faces a village green, now white with snow. A small sitting room basks in the heat from a wood stove. Alice, born in 1925, went to Smith, "across the river" from her undergraduate college, for her master's degree and then received her Ph.D. from Columbia. During World War II she dropped out of college to work in a war plant.

"I never married. I came very close to it once, and he stayed a very good friend. In fact, he died not too many years ago, and I read at his funeral.

"I told my mother at age eighteen that I was leaving town. And that I was leaving with a married woman. She simply said, 'Well, there are things you are going to have to do, and I'm just as glad if you don't do them here.'

"She was very accepting of me and what I had chosen and very honest, I thought, in that response. She took an interest, she started reading things about lesbianism."

Her mother, who had been widowed when Alice was five and her brother two and a half, worked in a bank with a woman named Clara. When Alice came home from New York to visit, she said, " 'Well, Clara and I are reading *The Well of Loneliness*. And I said, 'Oh, God! Don't think it's all like that.'

"She was not a 'sophisticated' woman, but a very direct woman.

I cannot account for my mother. I don't know where she came from. Her family did not have this sense of fairness, but she did. I say all this because I know it is awfully easy to capture mothers in stereotypes.

"And when I lived with a succession of women—sounds terrible!—my mother got to know them and liked them. But when a woman from town ran off with another woman and left her husband and several children, one of whom was very small, she was puzzled. 'How can she be a mother to all those children *and* be a lesbian?' It was a little hard for me to explain."

Alice's partner, Beverly—not her real name—who has sat back and allowed Alice, perched on the edge of the settee, to take center stage, adds in her soft voice, "Living in college towns, people are used to 'couples' of different women, different men, living together. My father and mother always had friends who were gay couples. But my brother and I were a different problem. My mother was not as accepting of that." Of the three children, two were gay.

"She was never one to share her children with other people very well. The men I went out with in my youth—if they were a real 'possibility'—were more of a threat to her than any of the women. Because then she would have lost me completely. We worked around a lot of stuff. My mother has died, but . . . we made peace."

In 1954, during her senior year at Mount Holyoke, Beverly discovered her capacity for loving women. She did not fear being caught and expelled. "Mount Holyoke was a small college. Once they took you in, they nurtured you."

At her school Alice sometimes went to sorority functions in a bow tie and jacket. "I did a Frank Sinatra imitation, and everyone thought it was just grand. We all danced together. Well, there weren't many men around in the war years, so it was a lovely excuse. But then I was also dating the boys, and quite frankly I think at that time I was trying to decide." At twenty-five she broke off relationships with two men. "I knew this other was the stronger pull. So, in each instance I told them, and they understood.

"When I was a child, I called myself a sissy-tomboy. I don't play sports, but I always looked as if I should. Later I had this woman say, 'Oh, you're such a bon-bon butch.' And I think that's a lovely expression. I wore silk shirts and lovely flowing ties. I would not have been caught dead in a flannel shirt and blue jeans. I rarely had partners who were gay. I'm afraid I liked to compete with men." Both of Alice's first live-in partners, now seventy and seventy-five, went on to have relationships with men; Alice is still in touch with them.

While in New York she knew little of the Greenwich Village

scene, but Beverly says, "When I was still in college, a bunch of us went to New York to a transvestite bar, and in the ladies' room I saw a woman in full drag. Completely dressed like a man. I cried for two days because I thought, 'I'm going to be like that.' But I wasn't like that. I tried but I never fit.

"The first thing I did when I finished college was run to New York. Right to the Village. But butch/femme scared the hell out of me, made me very nervous. I drank in those days. I'm an alcoholic. So, a lot of those years are lost."

"They're a little fuzzy," Alice says gently.

"I was in the Bagetelle, which was a famous bar, every night. Absolutely every night." Beverly would then go on to other gay bars, straight bars. "I never knew where I'd end up." She shakes her head at the memories. "I'm a lucky person."

"So am I," Alice adds.

"In New York you could not be sure of your safety around a bar. After all, it's a bar scene. Couldn't be sure about violence. The nightmare was the thought of being a headline in the *Daily News*." The only violence Beverly ever witnessed was a young girl beating up on a man. Beverly explains, "The young lesbian needed to be brave herself in this way."

Her basic belief is that "women have always been able to be quiet. We learn to be quiet and have gotten a lot done quietly," but she also thinks, "Human nature has not evolved to a higher plane. If a scapegoat is needed and no blacks or Jews are available, gays will get it."

Beverly drank throughout college and during her New York years; then in 1959 when she was twenty-six she joined AA and quit. "I'm convinced that alcoholics stop growing up while they are drinking. They are postponing the inevitable. I think if you unzipped a sixty-year-old who's still drinking, Peter Pan would step out. Until that's settled and you learn who you are, you're an adolescent."

While Beverly was floating from bar to bar, she worked in publishing. "That's where all graduates of girls' schools went. They could get us for nothing. There were a lot of lesbians in publishing then, the offices were humming with us. But you could not ever let the worlds combine. Not ever." A woman met in a bar at night was not acknowledged on the street the next day.

Alice adds, "Even when you had accepted who you were, you were still playing the game." Part of the game was talking in code. "You could drop the word *gay* into a sentence as a clue to someone. But now every kid, everyone who watches television knows it."

Beverly speaks of other changes. "In the old days we talked about 'rugged individualism,' but most of the world was very conforming; you had to belong to the right tribe. I think the individualism of today lets us wear what we are wearing." Beverly's gray sweatshirt and pants blend with the coziness of the book-filled room.

Alice agrees about styles. "I wouldn't dare to guess which of my students is gay. A woman who dresses very comfortably may be getting married as soon as she gets out of college, belongs to a sorority and is doing all kinds of conforming things. I used to think I went into the theater because of the freedom of wearing slacks. I can remember in the late sixties when a secretary in the speech department came in in a pantsuit and she was asked not to wear it. And within a year everyone was wearing those awful polyester pantsuits. Today in the area of the chancellor's office you are just as likely to see a secretary in blue jeans—very smart jeans, but dressed for her comfort. There was a tall, handsome secretary who, when it got warm, wore short shorts. And I was allowed to say to the heterosexual men, 'Wow, look at that.' "

"Wicked!" Beverly quips.

Back in the 1920s, 1930s, and 1940s Alice saw "women who really dressed like men—people would be fooled by it."

Beverly adds, "In the women's colleges there was always somebody. A man's jacket, a man's shirt, a man's tie, a short haircut, but with a skirt. If you saw them in a car, you'd say, 'Who's that guy?' "

"They may or may not have been gay."

Beverly says firmly, "Historically women who impersonated men usually had a relationship with another woman."

The women talk about the college campus scene in the late 1970s. Of a radical separatist theater audience Beverly says, "The women would come in and you'd hear *crunch, crunch, crunch* of work boots and *clunk, clunk, clunk* as every set of keys hit the benches. It looked as though there were a hundred workers!"

Beverly and Alice met in a gay male bar in Springfield, Massachusetts, in 1958. "Marvelous place. Run by straights, like a private club," Alice remembers. Both were with their women partners and gay men; Beverly's brother was part of her group. "This was a big, spiffy place, and there must have been three hundred people there, but only four women. Beverly gave me her New York telephone number because I was going down there to start graduate work." Alice did call, but the sounds of a wild party in the background deterred her. Three years later, when Beverly was at Smith working for her graduate degree, the two women met again. "But," Alice says, "I didn't get to know her until I fell down the stairs and broke my arm and *somebody* had to take me to the hospital."

"Some people will go to *any* lengths."

They began living together in 1964 and have been together ever since.

"I feel very fortunate," Alice says.

"Think we'll last?" Beverly jokes, a smile breaking through her Yankee reserve. "My brother's friend cannot understand which roles are which. Who is who in our family. I do all the driving, you see; then why doesn't Alice do all the cooking?" Of the two women Beverly has been more the homebody, involved in town politics and her small business.

"We divide things up, but not according to somebody's rules," Alice adds.

Their life has been a comfortable one. "The department where I taught," Alice says, "was half and half, gay and straight. Nobody made any pretense. We talked freely to each other. We had gay couples—both male and female—who had been together longer than the straight couples. More stable."

"A number of people in the academic world accept us flat out," Beverly says. "It doesn't have to be just theater people. But we still know of dinner parties where there has to be man-woman, man-woman."

Although Alice has been very open in her support of gays and lesbians in her school, she believes, "I would not be comfortable as a public spokesperson." When speaking or granting interviews, she feels she gives people adequate information when she says, "And then I went to New York and had my bohemian period."

"We never, ever, ever," Beverly insists, "dreamed of doing anything as 'lesbians.' My relationships are with people, not with a political group. If someone asks me to define myself, 'lesbian' is not the first thing I would say. I am first a woman. I don't need a sign that says, 'I am a lesbian.' It's relatively obvious."

"Lesbian is certainly a part of my life, but I don't want it to . . ." Alice pauses and Beverly interjects, "And that does not mean to say we are not lesbians. We know we are and are perfectly content to be so."

Beverly and Alice's friends include a wide mix of people. "Our dearest friends are heterosexual couples," Alice notes. "Beverly and I are at a good age for people accepting us. You're not as threatening once you get gray hair."

"When you are twenty-four, everybody wants to change you, but once you get past the childbearing years . . ."

"Old maids? Who cares if they live together, what they do."

"They don't matter anymore. A lot of it has to do with procreation." Beverly believes there is always pressure in that direction. "All the cute little 'Oh, you're still playing the field!' 'You'd make such a wonderful mother!' that women still get when they go to a family party. I think this," she waves her hand around the room to include Alice, the dogs and cats, bookshelves and wood stove, "is a most rational way of living."

4. WITHOUT MARBLES IN MY MOUTH

<hr/>

THE sidewalks of the Chelsea section of Manhattan flicker with yellow light in the windy winter darkness. Emily is five foot three, a nonathlete, a lesbian of earrings and mascara, but she traverses the shadowy spots with a determined bounce. "I feel strong physically within myself. I think I walk that way, like I'm nine feet tall. I give off the impression of 'don't mess with me.' "

Her apartment is one narrow room; kitchen at one end, sofa bed at the other. A friend from work, Trish Kele, is dipping into order-out Chinese. Emily, stocky, effervescent, with a full olive face and wild black hair, is, twenty-nine, a student at Adelphi studying for a degree in social work. Trish is a reserved, slender woman, her auburn hair bushy, her skin fair, her features fine and well defined. Both women were raised on Long Island in the original suburb of Levittown and both have Jewish backgrounds.

Trish, twenty-six, attended college in Buffalo, then moved to an apartment in lower Manhattan by the World Trade Center. She holds a master's degree in counseling and works with Emily at Big Brothers, an organization that matches volunteers with children who need an adult support figure from outside their families.

Emily noticed Trish when she first came to work because of her attitude. "I'm not sure it's always on a conscious level, but if I see a woman who is not panicking to be involved with men, I think she might be gay." When Trish told Emily she had done her thesis at Hunter College on "The Effect of a Gay Woman's Workshop on Homophobic Attitudes of Counselor Trainees," Emily volunteered the information that she was gay.

Emily settles into the couch and munches on an egg roll. "I worked in a corporation with two thousand people for seven years and I never met another gay woman. Now the chances of that are strange—I'm pretty friendly, so I get to know people and they get to know me. I never met one. I heard a rumor that one VP was gay, but I never spoke to her.

"I just don't think that you can walk down a street in the city and see a lot of gay women, as opposed to walking down Christopher Street and everyone on the block is a gay man. I don't think you can find them unless you join an organization or something."

Trish was a theater major in college. "There're a lot of gay women in theater. People don't seem to follow the same rules. Very famous women—everybody sleeps with everybody else."

Emily notes that the corporate world is "very, very conservative. I mean, if I didn't get asked a hundred times, 'And when are you going to get married?' I didn't seem desperate to meet a male and it bothered the shit out of them. I had my male director ask me outrageously inappropriate questions because my co-workers couldn't pin me. Which I probably take some pride in. I'd wear a typical costume—skirt, earrings, all that—with work boots. This used to drive them nuts."

Trish says, "It's fun. It's part of the mystique. Off-balance. I enjoy that about this life-style." Her blue eyes twinkle, giving that off-balance look to her serious face.

Emily nods. "In some ways being gay is constricting, but in other ways it frees you up. I can be all parts of my personality."

"It does free you up, because there are no rules. Straight rules don't apply because—we're not straight!" Trish exudes a calm acceptance of and joy in her lesbianism. "We always had gay people in the house when we were growing up. My stepmother's best friend was gay. I never consciously knew I was gay until I went to college and fell in love with someone.

"I was very much a recluse in high school, dreaming of being an actress, a singer. I remember trying to force being interested in boys, pretending I was in love with David Cassidy. I think I liked him because he was so feminine."

Trish believes that sexual preference is determined by genes. "It's a personal belief derived from my background. My brother and I are gay, but my stepsisters that I was raised with are not." Both her stepmother and father have been very accepting of her and her brother.

She says, "Being a lesbian is a twenty-four-hour-a-day role. It's not just having sex. You are your sexual identity—perhaps unconsciously. It covers everything—your personal relationships, your job, your plans for the future, the way you deal with people, what you talk about. Independence is so important for lesbians. We can't hide behind a man. We have to do it for ourselves.

"I've been very lucky. If I told my grandmother, I can tell anybody. No job is that important to me that I can't stand up for gay rights. And I think if this AIDS thing with Big Brothers comes up, if they start even in a subtle way ousting gay people, I'm going to challenge them in some way."

Part of the training Emily and her group went through when she joined the Big Brothers staff was to determine which people who volunteered to be Big Brothers should be accepted. A mock interview was set up in which Emily played the part of applicant being interviewed, while the rest of the group represented the staff deciding if she was qualified to be a Big Brother. "So I gave them my life. That I was a gay woman, went through the whole thing. Told them the truth except for changing my name and a couple of little things. And they rejected me! The basic reason was that they didn't believe I was telling the truth, because my life wasn't difficult enough. 'Oh, come on,' the woman said, 'all of a sudden you were straight and then you were gay? All of a sudden you met a woman and fell in love? That doesn't sound right.' There wasn't enough trauma. People want to see more of that kind of stuff."

Emily believes that lesbianism is a condition of environment and that "if we were a more accepting society, there would be some people who would be gay for five years, some people who would accept it for life, some people who would try it occasionally. A continuum."

She describes her family as "typical, liberal New York Jewish. If anything, we're too close. If anything happens, aunts and uncles you never heard of start calling up." Her parents are divorced. "My mother was in there struggling every moment to raise me." Her father had little to do with her upbringing, but she describes him as a sensitive man. "I like him."

"My mother lives in the city. She's very accepting of Raja, really cares for her. She's not comfortable with it to the extent that she says to her friends, 'Emily's gay, and this is her lover Raja.' " Raja, a forty-nine-year-old-Lebanese, has been Emily's partner for ten years, although they have not shared an apartment for the last eight.

Emily's mother is a therapist, as is her sister, who is five years older than she. "My sister does family therapy. My mother is into psychoanalytic therapy that is Freudian, long-term, and to me anti-women in a lot of ways—and definitely homophobic. So, my mother still feels, 'What did I do to cause my daughter to become gay?' She sees it as if something had gone wrong developmentally. Arrested development. That if things had gone right, you would go on, of course, to the next stage and be a heterosexual. She and Raja have a nice relationship, but she can't take it into the larger realm. And she gets nervous when I do."

Trish and Emily disagree about issues with the easy air of young friends. Whereas Trish would want her children to be straight because "it's easier," Emily says, "I actually would want my children, if I have any, to be gay." She tells the story of an older black friend who does not want her children to be gay, but would never wish that they were white. "It's interesting that she has pride in her color, but not in being gay."

Both women's lives are touched by AIDS. Four years ago Trish met a gay man, shared an apartment with him for a year and a half, then left to live with her lover, Nancy. After a year of overwhelming closeness in which she felt she was losing her identity, she moved out and since June has been living with her male friend again. If he developed AIDS, Trish says, "I'd be the one to take care of him, but I think if he knew, he'd disappear. He wouldn't want to be a burden. He doesn't have a male lover. He sleeps with people, but there's no one person.

"My grandmother hopes that someday we may get together as a couple, but she knows we're both gay and is okay with that. He considers me his lifemate. He told me that the other night, but I don't consider him that way. He's said he's in love with me.

"For a while it was difficult because he was very dependent on me, jealous of Nancy. He was too vulnerable to me, and I didn't reciprocate his feelings. So there's a part of me that's careful with him because I know he could fall into that again."

Emily's face sags with sadness when she talks about her friend, Richard. "I went through probably one of the most difficult periods of my life the year he was dying. I was there two times a week. Toward the end he lost control of his bowel movement, and it got very ugly and I helped." Emily believed that she herself would not contract the disease. "I also felt my help was more important than ever because so many people were shunning Richard in different ways. The board of his co-op apartment building left notes under his door for him not to use the washing machines. They were disgusting. So many people were backing away from him that it was more important for me not to.

"It's a whole group of people that are not supposed to be dying—some are twenty years old. I think that's what gets me. I had to confront death on a different level than I ever would have had to. My grandparents died, but . . . here was death . . . a person I couldn't call anymore. I think that was real hard for me. I know guys, five friends are dying around them. I don't know how they are making it. It was so hard for me that I can't imagine . . . you know, *all* their friends are dying."

Trish's voice is soft. "I feel removed from it, because how many cases of lesbian AIDS are there? Removed personally in that way." She pauses. "I'm worried about my brother."

Emily's hands flail the air. "I'm worried about my sister. I'm worried about my mother!

"One time I was sitting around with a group of my friends—Timmy and Richard, who's dead, and a couple other people—and we were talking about how many people we had slept with in our lifetime. Everybody else was pulling out calculators and I'm still counting on my fingers! Literally Richard was talking about hundreds of men, and, I mean, I just couldn't imagine being with that many people."

Trish says, "Obviously you would be if you wanted to. I don't have that need."

"But all women don't not 'have that need.' My sister pulled out a small calculator. It's just recently that it's been okay for us to enjoy sex without the purpose of procreation. Raja and I can spend a whole night cuddling and not have quote/unquote technical sex, and I feel like I've had sex."

Neither woman is involved either socially or politically in what would be called a lesbian community, although Emily has for years worked as an organizer of a women's weekend held in the Poconos.

"I have to say I feel guilty about it," Trish says, "because I feel that there are a lot of women out there fighting for my rights. And I might have particular things to say about those women like, 'Oh, God, that's not the image . . .,' but at the same time I'm not out there and I'm benefiting from it and I feel guilty."

Emily explains the intertwining of her social conscience and her lesbianism. "My whole family knows, my friends know—I just couldn't imagine being friends with someone who didn't. But at work—I was not out at work. I let them go on the assumption that I was a single woman. I got out of the corporation for many reasons—that being one of them. I was tired of having to wear a certain kind of clothes, little heels, having to say, "Good morning, Mr. C——," to my boss and having him say, 'Hi, Emily, how are you doing.' I wanted to feel I had done something in my life, on whatever scale, other than forecasting nail polish sales.

"I'm finishing up my Bachelor of Social Work and I'm going to be doing my master's in an accelerated program in a year, but I get a break between January and September."

With a somewhat deprecating laugh Emily says, "I have said I'm going to do an experiment. Trish introduced an interesting concept to me one day when we were discussing the different stages of coming out. I'd like to see what it's like to be totally out. And when I say that, I mean not having to put marbles in my mouth at all. If a taxicab driver says to me, 'So, do you have a boyfriend?' Instead of saying no, or whatever, I'll say, 'No, I have a girlfriend.'

"Now, of course, Raja has said we will not be going out much during this period . . ." Raja, a slim, stylish woman who has arrived at the apartment from work, admits she is afraid of social opinion, that her self-esteem is "not strong enough to take someone making fun of me."

Emily says that in the past when she told someone she is gay, she "always spent the next three hours making sure they are okay with it. Now I'd just like to try telling someone and walking away and letting them deal with it. And telling people that I haven't already made sure are accepting.

"I want to see what it's like not to edit my life."

Lesbians in all stages of coming out declare, "Well, I'm certainly not going to throw it in their faces." Now Emily is going to do just that. Talk "without marbles in my mouth."

PART 2

THE
SECRET

5. MY CLOSET HAS
A REVOLVING DOOR

A Boston therapist, Sarah Pearlman, said of her lesbian clients, "Throughout life there is the decision of whether to come out or not to come out, and that always is either a major or a minor crisis."

Coming out is often a difficult concept for heterosexuals to understand. An older woman said a college friend had driven a thousand miles to tell her in person that she was a lesbian. She could not fathom "why the woman had made such a big deal of it," until she found out her son was gay and experienced her own ambivalence and confronted the prejudice, ignorance, or patronizing silence of others. She phoned her friend and apologized for being so insensitive twenty years before. "Now I know," she said. Her friend replied that it was only the beginning and added, "You have a lot of experiences ahead of you."

Sarah Pearlman likens society to an umbrella that creates both the problems a lesbian faces in her contacts with others and also the ones she absorbs as self-image. "Heterosexuals don't have to deal with that unless they are minority or an interracial couple. That's where you start to see the similarities of what culture does to people. And it does terrible things.

"It determines, for example, how out one is able to be. I think there is a lot of ongoing fear of detection. Will I lose my job, will I lose my house, will I lose my children, will I be attacked? I've seen people lose a job. Even if you don't lose it, you become marginal, excluded either actively or through uncomfortable vibes."

Heterosexuals haven't developed the lesbian's antenna that constantly scans for subtle prejudice, so in blurting out statements designed to portray themselves as good liberals—like Kate's boss did—they sometimes endanger those they would befriend. Their courage is often glib. "Well, sue them if you get fired!" is a statement void of imagining what it would be like to have their own sexual life described on the front page of the local paper. "Ignore the adolescents, the drunks, the homophobics—they're just ignorant" implies that lesbians can stride through the world immune to hurt feelings, so secure that ridicule has no effect on their self-esteem.

Lesbians are aware that a very personal confidence can become a careless, "Oh, yeah, she's gay," said to a crowd in a lounge, or at a party, or at the water cooler at work. The information becomes common gossip, and then the lesbian, realizing her cover is blown, braces herself for what she knows has happened to others. A high school student shouting, "Dirty lesbian!"; a parent screaming, "I won't have you touching my daughter!" as she drags her child from a day care center; a drunk male acquaintance slurring, "Why does a pretty girl like you want to eat pussy?"

The fact that there is no simple definition of the phrase *coming out* is one of the problems. It may mean one thing to the listener, another to the speaker. When lesbian and straight attempt to communicate, bewilderment may result. Even lesbians have differing definitions. Dougal Haggart, a thirty-seven-year-old Smith graduate now a resident of Toronto, said, "I stick with the traditional definition. The first time you have sex with a woman is when you 'come out.' " Liz Pierce, a Minneapolis lawyer, referred to "coming out to myself" after she had lived with a woman for ten years. A New Hampshire artist said she is tired of coming out to someone every day.

Lisa's bewilderment at being out to others in her writing before she realized it herself is not an uncommon example of the difficulties with the term. A woman in Detroit said of her adolescence, "Everybody else knew, why didn't I?"

Lisa believes that in her first enthusiasm of coming out she told too many people and they now have a weapon if they choose to use it. Kate once experienced the sexual response of "Hey, will you teach me how you do it?" from a man in whom she confided. Taylor believes that if lesbians were born lavender they would avoid the agony of coming out to their parents.

Many gays and lesbians when asked, "When did you know you were gay?" answer with the question, "When did you know you were heterosexual?" That reply, however, begs the question. Boys and girls are so thoroughly gender imprinted from the time of their birth and so thoroughly schooled in compulsory heterosexuality that they never find out their sexual identity. They simply *are*. A boy. A girl. Lesbians *discover* they are different. Therefore, if they wish to separate themselves from the assumption of their heterosexuality, they must tell their therapist, doctor, employment counselor, visiting nephew, or any of the scores of people with whom they interact.

Unless the statement is a purely political one, the telling imparts the information that "I have discovered I have the capacity to enjoy intimate physical relations with a person of the same sex." Of course, the word *lesbian* may convey much more, depending on the listener's preconceived ideas, or, as the Spokane women believe, it "reduces you to a sexual thing."

There are ways other than direct verbal statements by which the women-loving woman "comes out." She may stop laughing at gay jokes, or cut her hair and put on a flannel shirt, or move in with a woman. She may justify these actions in terms the straight world will accept as "normal," or be noncommittal about them, or use them as blatant signals of her affectional preference.

A lesbian's degree of openness in regard to her same-sex relationships ranges from being scared to death others will find out, to observing a lifetime of caution, to informing a select few, to the feeling that although it is never discussed, it is generally known, to it being openly acknowledged. And each woman may be on a different place on the scale in regard to her neighborhood, her workplace, her parents, her siblings, heterosexual social groups, her own children, and the local media.

Because of the many levels of "being out," replies to the questions "Are you out?" "When did you come out?" "How many out lesbians are there in your town?" may obscure more than they reveal.

One woman expressed this complicated scenario by simply saying, "My closet has a revolving door"; another said, "The door to my closet is open, but my hand is always on the knob." The confusion is double-edged, for just as a straight person may be shocked to find out a friend is lesbian, so the lesbian may be shocked when a reporter calls up to interview her for Gay Awareness Week. Many lesbians spend much energy hiding what everyone already knows.

Sarah Pearlman, who in addition to having many lesbian clients teaches the psychology of women at Antioch College and has helped edit two books on lesbian psychology, says, "There is a tension that is not present for heterosexuals. You can talk about it as ongoing stress. You can talk about it as heartbreak when your mother won't see you. You can talk about it as anger when you go out and can't hold your partner's hand. You can talk about it as helplessness in a situation of a partner's illness. You can be depressed about the sodomy laws.

"A lot of the time people don't realize they are under tension. You see a couple start to go downhill and you realize it's holiday time." Lesbians become more conscious of how they exist on the margins of society when they are faced with racks of male/female greeting cards, when they are worried about how family members will receive them and/or their lovers, when the heterosexual partners of brothers and sisters are being welcomed into the family. "Couples start to fight, turn their own individual hurt on each other. It's pernicious.

"My partner and I are thinking of going to Greece. We have to deal with concerns that other people don't have. Should we write away for rooms and just say a double room, should we say single beds? I never had to think of these things when I was married. It becomes a consideration that parallels your life. And then you also have to decide—am I too paranoid? Or am I being realistic? Or am I denying that there's bigotry out there? There is so much wishing, so much denial."

Sarah knows lifelong lesbians who have so compartmentalized their lives, they are not aware of the damage done. "A woman told me her best friends didn't know she was gay. What is her definition of friendship? Superficiality. Now that's judgmental, but her translation of closeness is obviously so different."

One partner being more out than the other presents a problem to some couples. "Sometimes they admire the other's forthrightness but don't realize what that is eventually going to entail. Or if one partner is butchy, that that identifies the other."

She feels that the presence of children often creates serious problems: custody; children's feelings when they understand their mother is a lesbian; the father's behavior; adolescent children's problems concerning their own sexual identity, the stigma of being different from peers, and having the burden of a troubling secret.

Being closeted is, Sarah believes, the best choice in some cases. "But where there's a secret, there's a guard and there's a selection. There is also counterfeit secrecy: they know you know, you know they know, but you don't talk about it. You go through life with this monitor sitting on your shoulder. It's right there editing you. Editing your pronouns, your activities. It's got to have an effect. I'm not saying that people can't live good lives, but there's a toll that's unnecessary."

How out a woman is may be a factor of her personality. "I'm naturally a shy person." "It's nobody's business what I do in bed."

"I have to be up front. It would be very damaging for me to live a double life."

It may be a factor of circumstance. "My parents live five hundred miles away. It does not impinge on their lives." "I paint houses. Who cares if I'm gay?" "Toronto is a very open town. In Thunder Bay I'd behave differently."

It may be a factor of age and personal interpretation of age. "The habits of a closeted lifetime are very hard to change." "The older I grow, the more open I become. Probably because I have less to lose." "I'm out of the bar scene now. I don't drink or wear a leather jacket anymore."

It can depend on self-acceptance. Many women say, "I don't have bad experiences when I come out to people because I'm not confused. They accept me because I accept who I am." Or, "As we become more confident, we seek out lovers who are more out. Who draw us more into the visible community."

But lovers can also be a reason for not being out. A Detroit woman stated, "I don't meet the press, I don't march because I don't want to jeopardize Terry's job." Others must be sensitive to their partner's parents who do not know.

"Coming out" once had a very different definition. A girl came out at a debutante ball, which meant she was being presented to society as a woman starting on the quest of a mate. Instructions for her behavior and the behavior of males were known to all. She could measure herself by these standards, decide what was correct or incorrect for her in the way of experimentation. The goal, however, was very clear: a satisfactory, or perhaps brilliant, marriage, children, and a life adapted to her husband's social and financial standing.

For the eighteen-year-old with a clear primary attraction to women, coming out is a far cry from a debutante ball. Although the heterosexual girl may be no less terrified of hairy men and penises, she has the assurance of family, peers, church, and state that she is "doing the right thing." The lesbian has equally emphatic messages from those same groups that she is doing the wrong thing.

A lesbian's coming-out process may be difficult or relatively easy. Tara began looking for girls to love in second grade and "bumped around" through many same-sex and opposite-sex relationships before finding Lisa. Lisa struggled with depression during her twenties. She told of a secretary at her college speaking to her about a gay student who had just killed himself and adding, "Nothing is so important that you should take your life." At the time Lisa did not understand that the message was meant for her. Whereas Kate slid from husband to Taylor with relative ease, Taylor was subjected to numerous attempts to "adjust her to getting along with men sexually." Her one high school date was erotic agony; a therapist sent her to a twenty-four-hour Gestalt session, where she was inadvertently paired with a rapist; the father of her college roommate offered sexual "help."

Alice and Beverly have made their peace, both with themselves and with family and the world at large. They are, apparently, personally beyond anguish, because, as Alice said, "Old maids? Who cares if they live together?" but they do agonize over AIDS and the general omnipresent threat that exists for any minority.

Parents, children, neighbors, and friends of lesbians deny, or compartmentalize, or struggle with their knowledge in the same way the women themselves do. "My parents know I've lived with my partner for six years. She goes home with me. We sleep in the same bed there. The word *lesbian* has never been mentioned." "I told my mother and she said, 'Well, now that's over with. We don't need to mention it again.' She never has, and that was ten years ago. I don't know if she ever told my father." A husband may dismiss it as "just a phase," a boyfriend may interpret it as a sexual tease, a straight woman may believe "she's just saying that because she couldn't get a man."

The strong message is, "Keep it quiet." Many lesbians do that by becoming invisible. Because, as Dougal in Toronto said, "Lesbianism is about as socially acceptable as picking your nose in public," they leave their lesbian persona at home when they go to work on Monday morning. On Friday they don it again. That weekend at home, the flip side of the double life, is what most of heterosexual society never sees.

The house, situated in an executive Detroit suburb, is large. A Cadillac and a Honda sit in the driveway. Inside, the spacious rooms are comfortably furnished, some with family antiques.

Friday night Judith Hill attends a baby shower for a co-worker; Terry—not her real name—works late at her job. There are two bedrooms: Judith's, in which hang artistic sketches and pictures of nude women, and Terry's, with a huge four-poster bed, where the women sleep and sometimes make love. Saturday morning they arise by nine and move slowly in the midwestern heat, collecting laundry, writing shopping lists, and making phone calls; classical music plays. Judith has a meeting in the afternoon; Terry does errands. Friends, women-loving women clad in T-shirts and shorts who have been invited for dinner, drift in around six, talk about politics and brands of ice cream, and drink iced tea. The home-cooked meal is late and casual; by eleven the guests are gone. Late Sunday morning an ex-lover of Judith's comes by, and the three women leave for a day of picnicking and sailing at a friend's house. Monday morning, dressed in stylish summer business clothes, they kiss good-bye in the kitchen. Judith, forty-five, drives off to her management position, Terry, thirty-seven, to hers as an executive with an international company. Their combined income is over $100,000 a year. At the end of the day they will, as they have for seven years, return home to their woman.

Neither Judith nor Terry has ever experienced abuse, sexual or otherwise; has ever lived in a lesbian ghetto; been involved in drugs or molested a child.

Terry, a redhead with a peaches-and-cream complexion—a descendant of generations of Scot-Irish farmers—was raised on a farm in Illinois. From age fifteen to thirty she dated men, and was living with a man she planned to marry when she met Judith. Three years later the women moved in together. Comparing her years as part of the heterosexual majority and her years with Judith, she says, "I've gained more than I've lost."

Judith, a brusque, robust woman, is a doctor's daughter from a town of one thousand in Nebraska. At twelve she fell in love with the sixteen-year-old church organist. Although she was once engaged to a man—"I couldn't find any gay women on Long Island"—she identifies herself as a lesbian. She is quick to add, however, "Lesbianism is just one aspect of my life. It does not affect me as a person, except to someone out there who doesn't like that."

Neither woman has told her parents or employer. They are ordinary lesbians functioning in a heterosexual world.

6. BEGINNINGS: LIZ, SPYKE, JULIE, JACKIE

"**I** was asked, 'Are you a lesbian?' 'I don't know,' I said. Me who had lived with a woman for ten years! I didn't know."

Minnesota. Middle America. Family of five. Mother a teacher, father a professional. Liz, a loner in high school, quit college and moved onto a dairy farm. The life suited her: the bulky soft animals, the hay-sweet summer, the challenge of blizzards, the satisfying exhaustion of her body as she crawled into bed at night beside her best friend. The woman, call her Marge, was a teacher; Liz had fallen in love with her at eighteen.

As the years went by the farm, the daily solitary chores became a cocoon for Liz, then a prison; her only contacts were with her family. Marge, however, was content. Tired after her day of teaching, she did not want to go anywhere, see people, certainly not in any manner that would even hint of a sexual relationship with another woman. She did not acknowledge that even to herself.

Liz Pierce has a full, young face with brown eyes that smile and brown hair pulled back in a ponytail; her shoulders are broad. Against Marge's wishes, Liz began to attend National Organization for Women (NOW) meetings in Minneapolis, and in a consciousness-raising group she exchanged, for the first time in ten years, ideas with others. At the state NOW convention she saw two women kissing, and it took her breath away.

At C-R meetings, as her exuberant sexuality began to emerge, the other women backed away. One put her in contact with a feminist therapist. When Liz walked into her office, the therapist's first words were, "I understand you're a lesbian." Liz replied, "Who me?"

Although Liz's explorations were destroying her life with Marge, she continued. She joined a Coming Out group and gradually integrated her love of women with the other parts of herself. At rallies she found herself watching groups of lesbians and thinking, "These are my people!" At her first Take Back the Night march she sat with a section of lesbians, and when a straight woman asked her if she knew where she was sitting, Liz replied, "I know who I am and I know where I belong."

For twelve years she had built her life around Marge and the farm, and she describes the breakup as "horrible. I couldn't hang on to anything. In a move of desperation I told my mother. She was so wonderful, only wanting to know, 'Why didn't you tell me sooner? Didn't you trust me?' My brother and one sister were great. The other sister said, 'Oh, kinky sex.' I told her, 'No. *I'm* perverted. *You're* kinky.' " Liz's wry sense of humor is irrepressible.

As the oldest girl in the family Liz picked up strong messages from her young parents. "What I heard my mother say was, 'I got married and lost my career. To have children is stupid.' She would sing, 'I Wish I Was Single Again.' But she has no love of being a woman. There is a misogyny among women. I grew up thinking I was less than men." Her father said teenage boys were boring. "I think I was raised to be a dyke."

At thirty, Liz left the farm, and Marge and went to work in a factory. "I was grieving so for Marge. I went to a lesbian bar. I tried to talk to people, but no one there had ever been with one person so long and they couldn't understand what I was talking about." She shakes her head. "Total emptiness."

She returned to college. "I was scared. My vocabulary was so down from working on the farm. I dropped out at the end of a year." She rode her motorcycle to Maine, had affairs, and attended the Michigan Womyn's Music Festival. "Five thousand naked women! The women energy is so powerful that you don't want to leave. So many women!"

Liz tried college again, finished, took her LSATs, and was accepted at the William Mitchell Law School in Saint Paul. "I thought sure I'd get kicked out on grades, but when I graduated twelfth out of a class of three hundred, I figured, 'Hey! I found where I fit!' "

At college—her first close association with heterosexual peers in a decade—Liz had found herself laughing at gay and lesbian jokes. "I thought, 'And here I am! Not enough guts to stand up for myself.' So I decided I could never lie about it again. I am so terrified of their closet! People who think they are 'passing' are often not. It's the shame of pretending you're something you're not."

Joy and excitement infuse Liz's face and words as she talks about being lesbian. "The commonality is that women love women. I'm struck by the fact. Just overwhelmed by it. I love the drunken, stupid ones, the young and silly ones, the sad ones in the closet."

Liz applied for jobs at the big law firms but was not hired. "I couldn't pass—I don't look perky and straight." She went to work for a small firm as a lesbian lawyer and now drafts legal documents pertaining to tax, custody, and domestic problems for lesbian clients all over the country.

"A lot of lesbians are going to law school. I'd guess ninety percent of the one thousand people at the Women and Law Conference are gay. But they're not practicing law with traditional law firms. They're working for women's groups, et cetera. Some think traditional law is too macho, too masculine, too competitive, and the problem is to survive in that kind of legal system. It's so easy to lose the things we value, become hard. A number of lesbian lawyers I know are terrified to come out. You get killed if you come out and you're not *very* smart. Closeted ones will not associate with out lesbians. There is a tremendous fear.

"Having a lot of lesbian lawyers wouldn't make a difference in the system. They would take on 'male' values. Besides, lawyers can only help individuals—make the system less painful for them. Women judges would make a difference. They can do what's fair. I want to be the first out lesbian judge in Minneapolis."

When Liz found a new partner, she, in contrast to the total secrecy of her first relationship, insisted on a commitment ceremony in a public park. "We sent out invitations to a select guest list and received presents. My brother offered to take the pictures. Robyn and I exchanged rings and promised 'to be all that we could be to each other.' My parents each read something. My brothers and sisters were all there with their spouses. All the nieces and nephews. Two of my ex-lovers."

Robyn and Liz stayed together six years. "We parted with gentle loving. We had never said forever, we knew that wasn't possible. My incentive in relationships is to grow personally. Once I stop growing, it's time to move on. It's not bad. It's wonderful to share your life with lots of people. Help that other person reach another level of growth, of understanding. Changing partners is more a positive than a negative. I don't think you have to be lovers to learn from others, but straight women don't learn from their friends in the same way lovers do."

Liz defines lesbian as, "Total self. I can't separate lesbian from the rest of me. I'm a normal, healthy, middle-aged dyke lusting after women. But it's not just what we do in bed. That's not what it's all about. There is a connection. We can meet anywhere and our eyes connect and we smile. I've chosen to focus my energy on women. No, I'm not a separatist—I have five nephews and I love them all dearly.

"Positive role models are so needed for young women. [Parents, the system] are so perverse that kids think they don't have anything to look forward to except what the bad old stereotypes portray. Teenage lesbians determined to convince themselves they aren't lesbian are very promiscuous and get pregnant. I know lots of them. They are trying to find a way to belong."

Liz's way was to hide from the world and herself with a woman who did not want to admit anything beyond a "special friendship." And this was not in the thirties, forties, or fifties; Liz was born in 1949 of educated, compassionate parents. She was twenty-one in 1970, the heyday of "doing your own thing," of "letting it all hang out," but she lived her twenties in limbo, not acknowledging who she was or why she was behaving the way she did.

Heterosexual women may spend their twenties thrashing around in bad marriages or trying to "find themselves" through a series of relationships or jobs or life-styles; lesbians have no monopoly on confusion. Their struggles toward maturity are, however, exacerbated by cultural taboos that declare that their deepest feelings are wrong.

Liz's enthusiasms, her propensity for breaking into song, her idealistic view of lesbian life, are delightful and yet seem more apropos of a person in her mercurial twenties than a lawyer in her late thirties who aspires to be a judge. One day she says that she prefers the nastiest woman to the nicest man and then one of her own—an out lesbian lawyer—skewers her with a shabby legal trick and she is absolutely crushed; at the moment she is "madly in love" with a woman who lives in Chicago—with a man. Perhaps these traits are basic to her makeup, but measured by her mere seven-year experience as a lesbian in a heterosexual world, Liz may be said to be the equivalent of a twenty-five-year-old.

"To this day," she says, "I think I would have been better off if I had told the world at eighteen."

"Everyone thinks I'm a guy. My mother asks, 'Why do you want to look like a boy? You're such a pretty girl.' "

Spyke is twenty-one years old, tall and lean in a man's T-shirt and beltless jeans. Her spiked hair is black, her skin fair, and her eyes a very intense blue. She was raised in the San Francisco Bay Area, in a suburb "with pink houses and picket fences."

"From age twelve, people backed away from me, thinking I was gay. I had no role models. I became a 'newborn Christian' at the beginning of high school. One me made good grades. The other me was into pot, cocaine, real rebellious, against restrictions. It was part of my sexual-identity confusion."

Spyke acknowledged her lesbianism at nineteen. "I was really surprised when I went to a women's music festival, and outside of one twenty-year-old I was the youngest. A lot of older women— at least twenty-two or twenty-three. I'm lucky I came out so early. Now I've got a long time ahead of me." Her smile is warm and young.

"It's in vogue to be bisexual or gay. Everyone wants a token lesbian at a party. There are more true role models, like Eleanor Roosevelt. Also we see everyday people who are out. At summer camp over half the staff was lesbian, but I didn't know it. When I found out, I thought, 'These people are so great and they're gay!'

"I think it's that everyone is bisexual to a certain extent, and *we* live out our desires. I want to stay the way I am. I'm happy. I would say to my parents, 'You did a good job.' I told my parents I was going to college to be a doctor, but my goal is to be a police officer." She laughs. "My friends ask if it's because I want to carry a gun. I say, 'No, I like the uniform.' " She attends the University of California at Santa Cruz.

"My goal is to find one woman. I don't buy this bullshit over monogamy being weaker. Everyone is into one person. I would like the intensity of having one person all the way through life. I'm hopelessly monogamous. Nonmonogamy is good in theory but not in practice. One woman I know is such a dude—rejecting good things because they are associated with patriarchy. We should stop comparing everything to what hets do and say. Make our own judgments."

Spyke explains that she is in New York incognito. "I'm not out to my parents. They don't even know I'm on the East Coast. My parents were so freaked over finding out that my older sister was gay that my message was, 'You're straight!' "

Her sister told her parents she was gay while living at home and attending college. "They sent her to a psychiatrist to be cured. Every time she came home from a session, they'd ask, 'How is it coming along?' When she finally told them it wasn't, they said, 'Then get out!' They cut her off. She tried it on her own, but just couldn't make the money to finish college. None of her friends are allowed in the house. She's had the same lover for five years, but she's not acknowledged in the family, not welcome at the house. So I don't dare come out to them. They asked me and I lied.

"My dad is a fireman. He loves the guys he works with and

hangs out with them, not at home with a wife and three daughters. He goes along with what the guys at the firehouse think. He's very sexist, a gentle bigot. Hates homosexuals. He wants to put them on an island and then blow it up. Says AIDS is what they deserve. He said, 'I'd rather have a retarded child than a queer one.'

"When I broke up with my last boyfriend two years ago, they were really upset. I think he's gay, and he knows I am. When I was home last summer and said, 'I saw Paul,' my mother pulled the car to the side of the road and shut off the engine. She wanted to talk about it. She's afraid he dropped me because my sister is gay, because it 'might run in the family.' She's trying to educate herself.

"My youngest sister is sixteen, and I think she will be gay too. She shows the same signs my sister and I did. Doesn't date. Close to her girlfriends. She doesn't know about my older sister and me. My older sister is very different from me. She's conservative, doesn't like men—even gay ones. I know a family of five and they're all gay. I know twins who are gay.

"I internalized homophobia for a long time. When any girl showed real interest, I freaked out. Two years ago I was home and a woman was coming to pick me up to go to San Francisco. I had asked my mother what I should wear, and she asked me to describe my friend. When I told her about her job and sports, she was upset. 'Not another Lisa!' Lisa was the woman who was after my sister. No one liked her.

"When, an hour later, the woman walked into my house, it was tough. I saw her through my mother's eyes.

"It was a flash of the two worlds mixing."

A high school teacher, call her Julie, says, "Parents should not be so afraid of their kids exploring who they are and what they are. Kids should be able to try out a homosexual setting and, if they are not comfortable, drop out. But they have learned something about themselves. The homosexual adolescent experience does not set a life-style. And kids would have had experiences with puppy love in high school and maybe not have to glom on to one woman from the age of seventeen to thirty."

Julie, who as a teenager had been an exceptionally attractive blue-eyed blonde, a lover of classical music and star athlete, describes her own youth in the 1950s: "I dated in junior and senior high, and my junior year I went steady with a boy, Ed. I had a lot of fun exploring sex, but intercourse was out because I was concerned about pregnancy. My real fun was after school with girlfriends and teams. They were the folks I could share myself with. Males, being definitely the center of focus, made me feel like I was a part rather than my own being. I didn't want to be an appendage of someone. My feelings for girls were vague and crushlike, feelings of wanting to be held, to bare my soul to someone who would understand, then wanting to explore their body wherever that might lead.

"I had a crush on my teammate, Kay. She was shy, and I took the initiative—gently. We would study at her house, spend time lying on the bed reading, comparing notes, and then there was touching. Some gentle rubbing. It all progressed painfully slowly. We tried to get closer, but didn't know what to do. Finally I stayed overnight, and we explored each other's bodies.

"Neither of us had had an orgasm, so we didn't know what we were looking for. When I had my first orgasm late in my relationship with Ed, I went rushing back to share this wonderful information with Kay."

Julie's relationship with Kay lasted into Julie's freshman year at college. Kay had a few other relationships with women, then married and bore two children.

Julie continues, "My teenage image of lesbians—I still dislike the word because of it—was of tough, masculine women. I most certainly did not want to be that. But I never thought my feelings were wrong. In those days (the early fifties) there was no such word as *gay*. You were 'not all right,' had 'a problem,' were 'sick.' I knew I wasn't sick, I just thought the world didn't understand a good thing.

"I didn't experience self-hatred. I thought it was such a beautiful thing, so superior to other kinds of love, that I was just ahead of my time. Like a genius artist who at first is loathed for his or her work and is later recognized. I had faith in it.

"But in college, when I fell in love with Lea, who was much older than I, it got scary. This was the real world, and I had no one to talk to, no help. I was frightened, but it felt so good, so right that I just winged it.

"I remember approaching college teachers of mine in an attempt to deal with my own really troubling problems and having them go absolutely cold with me. Now I know why, and I think I do the same thing with my students. Gym teachers are a particularly vulnerable group. The straight world associates athletics with lesbian. And when you are and your job is on the line, you tend to present a highly developed false front to your school."

Julie's stable family life, acceptance by her peers, healthy sexual relationships with both Ed and Kay, had given her enough self-confidence to know that what the world condemned was right for her. Prejudice has, however, prevented her from passing on this strength to insecure and struggling teenagers.

She believes that the last place a teenager could look for sympathetic help would be from her lesbian gym teacher. "I could go in and tell my principal I'm gay and probably not get fired. And probably most of the faculty would not be surprised. The parents are the real concern. And the pressure they could exercise on the school board. And, of course, the kids too. No one can be more cruel than high school boys."

Jackie Brown is twenty-eight; she and her three sisters grew up in Detroit. "We had a home—barely. Well, my father was an alcoholic, so that caused problems in the family. My mother worked, my father worked sometimes. He drank all the money up. We had clothes and shoes that we had to wear for an extended period of time—they were bought too big, handed down. We thought clothes that came from Goodwill to go to school in were the greatest things because they didn't have holes in them, they weren't worn out. We lived with roaches, et cetera, but I didn't really think we were poor at the time. My oldest sister would cook dinner for us, and we'd have a plate of corn and that was it, or beans and a piece of bread and Kool-Aid. It was rare that we had meat. Mother worked at Oakland University as a cook, and when she brought home meat, we were like carnivores."

At first glance Jackie is an unprepossessing short, heavy black woman, but as she talks, her face glows and her voice takes on a rich, melodic power. Her laughter is large and comfortable.

"Mother always encouraged us never to depend on a man. That always stuck in the back of my mind. She always wanted us to get an education. 'Don't wind up like I did with a husband who has been committed a few times for his alcoholism.' We're talking really bad, bad alcoholism. From the time I was born until he died five years ago, he was always drunk, so I don't remember him any other way." He was verbally but never physically abusive to Jackie.

"My mother was so adamant about us getting an education that when one of my older sisters who was in high school became pregnant, she had guns for chasing the boy away from the house. She was really serious. 'Boys are no good' et cetera. My mother sent my second oldest sister away to Texas to a private college, but she got pregnant and married in college, so that still was not good enough. That sister now has four master's degrees. The oldest sister still is not doing all that well. The other sister also got pregnant and does not have a husband.

"My mother was such a strong figure in my life. Physically she was smaller than I am, but she was stern. When I was in ninth grade, I had a boyfriend, and when she caught me kissing him, she gave me the whipping of my life. And my mother whipped us with leather belts with holes in them. I mean you don't really kiss a boy after that. I was involved with men up to a point, but I always felt guilty about it, thought I might become pregnant.

"I got emotionally involved with a boy after high school. I thought he was the savior on a white horse, and then I found out he was being unfaithful to me, and that was devastating. All the guys I dated except one were black. The second guy I was serious about was also being unfaithful. So I went through a five-year celibacy before I made my transition. It's been three years since I've considered myself gay." Jackie's speech is careful, precise, but her body is relaxed and her smile bright and frequent.

"Sometime during that celibacy period when I was in college, I began to think about women. To get through school, I worked as a nurse's aid at a hospital. In housekeeping there was a really strong woman whom I admired. I began to have dreams about her and I thought it was so strange. Then there were other women in school. A teacher that I admired. I worked full-time and went to school full-time, so I was tired a lot. This teacher allowed me to take tests at other times, helped me with makeup work, so at the end of the semester I sent her flowers because I really appreciated what she had done. I considered it admiration.

"During that same time the people in housekeeping accused me of being gay, and I was shocked. It upset me, it devastated me. So then I began to think about that. I talked about it with a friend who worked with me. Someone introduced me to a magazine—the *Metro Times*—and I saw some ads in the back of the paper in the gay column. I answered one. I was so curious. What is this lesbian-type thing? What is my admiration all about?

"In retrospect I remember in the sixth grade admiring a lot of girls and then in ninth grade hearing a girl say that she had a crush on a guy and I remember thinking, 'Women have crushes on men? I've always had crushes on women.' And thinking, 'Is that the way it should work?'

"The woman in the ad called, and I talked to her for three or four hours about who we were. We met at a restaurant and talked. I was not interested in her, but just trying to find out what it was like. From her I found out about the bars, gay publications, and she took me to a women's bookstore. The one book I will never forget is *Coming Out Stories*. I read the whole thing from cover to cover. Wow, is this how they do it! I sort of coaxed a friend of mine who was straight and married and had three kids into going to the bars with me. We began going Friday, Saturday, Sunday nights, watching women. Did you see her kiss her? We were so amazed. So, over a period of about six months after we'd been going to the bars every week, we began to think, 'Well, we need to find out if I'm really gay.' " Jackie puts her head back, and laughter sings from her throat.

"I had a friend at work who had not come out at that time and I told her the story. We went camping. I thought she was gay and was going to bring me out, tell me the ropes, but she was not gay at that time either. We went to the bars and met women, and I finally did meet a woman and we went to bed, and it was like ecstasy. I melted. I had had so many fantasies about what it must be like, and so the story begins from there."

There are, according to Jackie, five women's bars in Detroit and no less than forty gay men's bars. "I think a lot of people come out through the bars, because that's the most accessible place." Through the *Metro Times* Jackie found out about a discussion group for bisexual women. "I went to their first meeting, and these women were into everything! It was such a shock! So I walked away from that rather dismayed. But I did get involved with a woman from that group, and she was the wildest woman I have ever met in my life. And me, this was my first real relationship. She wanted me to tie her up; she was into whips and chains and things. I could not comply; I do not like physical abuse. That's something I grew up with and wanted to get away from."

Jackie has just moved in with a twenty-five-year-old white woman from an upper-middle-class family whom she has been seeing for six months. Susan, who has one sister who is also gay, had her first affair with a woman at eighteen. When she subsequently fell in love with a man, she was enormously relieved, because she believed "lesbians were something that came up from the sewer." Then she went to bed with another woman and decided, "I guess I'm gay after all."

"I knew there was something there from the time I was very young—something funny. And I hated myself for it. As I got older, the girls became more attractive. The boys had funny voices and peach-fuzz mustaches. The girls smelled real good and they looked really pretty. The older I got, the more attractive they were. I hated myself for it."

Jackie says of her mother, "She is one of the old-fashioned types who would die if she knew I was gay—although she knows Susan, she's met her. She doesn't push me to get married, so I think she knows but she doesn't want to know." Mrs. Brown has always found it a problem that Jackie's friends are white. "This last holiday she said, 'I'm going to go where there's all black people and have some fun. You white people go and have your fun.' She said 'white people' including myself. She raised me to think they were not trustworthy."

Susan's mother is divorced, and her reaction to her daughter's affectional preference is, "I'm fifty years old, I've been through the wringer. You go do it, but I can't hear anything about it." Susan has not confronted her openly with the fact that Jackie is her lover and adds that Jackie's being black would add to her mother's distress. Susan also was queasy about the racial difference until she asked herself, "Are you going to let her go, going to lose her just because she's black?" She finally concluded, "I can't let it stand in the way anymore."

Jackie says she made a conscious decision to avoid the pitfalls of her background. "And so a lot of the things I did emulated white people. I thought a lot of them must be doing something right because they are successful. I didn't have any black role models, they were all white. Prior to my coming out, I knew a white-black lesbian couple, so I thought of that being the right way to do it." She has never been attracted to black women.

Jackie is a highly paid computer programmer and attributes her success partly to the fact that black women in the field are at a premium. They do not know she is gay. She lied and said she was married before and is now celibate because she is between relationships. Occasionally she talks about a man to her friend at work "just to please her."

Susan works in an office where everyone is married and talks about his or her partner all the time. "One time I came to work with a hickey, and everyone said, 'Oh, who's the new guy?' I decided that Jackie would be my new boyfriend and her name would be Jeffery." Jackie gave her a picture of a black man whom Susan thought was cute, and she put it on her desk. "I'm laying low now," she says, "because it got to the point of when we were having a work function, they'd say, 'Why don't you bring Jeffrey?' " The women she works with are black and are very curious.

"I'm to the point where I think I have a boyfriend. I forget. . . . So, as you see, it's gone too far. But I don't make up anything, I just say, 'Jeffrey,' 'he,' 'his,' and 'him.' It's kinda fun, but it makes you feel sad. And it's scary and it's dangerous. I have to constantly remember to say 'he' and 'him' even when it's Jackie I'm thinking about."

The necessity of hypocrisy makes Jackie angry. "Where I worked before, I had to do that, so when I changed jobs, I was determined I'd never do that again. Someday I'll get to the point where I'll say, 'I'm gay. Either you accept it or you don't.' I do believe we have a place.

"I hope we don't have to have riots, but I hope someone like Martin Luther King will come forth and help us come out that way. There was a gay march a few weeks ago, and I was heavily involved in that. I think we should stand up for who we are. We're human beings just like the rest of the people."

Susan compares the gay liberation movement with the equal rights amendment. "ERA will never be passed because of the real militant, Gloria Steinem types. Those few people push it down other people's throats. Personally I'm content with pretending I have a boyfriend, having to be careful. It's not that I'm ashamed, I love this life. But I don't want people saying, 'Oooo, you creep, I don't want to be in the same room with you.' The only part of my life where I'm in the closet is at work. But I won't march in any parade."

Jackie says, "Marching felt good. I was head of security this year. We had factory-worker-type people, executives, doctors, all kinds of people.

"It would take a Martin Luther King to let them know that we're okay. But I don't think it will happen in my lifetime, because there is no one out there doing it for us and I don't think we're doing it. We need a leader. Because I've had such a hard life, I know what a hard struggle it is to get through, to overcome something. I know a lot of the things it would take.

"It's reminding them that you exist. No, I will *not* sit at the back of the bus, take me to jail. No, I will *not* not hold her hand, take me to jail. Why aren't we allowed to be as free as straights? It's not fair. If someone spits on us, we should be able to have them arrested just as though they had taken up a bat and hit us. If I told my landlord I was a black lesbian, I would not live there. Laws would allow us to get our foot in the door.

"We need a heightened awareness. I'd like to make a fuss. I really would. I wish I had the know-how. I would almost like to be the one to get the movement going. Let me get up there on the podium and preach and start the revolution. Let's do it! MOHR has a great potential to reach the straight community. Maybe someday I'll see my name in print."

In 1987 Jackie Brown was named a vice chairperson of MOHR, the Michigan Organization for Human Rights.

7. PRIVATE OR SECRET?

LESBIANS are not alone in suffering from the secrecy that society imposes on those who violate its mores. They endure no more and no less than many others, but some groups and individuals have choices about defying certain cultural taboos. For example, a woman having an affair with a married man may keep it secret, but she has the option of demanding he get a divorce and legally marry her, thereby restoring her to society's good graces. Lesbians are denied that option.

The word *closeted* is frequently used by lesbians, the word *secret* seldom. The reason may lie in the undesirable connotations the latter word stirs. Mythologically, the opening of Pandora's box loosed chaos; historically, witches were burned for their secret powers; psychologically, Jung spoke of secrets as psychic poison.

Although Sissela Bok's book *Secrets* contains no reference to homosexuality, much of her thinking is applicable. She writes of the origins of secrecy, how it is part of forming an identity, of being separate and unique. At a very early age a child develops boundaries to her individuality by the realization, "I know this but you don't." The secret may be as temporary and delightful as Daddy hid Mommy's birthday present under my bed! Or as mysterious as masturbating. It conveys both a sense of power and a haunting desire to tell, a telling that would return the child to symbiosis with her parents and regain for her the attendant freedom from personal responsibility.

Throughout adolescence the young person experiments with what she should tell and what she should shield with silence. Secrets are often shared with peers, while the once-omniscient parents are excluded. Where did you go? Out. What did you do? Nothing. Gradually the young person develops discretion about what it is wise to reveal and to whom. But often the fear of parental judgment is imprinted for life. "The last person I would ever tell is my mother!"

Lesbians and others often confuse the terms *secrecy* and *privacy*. Bok defines the former as intentional concealment, the latter as controlling access to what a person considers to be her personal domain. The two most clearly overlap "when secrecy serves as an additional shield in case the protection of privacy should fail or be broken down."

For example, a teenage girl who is sexually exploring with a boy—or girl—might begin writing in her diary, which has always been assumed to be inviolable private property, in code. She may not be ashamed of what she is doing but, wishing to make very sure that her shield of privacy remains absolute, she also writes in symbols and allusions. The girl feels her parents would not "understand" and would attempt to squash her sexual growth by making her feel guilty ("That's disgusting!"), or fill her with fear ("You'll get pregnant!"), or worse ("They lock perverts like you up!").

Our culture has adopted no broad, comfortable way of addressing teenage sexuality in any form, but there are very different reactions to one girl, call her Audrey, who is doing some serious sexual exploring with her girlfriend, and another, Kendra, who is doing the same with a boyfriend. If both keep the sexual details secret, parents and peers will view Audrey as having a "best friend" and Kendra as "dating a guy." Both are acceptable. But in Kendra's case society acknowledges, however grudgingly or gleefully, that she is involved in kissing, probably petting, and maybe intercourse. Audrey is spoken of as more interested in sports, or music, or her studies than boys—*boys* being a euphemism for *sex*.

If the culture approved same-sex relations, Audrey would be granted a partial release of her secret as is Kendra. Her hour-long phone conversations would not be met with, "What do you and that girl find to talk about?" but rather a raised eyebrow and, "Sounds like you and she are getting pretty serious. Has she asked you to the prom yet?" Then Audrey could smile a mysterious half smile and feel a satisfying balance between her own need for privacy in establishing independence and intimacy with her parent. But that is not the way it is.

Because girls still believe that lesbians "are something that comes up from the sewer," what Audrey and her girlfriend experience goes nameless and securely compartmentalized. Secrecy becomes second nature to her and, as Bok points out, there are dangers to secrecy. If the secret is guilty or deeply embarrassing, it can "corrode from within." By shutting out criticism and feedback, people become "mired in stereotyped, unexamined, often erroneous beliefs and ways of thinking." Without realistic feedback from parents, friends, or media, lesbians remain "something that comes up from the sewer." And if that is so, how does she define herself? Certainly not "one of them," but. . . . Her sense of identity, always fragile in adolescence, is imperiled, and in her confusion irrational and even pathological ideas can take root.

Secrets acquired in childhood and adolescence become burdensome. The relief of a girl upon finding out that her best friend uses the same acne medicine creates delirious joy, as does the knowledge that her friend's parents are also divorced. She is not different! Secrets are both the means of creating uniqueness and the bane of the adolescent's frantic desire to be "like everybody else," which means behaving in a way acceptable to her special group of friends. Girls huddled together are often assumed to be "telling each other their secrets."

Sharing confidences with friends is one way of finding out about the invisible lives of other human beings. Another is the access girls have to adult female gossip, and there are also soap operas, books, movies, and women's magazines. They learn what is "good," what "unfortunately happens," and what—because it is never mentioned—is unspeakable. From these cues they know what to reveal with confidence, what to "confess," and what must never be uttered.

Confession implies having committed a sin, a behavior that can be changed. One confesses fornication, not pneumonia. The parent, priest, or, in these days of institutionalized confession, the therapist, "forgives," sometimes with the addition of a penance or punishment. Thus the secret has been brought into the light and its evil dissipated. To confess homosexuality implies a desire to change, whereas to state "I am a lesbian" with confidence exhibits a desire to restore intimacy with one's self and others.

This distinction is too seldom made. The youthful lesbian herself may be confused about her motives. Does she wish to become "normal"? To have her strange feelings validated? To share the discovery of who she is? Confusion also exists in the minds of those adults to whom she chooses to send signals or bluntly tell. Is this another sign of adolescent rebellion? Foolishness induced by reading the wrong book or hanging around with the wrong gang? A desperate cry for help? Does she want me to "fix it" or accept it?

The young woman is well advised to be cautious and carefully weigh the idea that "confession is good for the soul" against the concept of "self-betrayal." Because, as many lesbians have learned, an authority figure entrusted with her secret may initiate actions to "change" her by means that in any other context, would be considered barbaric and inhumane.

Frequently the lesbian can satisfy the very human longing to be completely known and all forgiven only in the arms of her lover. All sexual relations confuse the eradication of physical boundaries with those of the psyche—orgasm and "I love you!" become twins—but forbidden sex heightens this response. Therefore, the act itself—erotic relations with a woman—becomes part of the bonding that, of necessity, excludes the rest of the world. And thereby deepens the secret.

Heterosexuals like Kendra also keep the details of their sexual life private. They follow the pattern of parents who do not discuss a rollicking good time in bed at the breakfast table. But there are stages by which their sexual life is acknowledged and yet shielded by privacy. Dating, going steady, becoming engaged, living together, getting married, and obtaining a divorce have, in addition to other conotations, a sexual one. Details of sexual acts are considered private, and yet the world knows of their existence—they are no secret. At twenty-three Kendra does not have to add to her announcement that she is going on vacation with Billy that they are lovers. It is assumed. While the lesbian also wishes to keep the details of her sexual life private, she is denied a dignified, acceptable euphemism akin to "they are married."

If Audrey moves into her twenties continuing to find loving women more satisfying than relationships with men, she realizes that even as an adult her private life—unless she chooses to announce her lesbianism—must have the added protection of secrecy. Not only is there no diamond engagement ring to flash as a symbol of her entrance into the society of adult women, but adolescent cautions must continue. Notes to her lovers contain neither salutations nor signatures. Letters from them are immediately torn up and thrown away. Pronouns disappear from her vocabulary. Quips deflect questions about weekend activities. She adopts a double dress standard. Her house undergoes a transformation when work friends or parents—or even the plumber—are expected. She becomes concerned about her own paranoia—is she behaving as a rational person?

Fearful of losing the respect of long-time heterosexual friends, she has no one with whom to compare notes on what is going on in her life. No confirmation that yes, her feelings toward this lover appear solid and good, or that no, they sound destructive. Her secret begins to "corrode from within."

Society believes openness and sincerity are excellent qualities, and political lesbians insist she should be willing to march in a gay-pride parade, but Audrey is aware and constantly reminded that a world free of prejudice has not arrived. She hears the degrading jokes, reads about "queer bashing," hears lezzie used as a term of total dismissal. Courts uphold sodomy laws; Congress argues about funding any organization that believes the life she practices is normal and healthy.

She is also aware that others, her friends, her parents, society in general, hold conflicting views in regard to secrets. They simultaneously believe that leaving secrets alone avoids the suffering that knowledge might release and that bringing them to light dissipates their poison. A person who is fanatical about digging Communists out of government or exposing sin in a church congregation may at the same time be "oblivious" to his or her child's drug abuse because that knowledge would bring personal anguish. As a lesbian Audrey is liable to be the recipient of both responses. If she joins a branch of the military, they will go to great lengths to expose her, while her parents might frantically signal, "Don't tell me. I don't want to know."

This fear of knowing other people's secrets may be inspired by not wishing to have to take responsibility, to have to do something about the situation. Bok believes is it also caused by fear "of being hurt, or changed through them in ways one cannot control. To acquire any new knowledge is to be changed; but the change from learning secrets is less predictable, less in the power of the learner." To learn that you were born out of wedlock, that your husband is having an affair, that your mother is a lesbian changes your life in uncontrollable ways.

"The fear of secret knowledge, then, may be a fear of what learning it will entail—of being drawn into a guilty secret, perhaps, entangled in its protection, or polluted through mere contact with it. The change moreover may be irreversible. One cannot at will unlearn a secret, no matter how unpalatable or dangerous it turns out to be. It is hard enough to forget anything on purpose, but to forget a secret on purpose is even harder."

This explains much of what underlies that glib, overused word *homophobic*. It may not only be that some women fear lesbians because they are unsure of their own sexuality, but that they fear the secret itself. It explains why parents when directly confronted say, "All right. Now we never need to talk about it again." Why heterosexual people who "know" still don't ask, "Well, Audrey, how's it going with you and Sally?"

Because lesbians know that revealing themselves will create a burden for others, they are at least in part denied control over secrecy and openness. So, of course, are many others: parents of a mentally ill child, the wife of an alcoholic husband, the child victim of incest. For the lesbian it extends beyond the personal into the political, because "hating the homosexual" has been institutionalized. It has been argued that in a political sense lesbians are denied their right of free speech guaranteed under the First Amendment because revelation, an announcement of "I am a women-loving woman," may cause them to be harassed, lose their jobs, or be denied housing.

Bok wrote, "The person who tells [her secret] gains a measure of control over how others see it. The speaker establishes [her] identity in the eyes of the listeners. She no longer feels blurred and anonymous in their eyes; her life has taken on meaning, is set apart, unique through what is revealed."

PART 3

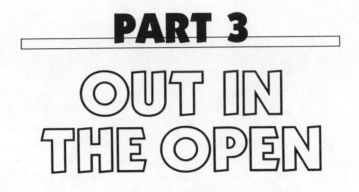

OUT IN THE OPEN

PART 2

OUT IN
THE OPEN

8. A WEEKEND IN SAN FRANCISCO

SATURDAY morning in summer. San Francisco. Gay capital of the country. The Mission District—imagined nirvana of lesbians everywhere. The south end of Valencia Street looks like an ordinary urban area in transition. The deteriorating dwellings of the working class, the poor, surround the enclaves of the upscale emigrants, in this case gays and lesbians. One of these buildings is new and solid with pass-card-only underground parking and buzzers outside the lobby. The corridors are deeply carpeted; the condo of a lesbian couple is young-upwardly-mobile comfortable and immaculately clean.

One of the women remarks, "When my mother was coming to San Francisco for the first time, she said, 'I want to see a eucalyptus tree and a homosexual.' In that order. No Golden Gate Bridge or anything like that. Just a eucalyptus tree and a homosexual."

"Lots of homosexuals," she explains, "live in every district, then they come to the clubs in the Castro." Just as Manhattan has its Upper West Side, Greenwich Village, et cetera, San Francisco has its divisions, districts that not only denote geographic boundaries, but also life-styles. In San Franscisco the Castro, which borders the Mission District, is known for its gay male population, although blacks, white straights, and poorer people live there too.

"You are free to show affection in the Mission District, but you may be heckled by Latino men. They have aggressions against all gays. Other places in the city you can experience violence. Not long ago an eastern boy was knifed to death—he looked gay. Talking back is not a good idea. Kids will yell, 'There goes a bunch of dykes!' But perhaps because of a greater preponderance of gay people here, you feel more free."

North of this area of families hurrying about their Saturday morning chores is the heart of lesbian-land. The Old Wives Bookstore buzzes. Business is reported to be the best in the store's ten-year existence. On display are small-press books found in few if any mainstream bookstores, and greeting cards are frankly for women who love women. The notices on the bulletin board assume feminist/lesbian patrons: Adrienne Rich reading on Tuesday night, apartments to share. The shoppers range from dykey to matronly. If lesbianism is a club, women's bookstores are the clubhouse.

Saturday noon. In the same block is the Artemis Café with lots of windows, pink woodwork, and white walls; fresh flowers decorate each of the cable-spool tables. Paulett, the server, says Artemis is open from 11:30 A.M. to 11:00 P.M., seven days a week, with entertainment on Friday and Saturday nights. "We do lots of comedy. The first five years we were totally closed to men, now we may even have two or three male entertainers a year."

The founder and owner of Artemis is Sara Lewinstein, who married a gay man, Tom Wedell. They have a three-year-old daughter. (Tom, an Olympic champion himself, organized the Gay Olympics of 1982, but a Supreme Court decision has since denied the group the use of the word *Olympic*.) Neither Sara nor her child is in the restaurant today. Paulett says, "Last Saturday a memorial was held for Tom at City Hall." He died of AIDS.

The clientele of Artemis is mixed: a biker in leather and bracelets, young sophisticates, a slouched-in-a-corner reader, and tourists. A teacher from Casper, Wyoming, is in town visiting her lover, Debbie Aquilar. Thirty-four-year old Debbie, who at eighteen was an activist in the fields with Cesar Chavez, says she had to leave Casper. "There is no gathering place for gay women, the nearest bar is in Denver, a five-hour drive. The isolation was overwhelming. I had a cut-off feeling, a split in my personality. There is also only one class—WASP." She took a job with Merrill Lynch in Denver and was later transferred to San Francisco.

In contrast to the thin, serious, olive-skinned Debbie, Ann—not her real name—is round with an open face, short iron-gray hair, and the pleasant air of everyone's favorite high school teacher. She stays in Casper because "I have a good job, good pay, and retirement. I get out as often as I can." She smiles. "I wait on the goddess."

Ann was married for twenty-three years, has two sons and a granddaughter. "I didn't know there was an option. I was not unhappy and I'm glad about the kids." Even after her divorce she kept thinking, "There must be a man here somewhere." Now she is sure that her place is with a woman, but her children dismiss the idea. One son says, "Mom, when are you going to find a nice man and settle down?" The other son shrugs and calls her "whacky." She and Debbie have talked of settling in Alaska, where Ann was raised, or in San Francisco.

Debbie's choice has always been women, and she loves living in San Francisco. "Eighty percent of the people I work with at Merrill Lynch are gay and lesbian, and most of the others are close to someone gay." As evidence of the company's acceptance of them she notes that " 'significant others' can have therapy sessions free on our insurance."

Debbie's serious demeanor vanishes when she talks about "parades and organizations and bars, the restaurants, the businesses—it's overwhelming! Numbers of people out are what makes the difference."

That difference is felt in Artemis, the craft shop, the bookstore. Women are assumed to be gay. The straight woman, if she wishes her sexuality to be known, has to be the one doing the signaling that she is different, and in this diverse mingling of women, that would be a difficult feat. She might, perhaps fearing condemnation, be content to blend. She might take off her wedding ring and smile pleasantly at everyone, donning for the time being an assumption of affectional preference that for her is false.

This is, of course, what lesbians experience every day of their lives. They are the one white person on a subway of blacks, or the one woman working on a construction site, or the American tourist in China ecstatic at the sight of one of her own. Lacking the identifiable traits of skin color or body build, lesbians have had to devise a means of conveying, "I am a women-loving woman," without using words or physical gestures that might arouse the ire of the majority. Their eyes are their signal. As Liz Pierce said, "We can meet anywhere, and our eyes connect and we smile." When women have felt the "starvation, hunger" that Debbie found in Casper, they are heartened by the thought, "Ah, there's another one!"

Saturday, early afternoon. Many lesbians move to San Francisco, some are born there. Twenty-four-year-old Donna Keiko Ozawa is a third-generation Japanese-American and a native of San Francisco. Her father, a civil engineer, was also born here; her mother, a registered nurse, was from a farming family. Her grandmother's brother and his wife were living in Hiroshima when the bomb was dropped. They survived, but Donna imagines what it must have been like for her grandmother, who was one of the last immigrants admitted in the 1920s, to go back to Japan and find all her friends dead, her house reduced to rubble.

Donna's grandmother and grandfather spent the war years in an American detention center. "The details of their lives I don't hear about," Donna says. "There was a lot of shame." Donna's body is small and neat, her face sturdy; she speaks with thoughtful sincerity.

In high school in the seventies Donna founded two clubs—one against the draft, one for peace—and was very active in the Methodist Church, "which helped me make connections about racism and sexism and what I had to do to make the world a better place. I'm still a driven person about issues."

Donna knew then that she was attracted to women, "but I didn't know how to find support and explore." Others she approached "hadn't thought about it, so they weren't clear, and that didn't help much." She found her first lover in a peace group in college. "Anybody can be attracted to anybody, but"—she smiles broadly—"when I was attracted to women, I had to *do* something about it." Her political activities centered on feminism, racism, and Central America. Of her college, Mount Holyoke, she says, "It is a place of privilege. The tolerance level for difference was not high. My race was the foremost issue."

Donna is still an activist. Her list of involvements is long and includes helping to organize the first Asian/Pacific Lesbian Retreat. "It made me really look at what I need from a community—just being Asian and lesbian is not enough, we need a common vision, common values. There was also a lot of relief and joy—'Oh, my God, there's a lot of us! Does your mother know my mother?'"

Her parents she describes as still being in the denial stage. "I said, 'Mom, sit down.' She said, 'Donna, I already know. I've known since high school.' She named all my lovers. Seems everybody knew but me. But she hasn't wanted to talk about it since." Nevertheless, Donna is glad she was open with her parents and with others. "Being in the closet does damage that we don't realize. Life can be so much fun out of it!"

Donna wants to be a teacher because she believes it is important for young people to have role models and "to give children alternatives so that they can choose. It helps their self-esteem. I felt really restricted growing up. I have a vision of a place where people are free to make choices. Both the oppressed and the oppressor are hurt—we need to be out of the closet on all kinds of issues, an ally to all sorts of people. It is good to know so many people are working on this. We move forward in little increments."

San Francisco, in comparison with the rest of the country, seems to move forward in seven-league boots. Gays and lesbians openly compete for political office. A lesbian, Mary Dunlap, took the "Olympic" case to the Supreme Court; another lesbian is a judge.

That morning Jean Kovalich, the woman whose mother wanted to see a eucalyptus tree and a homosexual, said, "Those people are out one hundred percent. A lot who are out are respected by city dignitaries."

Jean feels differently about the Bay Area Career Women, which is the largest lesbian organization in the country, with over one thousand members. "Confidentiality is a big deal with them. They come out to meetings and be gay and then go home and shut the door. I don't want to be part of people who are not proud of who they are. I don't like people in slices."

The Bay Area Career Women, a lesbians-only group, protested the opening to straights of another lesbian/gay organization, the Golden Gate Business Association Foundation, because that would destroy confidentiality. A columnist for a gay/lesbian newspaper commented, "It's all who's-watching-who-watching-who-doing-what." "Even in San Francisco," Jean said, "there are those who are very fearful."

Late Saturday afternoon. The streets of the Castro District are filled with people watching people. Jean's mother would have no trouble spotting young men in tight jeans holding hands with each other. Outside Francine's, a lesbian bar, exuberant young women clown and shout. Inside in the back a woman plays pool and whoops at the video; in the sunlight by the window one woman leans across a small table and caresses another's cheek; a big, soft-faced woman in leather hunches on a bar stool and cradles her beer.

Four women in creamy-white tails with turquoise bow ties and boutonnieres are gathered by the bar; the special warmth of their celebration is infectious. They have just come from church, where two of the women, Lynn Ferreira and Barbara Samaniego, have exchanged vows and rings in front of a woman minister. Linda Walker grins up from where she sits in a wheelchair. "I caught the bouquet!"

Lynn is short, firmly built, and her luminous light blue eyes twinkle as, after giving a description of the ceremony, she adds, "We haven't gotten to the garter yet." She drives a double bus— "You know, the two-body ones with an accordion pleat in the middle." She met Barbara over popcorn six months ago, and it was love at first sight. "I'm forty-one and I've had two relationships. One of thirteen years, one of six, and I never thought of getting married before."

Barbara is twenty-six with a lustily feminine body and dark curly hair pulled back from her rich, mobile face; her mother is Cuban, her father Puerto Rican. She grew up a street kid in the Bronx, joined the army to escape, served six years and played on the All-Army basketball team. She is still in the reserves. About lesbians in the army she says, "We were careful. I had a good position I didn't want to lose." Barbara was a drill sergeant and now manages a restaurant.

Carla Slominski, a husky strawberry blonde with a glowing face and smile is also a bus driver. Slim, witty Linda is a court clerk. If mainstream society, locked into the stereotype of sad, surly, tough, half-men with femmes at home, were searching for lesbian bus drivers and drill sergeants, they would look right past these attractive, warm, self-confident, good-humored women.

Nine o'clock on a Saturday night. San Francisco's lesbian bars range from Baybrick, advertised as "upscale, but not uptight," to A Little More, which features strip shows. Somewhere between the two in tone and clientele is Amelia's, located on Valencia Street a short walk from Jean Kovalich and Sandy Rowe's condo.

On entering, the long, narrow downstairs bar is a blur of women—one hundred, two hundred? Their impassive faces are difficult to read. Are they acting cool? Really scared? Just young? Cynical? Playing tough as they "cruise"? "Almost everyone," Jean says, "is single and looking. A few couples are out to celebrate something." The faces of the women-loving women, sharp near the doorway, fade into the smokey haze.

A New York woman expressed her feeling for the bar scene by saying, "The whole room full of women . . . it doesn't make me comfortable. I like boys and girls being together." But added, "Maybe it gets back to this feeling of right and wrong." People, lesbians included, grow up with one or two heterosexual parents and are exposed exclusively—in private, in public, and in the media—to male/female sexuality. Amelia's on a Saturday night smashes into those lifetime habits of perspective with such power that the world seems to turn inside out.

As is true for all nighttime entertainment, including tribal dancing around a fire, Amelia's is theater—costumes, lighting, music, posturing.

Upstairs—cover charge five dollars—the stage is set. A dozen or so tables sit between the bar and the large dance floor; the lighting, harsh at the bar, dims in the nether reaches. On the cue of pulsing music, women—silently single, in hand-holding couples, in laughing clumps—climb the stairs. Groups fill the tables, singles line the bar. In heterosexual lounges men's glances flick across women's bodies as they enter or leave, but here the tightly packed eyes focus more on faces. Jean notes that some women will hang out by the rest room door eyeing the passing women.

Donna Ozawa gave another reason for being in Amelia's on a Saturday night. "I don't drink and I hate the smoke, but I love to dance." When the music has thumped all other sensations out of the brain, dancers, two by two, step onto the floor, transforming it into a stage to those who watch.

Costuming is important, and eclectic, rather than butch/femme, is the style. Sneakers, jeans, muscle shirts, cotton skirts, suspenders and baggy pants, foxy tuxes, one miniskirt and spike heels, a few leather pants and leather vests. A lot of red, a lot of black, a little drab, and a lot of extremely short California blonde hair.

Performance, as in a heterosexual disco, is varied. Some women float, some bounce, and body types run the gamut. The athletes' movements are percussive, while the big women take small steps, keep their arms close. Although the slow dancing will come later, sensual suggestions are not totally absent—one woman dances with her hands in her partner's hip pockets. For others, partners are optional or interchangeable.

The floor fills and empties according to the popularity of the song being played. All of the music, however, has a strong rock beat that negates conversation. Sandy Rowe, who works as a lithographer, has to shout her opinion of life as a lesbian. "Be different. Isn't that what this world is all about—being different? When everything else gives way—where do you get your strength? From yourself. I get my strength from being different. I've always felt this way. I'm just so proud of who I love and how I love.

"It's difficult enough being a gay person without somebody asking you how you feel about it. They don't ask heterosexuals or Catholics. I live my life the way I talk. It doesn't matter if I scrub toilets. It's how you feel about yourself. I couldn't feel any different if I made two bucks an hour as opposed to twenty. I always told 'em [at work] the first day and put up pictures of my lover. That's being honest. Proud of who you are anywhere."

The air, thickened by an hour or so of electric guitar, gyrating women's bodies, and tongues loosened by alcohol, squeezes the occupants of Amelia's into friendly, possibly sexual, closeness. The drama extends from the dance floor to the bar to the rest room door. Eyes have met—not merely in lesbian recognition but in sexual invitation. As Simone du Beauvoir wrote in *The Second Sex*, "Lesbians don't want to be men, they want their prey." Most do not, however, view females as "prey" any more than heterosexual women view males as prey. The truth is that they do not wish to be men, they simply wish to make love to women. Amelia's is not a meat market. Overt sexuality is no more in evidence than at a high school dance or an office Christmas party.

On the way back down Valencia Street, Sandy grabs Jean's hand and holds it high. "This is what it's all about! Just this. We can walk anywhere in this city like this."

Sunday morning is a time of reflection. About place. About its importance in the lives of lesbians. When lesbians ask each other, "What's it like there?" they are not inquiring about ski conditions or available housing, but the tolerance level.

The women in Spokane had spoken of fear. "This is a scary place to live." They had spoken of a "macho, Old West mentality," of authorities "arresting gay men in Idaho, shooting them in Montana." A heterosexual, a member of the university community there, was surprised: "Fear? In Spokane?" She did not realize that lesbians, like other groups outside the perceived mainstream, live glancing over their shoulders, wondering, "Who's next?"

Emma Hixson, director of the Department of Civil Rights of Minneapolis, said, "There is a huge gay and lesbian community here. Hundreds of thousands. It is a mecca for the Midwest." It was one of the reasons she had moved there. "The reality of lesbians being in high economic and political positions is here now, but Minneapolis is a unique town. We have a very progressive mayor, and gays are very active and vocal. They have a lot of clout. In Duluth they tried to pass antidiscrimination laws in 1984, and there was a strong backlash, death threats, et cetera. Saint Paul rescinded their antidiscrimination ordinance by referendum in 1978."

Prevailing political attitudes are important, but so are individual perceptions. The codirector of the Spokane Peace and Justice League, Diane Jhueck, who moved there from Seattle seven years ago, said, "The Spokane community is too apolitical, too immature in its politics and its analysis of itself. They live very static lives: nine-to-five jobs, come home and fight with each other. They have dogs and cats and are poor. In Seattle you could have a strike of gay women, and the hospitals and schools and all the helping services would close down." Diane, who believes that being lesbian is a choice she made and that it is a political mistake not to speak out, adds, "But no matter what we do, we don't deserve harassment."

A woman with a different perspective of Spokane said, "I enjoyed the small, close community. It was just right for me then."

A Detroit woman considers her town "strange politically—very closeted. Maybe it is due to Midwest or blue-collar influence. Only twenty-five hundred showed up at our gay-pride parade." In Toronto Dougal reported that ten to fifteen thousand marched.

"I go on vacations," a rural woman said, "where I can hold hands with my lover in public. Provincetown [Mass.], Key West, Toronto, San Francisco."

Sunday brunch. Karen Strauss, fair-skinned and dark-haired, a gracious young woman whose speech is soft and deliberate, shares a wonderful old apartment in the Mission District with a gay man. Raised in a New York Jewish family, Karen lived in Boston after her graduation as a dance major from the University of Massachusetts. "In Boston it was hard to feel like it was okay to be a lesbian. I felt terribly harassed just as a woman. There is sanctioned racism there." She finds San Francisco "definitely a much calmer city," although she acknowledges the violence between the Mission Latino and Castro gay.

Karen's eyes are troubled as she speaks of her concern for her housemate. "If he got sick, I couldn't possibly take over his care. I would do all I could, but. . . . We are not even best friends, we just share space. He recently broke up with a lover, but he probably would come back to help. After a while I would have to call in a support system. The financial costs are so great." Family help is not even mentioned. Karen's fears are all for him, not for any danger of being infected herself.

Sandy Rowe spoke adamantly about the first priority of gay and lesbian organizations. "Every cent goes to AIDS! That's where it should go! Three men die in this city every day!" At intervals she morosely repeated, "Three men every day."

Jean, motioning to one door in her building, said, "There is always a smell of medicine. I think someone is sick in there." Everyone on her floor is gay; sick means AIDS, and AIDS means dying.

"No woman in San Francisco," Sandy said, "will have sex with a woman who has had sex with a man in the last five years."

Midafternoon. Maud's, reputed to be the oldest gathering place for lesbians in the world. The room, shaded from the bright Sunday sun, is long, dim, and dingy; pictures of the owner, Jackie Stricker—with her softball teams, with Gloria Steinem in the seventies—decorate the walls. Maud's is "a second home to some," the bartender, a woman in her thirties, says. She herself has "had enough of this," is taking forestry courses, and wants to move to a quiet, empty place—"probably Oregon."

Only one person sits at the bar, a biker with large, colored tattoos on each arm, gloves, black leather jacket, blond crew cut. She shakes her head, refusing conversation because "the wind's still in my ears."

Out on the patio the scene is stereotypical San Francisco. An Asian woman has her radio tuned to classical music; a couple of gay men are having a drink. A very fit woman in her forties—she rides her bike four hours a day—clad in short shorts and a pink muscle shirt, offers around a joint saying, "Beats Valium." The air is clear, the sun bright.

In San Francisco the habits of a more closed culture seem easy to dislodge. Jean said of the city, "It has a greater feeling for personal freedom. People can express themselves in any way they want to. If they want to do things differently, they can do it here with respect. The very presence of some of these people would cause arrest in Columbus, Ohio. When I lived there I was in a duplex closet. Not part of the community. There people look at anyone different as a threat, a bad influence. They are living by rules they have not even examined. They are being what someone else carved out for them.

"Here people realize there is more to life than the way they have been taught and that difference can flourish here. Even in New York there is still a feeling of status quo. Here *human* behavior is proper."

San Francisco is not nirvana, but rather a different place and a place of differences.

9. NEVER IN MY WILDEST IMAGINATION

JEAN Kovalich said, "There are no answers to why. If you're gay, you just are." And some women come to a place where they are no longer willing or able to keep it a secret.

Emma Hixson, the thirty-seven-year-old director of the Minneapolis Department of Civil Rights, was identified by the media as a lesbian when she accepted the position. "It was scary at the time," she says. "In grocery stores everyone stared at me. They looked when I walked down the halls [of city hall]. There was a little graffiti in the bathroom. Perhaps I was projecting paranoia. Since then it's been comfortable. I prefer being out because then I'm not one-on-one constantly coming out. Now it's annoying when I encounter someone who doesn't know."

Portly in her business suit, she leans back in her office chair and laughs. "When they write about me, they always say, 'Hixson, an admitted lesbian,' as though to make sure people take that into account when weighing what I say."

She had told her parents long before, "but they live in a small rural Kentucky town, and the *USA Today* release was a little uncomfortable for them. But they care about me. People have always looked on my mother a little strangely for *her* ideas"—she was a strong supporter of civil rights—"so I suppose they think, what's one more?" Emma, in addition to having a role-model mother, possesses a law degree and a passion for civil rights, factors that make it easier to live with the hyphenated last name of Hixson-Admittedlesbian.

Diane Jhueck, codirector of the Peace and Justice Action League in Spokane said, "I'm a totally political person. Being lesbian has not handicapped me. It's even a help in my profession."

Jean Kovalich, the thirty-four-year-old woman who lives in the Mission District of San Francisco, became a public lesbian not to enhance her professional position but to try to save it. Jean works for the Department of Defense and is suing them for discrimination.

Her coast-to-coast public exposure was a shock her mother has not gotten over. Jean was raised in a Catholic Eastern European family of three brothers and two sisters; her father worked the mines of northeastern Pennsylvania until World War II. Jean describes her teenage self as an "attractive kid with long hair, a perfect heterosexual appearance." Around her hometown, *lesbian* was like a swearword.

Now that Jean is involved in an open legal battle, her mother is in turmoil. " 'Why do you have to do this to me? I don't go to any groups because of this. What am I going to say to the relatives? I went to the butcher, and someone was staring at me.'

"I was by her side all the time growing up. Now we have nothing in common. I haven't been home since the court case began. I haven't been invited by my mother. She says she has to go to church and pray about it. Her big thing is to keep up appearances. I had helped her out financially before. Now I offer my retirement-money refund and all of a sudden she doesn't want to touch my money. She's attacked not my faults but my strength. It really gets at the core of me."

In the fall of 1974, when Jean was in graduate school at the University of Arkansas getting a master's in judicial administration, she received a job offer from the Defense Investigative Service, an agency of the Defense Department. Her starting salary was $8,000; with her last promotion to supervisor of investigation of the San Francisco field office, it was $37,000. When the ruling came down that federal employees who were homosexuals should self-report so that they could not be open to blackmail, Jean did. She was then denied an update of her security clearance "because you are an open homosexual."

After a nine-month investigation by the department, Jean received a letter reassigning her to Washington, D.C. According to Jean, "The letter said, 'We can no longer use you as an investigator' because I could 'not be objective with other homosexuals you are investigating.' " Jean adds that she "had been unwilling to provide identification of my former lovers to them.

"Subsequently they said the reason for demotion was 'poor office procedures.' " Jean claims, "Once I had acknowledged I was a lesbian, it was a question of 'How are we going to get rid of her?' I don't want to go to a reupholstered closet in the statistics section in D.C. that has nothing to do with operations. I said, 'I'm not going to stand for this.'

"I'm not one to take on causes, I'm not into a martyr role. I'm doing it for Jean Kovalich because it affected my primary relationship at work. I'm not going to pay the price for those closet lesbians if someday they get caught. I'm on the front line." Jean is paying the court costs out of her own pocket, with the exception of one hundred dollars from a gay organization, because she does not want to become a major media event in exchange for someone paying her bills.

A year and a half after her security clearance was lifted, Jean says, "What people don't realize is that I go to work every day. It's like being a POW, but I'm very stubborn. I won't get worn down. I'll be damned if I'll resign. Now that I've done what I was supposed to do [report herself], I'm fired. I should have a stamp on my forehead: 'She came out and look what happened.' The Defense Department said that if I 'got reformed and went straight, things would be better for you here.' The innuendo is, 'Would people take orders from a known lesbian?' Now that I'm out in the open, people have to react.

"They say, 'Homosexual conduct is not protected by the Constitution.' You think you have rights. Gay people need to be told that they don't! I never would have thought of suing the government. Never in my wildest imagination. Never thought Jean Kovalich would be in the law books forever and ever."

On December 13, 1987, an out-of-court settlement was made, Jean was returned to her government pay grade and received back pay, attorney fees, and "the symbolic victory of entitlement to the supervisory position when it is vacated."

Onalaska, Wisconsin, a town of three thousand on the east bank of the Mississippi River, shimmers in noonday silence. Two flights of steps, one concrete, one wooden, lead from the sidewalk up to the porch of a modest old-style bungalow. Inside, a lean woman in a golf shirt and jeans bends to tie a small boy's sneaker, then pats his backside and sends him off to play. "See ya' later, Aunt Joy."

Joy Holthaus was born in 1928 in a house in this same block; her father worked as a security foreman on the railroad; her mother bore and tended seven children who stayed in the area, raised families, and remained a close-knit group. Joy, however, did not marry. She went over to Madison to the university, earned a degree in geography, lived in Sparta for a while, then came back and settled into an administrative position at the military base. At fifty-five she retired.

A unknowing visitor would cast Joy, as she sits with her hands folded and locked in her lap, her speech larded with old-fashioned courtesies, in the role of the gray-haired spinster who will one day merit a bland obituary in the local paper. The obituary of Joy Holthaus will, in fact, read very differently from any ever printed in Onalaska.

Joy has been a secret lesbian all her life. "I always managed to know someone because I worked for the army. Either military personnel or civilians. People are always being transferred in. I was *never* out on the job. I had security clearance, and they could pull clearance and there goes the job. In effect I would have been fired. But . . ." and a small smile touches her lips, "my boss and I were lovers for sixteen years."

Fans drone, outside children shout at their play. It is not difficult to imagine a slender Joy clad in the obligatory skirt exchanging smiles in the ladies' room mirror with her lover, nor is it difficult to imagine her editing her pronouns, her activities, paying, in Sarah Pearlman's words, "an unnecessary toll."

The people at work "knew we were always together. They didn't think beyond that. They were mostly concerned about how you did your job. They never even consciously said to themselves, 'I don't care what their lives are.' "

Joy has never lived with a lover. "Somehow," she says quietly, "it never worked out." After a pause she adds, "I'm having trouble finding someone at fifty-nine. Most are younger women. I know hardly any in their fifties."

Even though this is small-town Middle America, Joy knows, by sight and name, at least one hundred lesbians through bars, women's activities at a nearby university branch, the softball league, and potluck dinners. "I've always," she says, "been out to the lesbian community."

In 1982 Wisconsin became the first and still the only state to add sexual orientation to the list of differences for which people may not by law be discriminated against in housing, employment, municipal labor organizations, and the national guard. The statute defines *sexual orientation* as: "having a preference for heterosexuality, homosexuality, bisexuality, having a history of such a preference or being identified with such a preference."

One provision requires that "the equal rights council shall disseminate information and attempt by means of discussion as well as other proper means to educate the people of the state to greater understanding, appreciation, and practice of human rights for all people, of whatever race, creed, color, sexual preference, or national origin, to the end that this state will be a better place in which to live." To expedite this provision the governor formed a state gay and lesbian rights council, which then sought representatives from different parts of Wisconsin. Joy smiles as she says, "At first no one in the La Crosse area was willing to serve."

A council member met Joy in the bar one night and afterward contacted her. The thought of being out to the world staggered Joy, but she agreed to think about it. She had retired, so work was no problem, but she had never in her life told a straight person. "Being on the Governor's Council is a *public* office," she says. It meant not merely coming out to selected people but allowing anyone and everyone in on a lifelong secret of a very personal nature. It meant walking down the streets of Onalaska with a sign around her neck.

After a week of weighing each pro and con, Joy decided to tackle what many lesbians like Tayor confess to "not having the guts to do."

"I was appointed in April, and they said they'd do a press release at the time of the first meeting on June first. I thought I had plenty of time to tell everybody quietly. I had never talked to my family. This was Saturday. On Monday I got a phone call from a radio station—'We just got this press release.' " Joy hung up the phone and began dialing her brothers and sisters. "I've got something to tell you." In the few hours remaining before the six-o'clock news Joy reached them all.

"I had the reputation of being the family radical, so they took it with 'Oh, we always knew it anyway.' One brother was actually relieved. He had thought I was going to say I had cancer."

After that frantic flurry, this private, soft-spoken woman of fifty-seven sat in her living room waiting as neighbors, friends, and family picked up the evening newspaper, turned on the radio, and heard that Joy Holthaus from Onalaska had been named to the Governor's Council for Gay and Lesbian Rights.

"There were no adverse reactions. Not one single bad reaction from family or people I grew up with. After I was on TV, I got a few phone calls, but never anything threatening or obscene. I never heard of anyone being harassed here, even though the bar is close to two redneck ones."

This, in "very Republican" Onalaska. But then Joy Holthaus is one of their own, and if her mother is typical, the townspeople respect individualism. Growing up, Joy says, "I *never* heard, 'You can't do that.' My mother *never* pushed me to get married. I was *never* guilt-tripped."

As Joy traveled around the state gathering information for the

MARTHA BARRON BARRETT

Governor's Council, she heard "of fear more than anything else. Fear of exposure to family and friends, of harassment. In small towns fear of the police. Men on the council were much more liable to say men had been beaten up. I never heard of a lesbian who was. I heard one story of a woman who claimed she was raped because she was on the Gay and Lesbian Council. She was called the governor's dyke. She tried to sue the city. Kathleen, the head of the council, was harassed, but she believes she will be, therefore she is vulnerable."

The council resigned in protest—"before we were disbanded" —when a conservative governor was elected, so Joy once more operates in a smaller sphere. Now that she is retired, she can say, "as an individual I feel totally protected. I'm safe, I'm free. I see things changing. Imagine, *Waiting for the Moon* on public TV!" Joy perceived the honest portrayal of the partnership of Gertrude Stein and Alice B. Toklas as a major media breakthrough.

She continues to be a mainstay of potlucks as she has every month since 1978 and helps with the *Leaping La Crosse Newsletter*. "I have a commitment to others. And that is important to me as a person."

It was for those others that Joy acknowledged to her family, lifelong neighbors and friends, and strangers all across Wisconsin, "I am a lesbian." A word that did not even exist when she was growing up in the thirties—"*Homosexual* was all we had."

That Joy Holthaus not only survived in a society that condemned her deepest feelings but did so with intregrity and without bitterness is deserving of Emily Dickinson's accolade:

> We never know how high we are
> Till we are called to rise.
> And then, if we are true to plan,
> Our statures touch the skies.

10. HOW DARE YOU!

THE first church trial in over one hundred years, and the first church trial in modern times on the issue of homosexuality, took place on August 24, 1987.

The Reverend Rose Mary Denman and Winnie Weir, who have known each other for eight years and lived together for three, share a cozy upstairs apartment in a Portland, Maine, working-class neighborhood. Winnie's tall, angular body aligns itself with a straight-backed dining room chair; Rose Mary, like a bouncing ball come to rest, curls against one corner of the couch. Winnie's expression is unchanging, Rose Mary's a mirror of her lively emotions.

After high school Rose Mary joined the air force; she married in 1967 and divorced in 1971. Her father's family had immigrated from "little farms in Portugal, where they just barely had enough money to make ends meet. They came to America, worked in factories for big money, and within ten years had enough to buy a home—cash, mind you—and cars." Rose Mary's mother, French/Irish/English, "became Portuguese by osmosis. It came with getting married. What John said went. He used to love to brag that when he picked her up for their first date, she had no stockings on, just sandals—it was summer. And he said, 'I don't take half-naked women out. Go in the house and put something on your legs.' And she did."

At the time of her divorce Rose Mary's son was two and a half. While raising him she put herself through college, graduate school, and theological seminary. "I knew I was heading for the ministry. I took the detour through graduate school because I didn't feel I was holy enough for seminary yet. Then when I went I saw all this wife-swapping and drugs . . ." But if there were lesbians at the Bangor Theological Seminary, Rose Mary did not recognize them.

"She'd have probably had a stroke," is Winnie's comment.

"Lesbians drove me crazy. Now I understand that they confronted my sexuality. I liked gay men. I once said to a woman friend of mine, 'If you were a man, I'd marry you.' I even said that to Winnie before I began to understand. I always had to translate it into the personality of the person because I couldn't say it was a woman I loved. Socially, culturally, denominationally, you name it, I had been conditioned that this was not an option. Now looking back I know Aunt E——was a lesbian. It was always Aunt E—— and E——. They came together. Aunt E——was a widow, she 'was lonely so wasn't it nice she found somebody to share an apartment with.' I didn't realize I was a lesbian until 1984. I was heterosexual as they come, homophobic as they come. I would have these great men friends, and when it got romantic, I would mess up."

At her first assignment in a small Maine town she met Winnie, who owned the Christian bookstore in town and whose husband was the minister of the adjoining church. "At the end of the first year I knew her, she told me she was a lesbian, and that was weird because she was planning on being a minister. I believed that lesbians couldn't be ministers and ministers couldn't be lesbian." Rose Mary's fears about Winnie were allayed by the fact that she was married and was resigned to staying married. "We could be friends."

Winnie did decide to leave her husband, however, and circumstance made it convenient for the women to live together one summer. "She finally told me she was in love with me, and I said, 'I don't want to deal with this. I'm straight. Let's not mess up the friendship.' Then when I came back from dropping her off at the seminary, here were flowers from the florist, and I cried. I started reading Mary Daly and all this other stuff. I'm thinking, 'I wonder . . .' Lights were beginning to dawn." For Rose Mary the rest was easy; her trauma had been "making the decision to be open to discovering whether or not I was a lesbian."

Winnie came to Rose Mary's house in Conway, New Hampshire, for fall break. "That's when I had my lesbian birthday," Rose Mary says. "It was like a huge part of the puzzle 'Who is Rose Mary?' fell into place. There was never any doubt, any guilt after that. How can I possibly feel guilty about discovering who I am?

"See, my father's main objective in bringing up his kids was— you tell the truth, you be who you are, you know what's right in your life, and that's what you do. Of course, he didn't realize . . ."

"He didn't list the exceptions," Winnie adds dryly.

"So, when I discovered I was a lesbian, my attitude was, 'Of course, I can't be in the closet.' That wouldn't be being who I was. That's just not a possibility for me."

Rose Mary chose to avoid a possible split between the churches she served and the Methodist hierarchy, which has the power to remove and assign ministers, by requesting a leave of absence beginning the following June. "If I had come out while I was still in the church as a pastor, the bishop would have said, 'Get out of there now!' In any denomination—Presbyterian, Unitarian—where the individual church does the interviewing and hiring it would have been okay to take my chances [that the congregation would have voted to retain me]."

Winnie moved in with Rose Mary in January. "It was an uncomfortable time for me. There were some nosy people in the congregation. I never actually had to lie, but I hated it."

Feminist books also influenced Rose Mary's theology. "I couldn't deal with a patriarchal, Christo-centric religion any longer. For six months I went around saying under my breath, 'They lied to me. The church lied to me. Why were they so afraid to let me make a choice? Why didn't they tell me there were other names for God? That God had a feminine identity long before a male one?'

"All the thousands of dollars and sweat and tears I put into my education and I find out it's all a crock. That I had learned to perpetuate lies. That I'd gone around telling people that's what *they* ought to believe! If I've felt any guilt in my life, it's in passing on books that propagate the fundamentalist viewpoint. I should have burned the suckers!"

In June she and Winnie moved to Portland, Maine, and she found a Unitarian Universalist church in Portland "that was a different animal altogether. They are so wide open. They have a different program every week—Native America spirituality one week . . . they just run the gamut. It felt like a warm bath."

Once she acknowledged her sexuality as lesbian, she discovered that "all of a sudden I became a second-class citizen, or less maybe. For instance, my parents were so proud I was a minister that they addressed everything they sent to 'The Rev. Ms. Denman.' As soon as I let them know I was a lesbian, 'The Rev.' was dropped. I didn't deserve to be a minister, I had nothing to give to anybody. I said to my parents, 'I'm still the same person. I still give to people the way I used to give to them.' "

In 1984 the United Methodist church passed a rule that homosexuals could not be ordained ministers. "Before, it was never an issue, because nobody came out. My bishop had said in a conversation with me in Boston, 'Rose Mary, what you don't tell me can't hurt you.' I said, 'George, you are asking me to climb into a pulpit on Sunday morning to preach truth, to ask people to live truth in their lives, climb down from that pulpit, and for six and a half days of the week live a lie. Can you see the inconsistency in that, George? Can you see the fragmentedness in that?'

"He couldn't see it. Most of the women who stay in the closet can't see how that's fragmenting. Winnie had a woman rake her over the coals for what I was doing. 'The Methodist church is not that bad, you can live in the closet and be a minister, and what's wrong with that? Your lover is going to break it open and ruin it for all of us.' They don't see the duplicity.

"If the lesbian ministers in Maine ever came out in force and the bishop had to dump them all, there would be such a shortage of clergy in Maine!"

Rose Mary's request for a third year's leave of absence to complete her transfer into the Unitarian Universalist system was denied. "The bishop's attitude was that the Book of Discipline, which is the law of the Church, said you have to be a minister in good standing to transfer from one denomination to another. 'And we can't consider you a minister in good standing, so, no, you may not have the additional year so you can transfer.' And then he said, 'Send in your ordination papers.' Throwing down the gauntlet, I wrote back, 'No, I have no intention of sending in my orders. That would be allowing the United Methodist church to tell me I wasn't a minister because I was a lesbian.' And I continued to ask for an extension of my leave of absence. That's when he filed the charges."

The Unitarian Universalist church had already agreed to accept her as an ordained minister with or without her credentials. Her defiance was an an act of conscience. "Don't you dare tell me I can't be a minister because I'm a lesbian! How dare you ask me for my ordination papers when you are the man who ordained me? I've ministered to you and your *family*! At *your* request, in *your* home. And you're telling me I'm not a minister because I'm a lesbian?"

Theoretically there are other reasons a minister may be removed. "Supposedly, you could get thrown out for messing around if you're married. But typically the minister is told, 'We're going to put you in a different church, and you keep your fly zipped up!' And it's all done very quietly and nobody knows, quote/unquote. Supposedly, you could get kicked out on heresy charges—it's been several hundred years since one of those. Mine was the first church trial in over one hundred years. And it was the first church trial of its kind—ever."

A few days before the trial began, Rose Mary attended the 1987 United Methodist Women Clergy Conference. She received a standing ovation when she spoke in the afternoon, and that evening she and three other women read aloud the words of thirty unidentified lesbian ministers—"our sisters who cannot speak for themselves."

The quotes were included in the conference record:

"I am a woman who has been in ministry for twenty-three years. I acknowledged my lesbianism to myself twenty-three years ago. I ache to be free, to be creative in my wholeness . . ."

"My congregation treats me like a princess. How kind I am. How approachable. How pretty. Kids like me. Parents like me. Grandparents adopt me. But nobody knows me. And when they do . . . ?"

"I am an elder in the Midwest, serving my third appointment. I am a good pastor—and so far back in the closet that no one can see me."

"I am an elder in full connection serving an upper-middle-class congregation. I am mostly who I am; I am partly defined by my culture and my congregation. I am female and feminine; strong and capable. I function in a largely straight and mainstream community, but I am Lesbian. When my lover died of cancer, there was no one to tell, no one to grieve with me. When a subsequent relationship ended, there was no one to give support. Now I am growing older and I often wonder where and even if I will meet someone again. The closet is silent, dark, and lonely."

As the readings continued, pockets of women rose, stood silent.

". . . I am choosing to leave . . ."

". . . I can no longer live a lie."

"My partner of four years dialogues with me when I'm preparing sermons and we also meditate together. Yet, when it comes time to give voice to my spirit with my congregation, the part of her that she shares with me is expressed with a deafening silence."

At the end of the readings the entire audience of nine hundred women were standing in a sad, silent tribute to their sister ministers.

On the final day of the conference one of the ministers asked for permission to lead the service. She spoke of her love for women, distributed what she said she believed would be the last communion of her ministry, and then laid her stole at the foot of a fountain, the Well of Hope, which had served as a theme for the conference.

The following Monday the Reverend Rose Mary Denman went to trial.

Rose Mary had asked three witnesses to speak in her defense at her trial: a theologian, an ethicist, and a biblical scholar. The judge held that their testimony had no relevance. "So here we were," Rose Mary said, "in a trial in a Church that would not allow us to talk about theology or the Bible or about ethics. All we could talk about was whether I broke church *law*. It was Pharisee-land, I'm telling you, Pharisee-land from top to bottom. The guy who brought the charges, the bishop, was the guy who chose the judge, and he's the boss of all of the people who were on the jury. They are clergy, and he's the one who appoints them to their next church.

"They were scared, but they were not intimidated. They came through."

"They came through within the guidelines," Winnie adds.

Rose Mary agrees. "No one said we will *not* put up with this bullshit. First they had to decide whether or not I was guilty. That took them forty minutes. The chairwoman stood up and said, 'We find Rose Mary Denman to be in violation of church law.' And the presiding judge said, 'Does that mean you find her guilty?' She looked at him and said, 'We find her to be in violation of church law.' 'In other words you find her guilty?' And she put her teeth together and said, 'Yesss.' Then they had to deal with the penalty. He read off the three penalties they could choose from. It was like a Chinese menu. One juror said, 'Well, couldn't we extend her leave of absence?' 'No. I gave you the three you can choose from.' He was very angry. They were gone for three hours."

Winnie groans. "Three hours."

"They finally came upstairs and they were brilliant. First they read the social gospel and said, 'We want to remind everyone here and in the Church that our social creed said that *all* people are people of sacred worth. Secondly we want to reprimand the Church for not ministering to Rose Mary in any of this.' And then they gave me the least restrictive of the three penalties."

Rose Mary is now a minister in the Unitarian Universalist church, but she says, "Who knows how long it's going to take me to find a church?" She believes 50 percent or more of the churches will not be receptive to her. While waiting, she works as an office temporary—filing, typing, answering phones; once she experienced discrimination. "I was sent to a job for three days. Midafternoon one of the people recognized who I was, went into the boss's office, and closed the door. There was a lot tittering, tee-heeing, and I was asked not to return. I called up the Human Rights Commission, and there was nothing they could do about it. Equal rights has not gone through in Maine. My boss could have come right out and said, 'You're a lesbian, we don't want you, get out!' We could have put that on a tape recorder, they could have signed an affidavit, and there is still nothing the Human Rights Commission could have done about it. Our landlady could have asked us to leave." She hasn't. "She's an old Jewish lady who doesn't understand why we're doing it, but she thinks we're wonderful."

A few days after the trial the two women were having dinner in a New Hampshire restaurant, "expecting someone to come and spill a drink on us," as Winnie says. Instead, a married couple in their early twenties came to their table and congratulated them on what they were doing.

"I have gone to a toll booth and had the kid ask, 'Aren't you Rose Mary Denman?' I say, 'Yes,' and it's 'Oh, great!' Last week when I flew in from New York, two little baby-dykes [lesbians in their late teens or early twenties] coming back from vacation in Florida recognized me. One of them approached and said, 'You're the minister, aren't you,' and shook my hand."

No strangers have been rude to her. "The only thing that is uncomfortable," Rose Mary says, "is that one of the line managers in the supermarket points me out to the people she is chatting with when I come in." Her name is still in the phone book, but outside of a few 4:00 A.M. hang-up calls at the time of the trial, she has not been harassed.

The first day Rose Mary's picture was on the front page of the *Portland Press Herald*, she asked Winnie to accompany her to the supermarket to get cigarettes. "I had no idea what would happen." As she was going through the line, "the checker looked at the paper, looked at me, and said, 'That's you. My brother's gay.' That's all she said. It has given so many people permission." Since then she has done many interviews and TV appearances.

When she speaks to United Maine Methodist groups, she tells them, " 'You invited me here, but don't sit back on your haunches and think you're wonderful. If you're not part of the solution, you're part of the problem. Don't think that because you are being neutral and letting a gay or lesbian in your door, you ought to win some kind of peace award.'

"When I spoke in Boston to a lesbian group, I called the Church a rapist. I talked about how a rapist will try to blame the victim for the incident. And here is the Church raping gays and lesbians and blaming them for the incident."

Although she believes that closeted lesbians are part of the problem, she would grant everyone their own timetable. "When I was at Boston University last week, I said, 'What do you mean, should we all come out? Some of us are not emotionally ready to come out. It would be the worst thing we could do for ourselves or anybody else. It's just not good. We each have to respond to the situation as it is best for us. Now, if we're doing it because we're chicken-shits that's different from being just not strong enough emotionally.'

Rose Mary loves the full array of clothes. "I love my jeans and sweatshirt and I love to get dressed up in a gorgeous dress, makeup, the whole nine yards."

She tells the story of a church meeting at which a woman said, "I thought if we were going to talk about 'them,' one of 'them' was going to be here." Rose Mary replied, "One of 'them' is." "Who?" "I am." The woman looked at Rose Mary in disbelief. "She wanted leather. She wanted the DA, a cigar maybe. She had this image in her head that she'd know a lesbian if one walked in. I love to break that stereotype."

Rose Mary explains that she had been prepared for being a public lesbian. "When you're a minister in a small town, everybody knows who you are, and many people don't know you as Rose Mary Denman but as 'the Methodist minister.' I already knew what it was to be singled out. There is actually less isolation with this than there was with that because I have a lot more opportunity to be with other lesbians than I had an opportunity to be with other clergy. I live with a lesbian, I didn't live with another clergy person."

"I did," Winnie mutters, "it's no fun. But then I still do—I must be specific."

"To go from everyday normal life to this might be much more of a trauma. But I had a stepping-stone. As a minister people scrutinized and commented about everything I did."

"I always wanted to be public," Winnie says, "but I had no vehicle."

Rose Mary smiles. "She loves this stuff! Sometimes I get real tired, but she doesn't. She'll say, 'You know what you ought to do next?' 'If it was me, you know what I'd do?' "

Winnie Weir grew up in Brooklyn, where life was supposed to be: graduate from high school, get a job, get married, have children. "I knew I didn't want that, but I didn't know what else to do. I was very shy, not from a very sophisticated or intelligent family. I did have two gym teachers I was in love with. I took four gym classes a day. In my senior year they both got engaged, and my heart was broken." She spent a lot of time with her best friend, and once her mother shouted in anger, "What are you, some kind of homosexual?" Winnie looked it up in the dictionary. "So I just buried that. I married because I knew a homosexual was a sick person, ostracized by society.

"After Adam was born, my husband and I didn't have any sexual contact for the next twelve years, but we slept in the same bed together." Although "a lot of ministers have affairs with their secretaries or choir directors," her husband did not. "We were good friends, we worked well together. I covered his ass when things would get rough in the Church." She wrote grants, started a Food Cupboard in Skowhegan that served hundreds of the needy. "I did the typical and then some. I had preached sermons, put services together."

Winnie lived with the knowledge and frustration of her attraction to women until "not too long ago"—she is forty-four now—she had an affair with a woman in the choir. "Alto. Oh, what a voice. I would have left my husband for her if she had been willing to leave hers." Winnie had other lovers and became acquainted with lesbian ministers.

She is very out everywhere, even at work. "At lunchtime women will be sitting around bitching and moaning about their husbands, and I'll say, 'Oh, I'm so glad I'm a lesbian.' "

At the October 1987 March for Gay and Lesbian Rights in Washington D.C., Rose Mary, as did six hundred thousand others, basked in "the unbelievable feeling of warmth and acceptance. At last we were the majority in this great town." In a Unitarian church people stood and applauded when she came forward to read Scripture. "You go to this march. You are so hyped—Oh, my God, 'My country—community—'tis of thee.' "

After the march the members of Affirmation, the lesbian group of the Methodist church, held a potluck supper. Rose Mary had been asked to give the sermon. "I felt like I had stepped into a prison where all the inmates were sitting there trying not to feel. During the dinner you could notice it, and it built. At the service it was like an invisible wall between me and them. I don't process very quickly on my feet, and I was standing there trying to give a sermon that was collapsing—whewwwww. Just missing. I knew what was wrong, but I didn't know how to address it. I should have told them this story. 'We're all in prison, but I just discovered something. The doors aren't locked from the outside. They are locked from the inside. And you have the key and I have the key. I've been out there, and I'm coming back to tell you how you can walk out of this place, because you have the key.'

"You could see in their faces, in their body language that they were so grateful for the little scraps the Church was willing to give them, that some individual ministers would *allow* them to use their buildings, that some individual churches thought that maybe homosexuals might be okay. I wanted to say, 'How dare you accept so little? How dare you settle for so little?'

"I went home angry and frustrated and sad. After that huge exhilaration—I think they saw the contrast, and although they were not able to verbalize it that night, they were feeling it. 'There we were, out there being proud, and here we're . . .' The body language was like some kid who has been whipped and whipped and whipped and is just so afraid."

Winnie adds that it is difficult to understand this about the laity, because the Methodist offical position is that the homosexual is a person of sacred worth. "But they don't want to run the risk of being known in their local congregation because of being personally shunned. A district superintendent told us that some ministers and laity believe that if homosexuality is incompatible with Christian teaching, then lay people who are homosexual should not be allowed to hold certain positions in the Church, period. Not teach church school, be on boards, hold important positions. He was surprised at that. He was surprised! I said, 'Hey, Cliff, welcome to the real world. What did you *think* you guys were doing to us?"

What, indeed. Or as Rose Mary would say, "How dare you!"

PART 4

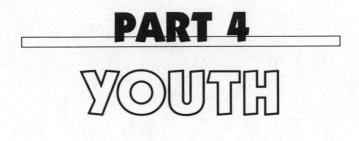

YOUTH

11. BOYS AND GIRLS ARE SUPPOSED TO BE TOGETHER

AT thirty-two Sue is an independent producer of TV commercials and owns a brownstone in Brooklyn. She and her lover, Gretchen—not her real name—occupy two floors of huge, high-ceilinged, sun-bright, uncluttered rooms. The wood floors gleam, and an air of artful taste prevails, although Sue insists that almost all the furniture and rugs have been gleaned from the Salvation Army warehouse. The garden out back is secluded, and brick walks circle winter-empty flower beds.

The setting is a fitting extension of Sue's private-school days, of a Greek-columned main building and rolling acres of lawn, of field hockey and demitasse after dinner on Thursdays.

"I did have my first experience with a girl at school when I was fourteen, in ninth grade. I remember the uproar over drug use on campus that year—1969. One girl was kicked out, one or two were suspended."

As a student Sue was unaware of the thick silence on homosexuality among private-school adults: a gym teacher's shocked whisper, "You mean unnatural acts?" a faculty turned to stone by a new dean's mention of "homosexual tendencies," the unpublicized expulsion of two girls several years before.

"I fell madly in love with Sandra Smith [not her real name]. And Sandra Smith came from a broken home. She was half Hispanic, a tough little New Yorker, born and raised in the city. Her mother was living with a male model who was years younger than she, and Sandra was dropped off at school by her mother and a band of friends—pot-smoking, drinking, freewheeling people. She and I could not have been more different."

Sue's family was living outside Washington, D.C., at the time, but shortly thereafter her father received a diplomatic appointment abroad. Being at school, away from home for the first time, "was great. Home was volatile, my mother has a temper. I was much, much closer to my father, and I think that was hard on her, created jealousies."

Both Sue and Sandra had gone steady with boys, but neither had had an experience with a girl before. "I was totally in love with her." Because Sue's roommate failed to return after Thanksgiving, she and Sandra became roommates.

"When I look back on it, we were such prudes. We never saw each other dress. I was still incredibly modest at fourteen years old. I had these tits that I didn't know I had. Rarely did Sandra and I sleep in the same bed. We would be intimate in one of our beds, and then she would go to her bed or I would go to my bed. All we did was kiss and hug. Not even French kissing! It was chaste.

"I remember being emotionally in a swoon. But I'll just add this—I did not know what an orgasm was until I was twenty-six. I was a late bloomer as far as orgasms were concerned. I remember an article in a news magazine years ago and it quoted one nineteen-year-old lesbian as saying that men are taught from the time they are babies about their sexuality, but women go through this process of finding their sexuality. I thought that was very true for me. I didn't know at all—no idea what it was all about.

"All of our classmates, I think, pretty much knew what was going on [between the two girls], but late in the spring there was quite an uproar because Nancy L——had seen Sandra and me either kissing or holding hands. I remember being incredibly defensive. I would deny that anything had been going on.

"Miss D——confronted me, and Mrs. K——was onto it. It was not a healthy relationship, because Sandra was a very depressed girl and had a lot of emotional problems. She attempted running away at least twice that I know of. There were these very melodramatic scenes of me chasing her down the back road, the rest of the class chasing after me.

"Because of the story Nancy had spread among the kids, I think I felt as though I wore a scarlet letter for a day or two, or however long. It was not a comfortable feeling. Miss D——thought it was just a rumor, and I assured her that it was. I remember Mrs. K——'s almost exact words, 'Don't let Sandra's despondency make you depressed.' I didn't know what the word *despondency* meant, so I had to go and look it up. I think Mrs. K——was savvy that there was more going on than just being good friends."

Sandra and Sue's affair lasted from Thanksgiving through the spring and into the summer. "Once away from her, I felt I really began to grow. Something clicked in my head, and I realized that although the time spent with her had been great, it was not healthy for me. She came to visit me once during the summer, and I felt very different. And as it happened, she didn't return to school because of financial problems."

Sandra Smith now lives in Queens. "She has two boys. After our relationship she took up with a man fifteen years older but has never married him. He works in construction. I went out to see her, and we reminisced, and that was it. I'm glad to know what she's doing. She told me that she felt, after our thing in ninth grade, that she knew I was gay.

"How can you know something like that? Because, frankly, I don't know that about myself. I am not that sure about my sexuality even to this day. It's like a day-to-day thing.

"I won't say there are men I find attractive. But there is a man, singular, that I find very attractive and that has caused some problems with Gretchen. He's married and lives on the West Coast. My problem is—is my fantasy better than the reality? Probably much better than the reality." Sue has slept with other men but not this particular man.

After her affair with Sandra she "felt different. I don't think I thought what I felt was *wrong*, but it troubled me. It made me feel exclusive and unique, but occasionally I sensed, 'This is not a cool thing to do.' And of course, if I hadn't felt that pressure, it wouldn't have been so hush-hush. But I did not feel shame, guilt. I grew so much that summer and came back to school feeling really good about myself. My classmates picked up on it and voted me class president."

Sue felt that "all the blind dates at school were just such stupid stuff." Before a big dance a girl would put her name and height on a sign-up sheet; the list would be sent to a private boys' school. Before the dance the girls, all gowned and scented, would line up; their names would be called and boys would come forward to claim them. "What really annoyed me was that it was so artificial. The guys only wanted to get in my pants, and it bugged me. I wanted them to get to know me.

"I regret the lack of confidence in myself to say, 'No! I don't want this!' I made out with the boys from Valley Forge in the bushes. Nothing under the clothes—I was not that kind of girl. It seemed to me most of the girls were into it. Let's get in the bushes, let's get drunk. There was only one guy I really liked. . . . I don't know, but I think dating would have been more natural in a public school.

"After ninth grade I was not involved with any other girls, although junior year an epidemic of lesbianism broke out in my class." She names two couples. "They were so open about it in the cottage! But that was after our sophomore year, when we went through six housemothers because we freaked them all out—girls huffing Carbona [cleaning fluid], cutting campus to meet guys in the Square. Drugs were a major part of '70 to '71. Everyone was wild."

"I had no feelings for any other girls. I wonder if after my experience with Sandra I decided not to do that because, even though it was great, it was not a comfortable feeling. I felt like the head-master trusted me, teachers trusted me, so I elevated myself because I had all this trust in me.

"I don't think I'd call it a crush, but I knew almost from the beginning that I cared very, very much about one of the teachers. I loved her very much. She was more a substitute mother for me because I was having a very bad time with my mother then. It wasn't a deep, emotional crush, but I knew that I felt very good when she touched me. It didn't happen often, but when she'd come over and give me a little pat, that was nice."

No girls made advances to her. "L——would come back from a date and show R——and me how she and her date had laid on top of each other, so yeah, I guess it was pretty strong stuff. Very innocent or maybe not so innocent. But there was nothing more to it. We'd all laugh and giggle, and that was it.

"If lesbianism among the teachers had been staring us in the face, I don't think we would have noticed it. We were so self-absorbed."

Although Sue is successful in a demanding business, she retains the wholesome look of a private-school girl in navy knee socks and plaid skirt. Her round eyes fix people with an open, questioning gaze, and her curly hair is short in what was once called a poodle cut. Her first sexual experience with a man occurred in her sophomore year in college. "We cared about each other. But it was like—so what's the big deal? I don't get it." She pauses, then says, "Let's fast-forward.

"It was either junior or senior year in college that I met a woman who lived in the female dorm. I was living at home. Through her I met T——, who had been living with another woman for three years, but they'd been having problems. I was interested, but very tentative. We ended up having an affair that lasted maybe a month and continued to be friends beyond that. She was so experienced, and I really didn't know what I wanted from her. But I knew I was attracted. Sex was a disaster.

"She is a brilliant woman, a poet living in San Francisco. She has not been with a woman since me, but my own judgment of her subsequent relationships is that she has not been involved with healthy men. One was a fifty-year-old alcoholic who lived in a dark room." Sue considers a society "sick" that accepts any opposite-sex relationships with at worst a shrug and shake of the head and yet places lesbians in the same category with those who commit incest, sell drugs, and rob and murder.

After graduation Sue moved to New York and dated men. She and "a very sweet guy, more of a buddy than a lover" contemplated living together.

"At twenty-seven I fell in love with another woman, a friend. A really nice hug naturally went on to become a kiss and so on. I was in love with her for a week. A week of bliss. She said she always knew that being intimate with a woman would happen in her lifetime." The other woman was, however, involved with a married man, who subsequently divorced his wife and married her.

Raised to be a good girl, a follower of rules and also perceived by others as a self-confident leader, Sue has turned her conflict inward. On the phone arranging a high-powered dinner party, she is at once gracious and decisive, but the topic of her personal life puckers her forehead with worry.

"I have never been in love with a man the way I have been in love with women. I don't know if I ever will. I tried. I felt back in high school that I had to submit to men to a point; I thought that way even as late as twenty-one or twenty-two. I didn't know I could say no, so I continued to submit unhappily. Not that I dated that many people, but always thinking men. It's just an unstated social pressure. Boys and girls are supposed to be together. That's what everyone does. I've got this internalized."

Four years ago she reluctantly agreed to house a friend of a friend from Europe for a month. Gretchen arrived. A twenty-two-year-old "very cute, bright-eyed, bushy-tailed, little tourist," as Sue describes her. Every night Sue came home to a lovely dinner and wine and an opportunity to growl about work. After a Philip Glass performance they bought his tapes and in the evenings told each other their life stories to the background of his music; Sue included her romances with women in her story.

Gretchen had had fantasies about loving women, but had never been involved; by the end of the second week she realized she was in love with Sue. The last night of her stay, as the two women relaxed over wine and a joint, Gretchen told of her days at Catholic boarding school—the frigid sponge baths, the strict rules. The tale of adolescent loneliness moved Sue to give her a hug. "A really, really good hug." After moving back to her chair she realized that it was going to take more energy to repress the desire to kiss Gretchen than to just do it. "Would you let me kiss you?" The answer was yes. Gretchen never left.

At thirteen Gretchen had been accused by her mother of lesbianism, and during her teen years her mother had opened her mail, read her journals. Gretchen's four-year relationship with Sue has been a carefully guarded secret, and in addition to that weight, and the resentment of Gretchen's family over her choosing to remain in America instead of returning to run the family business, are the immigration problems. There have been times, Sue is certain, that even a hint of lesbianism would have tipped an immigration official's decision against Gretchen. The relationship of the two women appears to operate under severe handicaps of sacrifice and societal pressure.

"I love my house," Sue says. "I like having nights at home alone or with friends. I have been to lesbian bars, but there is something so unbalanced about this whole room of women who are actively engaged in cruising each other, being physical with each other."

The first lesbian friends Gretchen and Sue had were part of the bar scene, but they have not stayed in touch with them. Most of the people they socialize with are Sue's straight business friends. "They all know about Gretchen and me. I think maybe I'm in a little more liberated business than most, but there is a company that I worked with only once—Gretchen was with me on that job. There were major logistical problems, but things worked, and everyone was saying what a great job we did. I suspect I have not been rehired there because the executive has picked up on the two of us. She's very neurotic and was threatened by us and the fact that we did such a good job. She may be a closet homosexual, although she's married."

Sue feels that living as a lesbian takes more energy, "because I still have this idea I'm not doing the right thing. Maybe there's a man out there for me somewhere, and my biological clock is ticking. Will I ever have kids? I love kids. I don't see how it's going to fit in. Gretchen wants to have a kid. I have no idea how it will work. It's not so much that I want to be married, but I've had very strong feelings for this guy, so there is this question in my mind, 'Could I fall in love with a man?' "

In his 1950s study of sexuality Afred Kinsey used a scale of 0–6. Zero represented the pure heterosexual, 6 the pure homosexual, and 3 a bisexual middle. Sue believes she is a 3, "although I think it varies from day to day. Being a bisexual opens up a possibility. Maybe there is a part of me that is a little homophobic too. Even though I'm in love with a woman—I can't even explain it really—there are so many lesbians out there that intimidate me—wow! That's an extreme, sure.

"But I don't know whether I'm saying 'bisexual' because there's a part of me that wants to keep this option open or there's a part of me that uses this to reject who I really am. If I felt more like a 6 and if I were more out with my mother and my friends, my guess is that I would enjoy the validation and enjoy having openly lesbian friends."

When Gretchen and Sue work together, which they do only occasionally, it is, as Sue says, "difficult. There is an extra weight there, an extra heaviness. There is this facade that we both present to the world that we are 'normal heterosexual women.' "

Sue describes Gretchen as "an opinionated, independent thinker who has real strong ideas about herself and what she does and doesn't want to do. I have supported her for a while—off and on. Because I was the prime breadwinner, we fell into the heterosexual husband/wife roles. She resented it and rightfully so. She's a very shrewd businesswoman, so she played a key role in negotiating with my partner [a real estate investor] about buying this building. I did not have three hundred and fifty thousand dollars, I could not have done it without her, but . . ." Sue sighs and is silent. December sunlight whitens the tall plant-filled windows.

Like Gretchen, Sue is the middle child in her family. Her older sister is now enrolled in a theological seminary. "She tells me that well over fifty percent of the women there are gay. Now that she has been confronted with women-loving women, she questions herself. It hadn't been an issue for her before except a couple times being very close to a girlfriend." Sue's younger sister is "very straight" and soon to be married.

"If I were to come out to my mother, there would be this great weight lifted, because it's like at school, I'm still not doing the right thing. So, even though I know that she knows, and there are also people at work who know . . . But if I could just say, 'I know that you know and I'm glad that you still like and accept me.' If I could just say that, it would take something away from the illicitness of it. But I've felt my mother doesn't want to hear.

"We were in this very room looking at photographs." Sue pauses, clears her throat, then continues in a husky voice. "Gretchen is sitting next to me. When I was very young, my mother gave me a ring that she was given when she was very young. Since I've become involved with Gretchen, she has worn it. When my mother's here, Gretchen always gives me the ring, but this time I completely forgot. So we're looking at pictures, and my mother looks over and says, 'Isn't that my ring?' Gretchen says yes. My sisters are also here and they are wide-eyed. They know. My mother asks, 'Why is Gretchen wearing my ring?'

"In that moment of hesitation I thought, 'She doesn't want to be told.' And the answer I gave her is so classic and so ridiculous. Like a four-year-old I said, 'Because.'

"That was it. End of the conversation. But that has not taken away the feeling that I'm doing something wrong as far as my mother is concerned. There is that pressure."

Sue would like her mother to sit down someday and say, "I know, and it's okay." "That would be nice. I'm closer now to my mother than I've ever been, and our relationship continues to get better. My sisters have gone off and gotten religion, and she's left with me—" She laughs.

Her gay daughter.

"Yes, yes."

12. THERE AREN'T ANY GAY OR LESBIAN KIDS

"I thought I was enchanted," Randon T. Eddy, a forty-year-old blond craftswoman, remembers. Not enchanted with someone, but as a person. She was seven when she had her first crush on a woman.

Randon's camp counselors might have described her as an exceptional girl—tall, athletic, creative, and in possession of special talents, and those who knew Marty Alinor—not her real name—as a young flyer might have used the same words. But enchanted?

Marty and Randon's growing-up years, which together spanned the 1920s to the early 1960s, took place in an America obsessed with science, war, and business. Society reserved its accolades for persons and activities that furthered these ends by conforming to the pragmatic "norm." This society had even, as Jonathan Ned Katz points out in *Gay/Lesbian Almanac*, "institutionalized a response to the erotic whose dominant terms were 'womanhood' and 'manhood.' " The mystical, the magical, were soft and fuzzy; they had no place in a Western industrialized nation.

In a culture that honored the enchanted person as a bridge to supernatural powers, a Marty Alinor, instead of lurking lonely and puzzled in the halls of her high school, might be acclaimed Fairy Queen in acknowledgment of her innate gift, just as the prom queen is crowned in recognition of her feminine beauty or a football player acclaimed for his manly physique. Her family, her town, would encourage the early signs with hope and awe. She would be told tales of other great women who had been enchanted in this way, been given their poetry to read, their biographies to study, been taken to sacred places where their music was played. She would be encouraged to hone her intellect and body so that one day she, too, could be honored as these women were. Her attraction toward a certain girl would have been greeted with smiles, or cautions of "suitability." The recipient of her young love would have rushed home to tell her parents that she and the enchanted girl had exchanged amethyst pinky rings.

But even though girls like Marty and Randon existed in a culture where science had become so pervasive that the aesthetics of loving were defined as healthy or sick, these enchanted girls silently, secretly, without a name for their desires, found their heroes. As they sat in their schoolrooms longing to be free of their obligatory skirts, hair ribbons, and destiny as wife, they gazed at the painting of Joan of Arc in armor, her white horse nuzzling her shoulder. Surely they felt a deeper, more spiritual connection with this fair-faced woman than any picture of a wigged George Washington or a crucified Jesus.

Judy Grahm wrote of Joan of Arc in *Another Mother Tongue*, a book that searches for the mythical roots of gay and lesbian culture. "This ceremonial office of impersonating the goat-god (in butch drag) was last acted out in the grand public manner by Joan of Arc . . . the quintessential ceremonial dyke, the warrior maid who listened to Fairy spirit voices under a sacred beech tree, who cropped her hair at age sixteen and put on men's clothing and armor." She notes that if Joan had taken the trial court's suggestion that she put on woman's dress, she probably could have saved herself from being burned at the stake—but she refused.

And how many girls felt a thrill of spiritual recognition as they studied World War II photographs of pilots like Marty Alinor, a modern Maid of Orleans in a Women's Air Force Service uniform with an airplane behind her shoulder? If the mystery of a call to serve God is accepted, as is love at first sight or an obsession to fly an airplane or paint pictures, why not the mysterious lurch of a girl's heart when she gazes at Joan of Arc or reads the Bible story of Ruth and Naomi?

As with any call to destiny the sacrifices—Joan chose death over conformity, Ruth chose loss of family and homeland to follow Naomi—become part of the glory. The young Christian is scorned by her peers, the young lover by her family, the pilot or painter by anxious traditionalists, but usually enough personal mentors and universal role models are found to sustain the determined adolescent in pursuit of her destiny. Marty and Randon, as was the wish of their culture, found no stirring biographies to read and close-to-home heroes—teachers and professors, unmarried aunts who ran farms or businesses—gave them no encouragement, only messages of celibacy; the people called lesbian they perceived as frightful male-women. The adolescent could float for only so long in that never-never land of enchantment, of crushes; then she had either to deny her destiny or to embark upon, as Simone de Beauvoir said in *The Second Sex*, "forbidden ways."

From the 1920s to the 1960s adults frequently tossed their hands in the air over this strange new period of growing up in which children had gym classes instead of farm chores or city errand-running jobs. Other parents wanted these teenagers to keep their noses to the educational grindstone so that they could "better themselves." Sexuality was cast in terms of avoiding a shotgun wedding. Homosexuality had something to do with Freud, they supposed. These attitudes persist.

"There aren't any gay or lesbian kids. Only seven in all Minnesota." Leo Treadway, a ministry associate at Saint Paul–Reformation Lutheran Church, laughs. "In a flippant way that says it all. The popular notion is that gay and lesbian people are all adults. We sort of appear at age twenty-one and die off at age thirty-five or something."

But of course, all lesbians were once kids with parents and siblings and questions about sexuality. Some of them, like Julie and Sue, actively explored with other girls; others, like Liz Pierce, "didn't have any close friends growing up because they didn't know how I felt."

Has anything changed for high school girls in the last fifty years? Women remember the year they were sixteen.

1938. Marty Alinor. "I was very mixed up. I was afraid to check *The Well of Loneliness* out of the library. Straights could, I couldn't."

1958. A Baltimore working-class girl, Geri Cox, said of looking ahead to life as a lesbian, "You didn't see anything. You lived day by day."

1971. Chrisse France, the daughter of liberal midwestern parents. "If I had had any kind of socialization or education, I would have known in high school that I was gay. When I was married, I used to lie in bed and cry and cry."

1980. Cindy, a Lawton, Oklahoma, girl. "Because my life centered around the bars, I thought that's what gay was about."

1982. Spyke. San Francisco Bay Area. "From age twelve, people backed away from me thinking I was gay. I had no role models. One me made good grades. The other me was into pot, cocaine—part of my sexual-identity confusion."

A Chicago social worker said in a *Chicago Tribune* interview,

"Society's disapproval of the gay life-style makes it almost impossible to be a gay adolescent. Everything is against these kids. There are no guidelines for normal growth. There are no positive role models, and there is little that teachers or schools can do to help students without incurring the wrath of the community." In the spring of 1988 "the wrath of the community" shook New Hampshire.

In a sex education guide for teachers called *Mutual Caring, Mutual Sharing*, the authors "made the assertion that gay and lesbian adolescents were perfectly normal and that their sexual attraction to members of the same sex was healthy."

A right-wing group spotted the heresy. The *Manchester Union Leader* trumpeted, SEX ED COURSE OK's SODOMY, NOT PARENTS.

"I'm not against sex education," a county commissioner announced, "but when teachers start telling impressionable kids if you are lesbian or homosexual, then you're all right, normal, and healthy, that's not okay. At one time they were in the closet. Just because we let them out of the closet doesn't mean we have to start glorifying them. Now they're trying to justify homosexuality as a norm in society." County funding for the Prenatal and Family Planning Clinic, which had developed the manual, was frozen.

The New Hampshire Department of Health and Human Services ordered the clinic to surrender all copies of the manual by 5:00 P.M. that same day and hand over within thirty days a list of the seventy-eight organizations that had ordered copies.

An irate Governor John Sununu asked the state attorney general to see if distribution of the manual could be blocked. "It is not the kind of document that I would like governing any kind of programs that my kids are exposed to."

Senator Gordon J. Humphrey asked for a federal investigation. "The program deserves an F. It should be expelled from New Hampshire."

The U.S. Department of Health and Human Services moved to block the clinic from distributing the manual.

A Baptist minister advocated a public burning of the manual and called for "reestablishment of the death penalty upon them [homosexuals]."

In September 1986 *The Advocate*, a national gay newsmagazine, noted, "One of the most frightening and hostile environments is, unfortunately, the place where they [gay and lesbian youth] spend the majority of their time outside the home—their schools. Even in San Francisco, where their jobs are protected by law, there are virtually no openly gay teachers." A seventeen-year-old girl was interviewed: "In Minneapolis, where she used to live, the other students at school knew she was a lesbian 'and it was horrible.' She got hit, teased and spat on. She wasn't even allowed in the girls' locker room."

The *Chicago Tribune* (May 27, 1984) quoted a Chicago public high school English teacher: "The gay students are virtually stranded; they are deserted. They lead invisible lives, the most ostracized minority. If a black child is having trouble or being harassed about being black, he can go to his black parents and talk about it. But parents are often the last people gay students can talk to."

Leo Treadway is a rare example of a person reaching out to the gay or lesbian teenager. Lesbian and Gay Youth Together, a social group consisting of boys and girls aged fourteen to twenty-one, meets in Saint Paul, Minnesota, every Sunday afternoon.

Leo, a husky, relaxed gay man in his early forties, believes that teenage lesbians are more invisible than the boys and for that reason are less impacted by homophobia. "But the down side of that is that it keeps them pretty isolated. Finding other people like themselves is a godsend.

"Both boys and girls come to the group scared to death. The girls with the additional burden of believing that this will be one more group dominated by boys, and to an extent that's true." Usually boys outnumber girls, but at half the meetings the sexes are separated. Leo has also found that these boys are quite sensitive to the issue of sexism. "They are a few notches beyond their heterosexual peers in terms of awareness. Both the boys and the girls are very nonjudgmental."

The congregation of the Saint Paul–Reformation Lutheran Church, which sponsors the group, were early advocates for black civil rights and in 1977 took a stand against the abolition of the city's gay and lesbian rights ordinance. That action attracted more gays and lesbians, but the vast majority of the five hundred members are heterosexual. Their Wingspan Ministry has been actively involved in gay and lesbian activities since 1981 and, feeling, as Leo said, "the need to work in areas where others are not," have concentrated on youth.

Five adults, two lesbians and three gay men, are advisers to the teenage steering committee and are present at every meeting. "We screen our adults very carefully. Sex is not what adult-youth relationships ought to be about."

Unless the weather is very bad or very good, twenty-five to thirty teenagers show up every Sunday year-round. The boys and girls arriving for the first time "are very nervous but clearly feel that they need to touch base with these people. You can sometimes watch magic happen in one two-hour Sunday session. Or over a

115

few sessions, you watch people go from being shy, withdrawn, to opening up and developing relationships. It's probably one of the most energizing and rewarding things I do, because the benefits are so clear.

"I have fought, literally, with other professionals who have thought the group should conform more to a therapy model, and I have argued vigorously against that. The kids don't need therapy.

"They need to meet other kids like themselves, they need a chance to be themselves, do the same groupie things that all other kids do. Fall in love and have little romances, break up and pick themselves up and go on again. That's what they need.

"Some come out of homes where there is trouble—sometimes it has to do with their identity. Some lesbian girls in the group have had very difficult times with their parents and siblings and kids at school, and others have been blessed with a more humane setting. Some are not out to their parents, some sneak to group meetings."

Coming out, according to Leo, is different now than it was for him because "today the kids in the Minneapolis–Saint Paul area can read about a vital, visible, positive gay community in the newspapers and see those people on TV. In fact, they can read about themselves in the newspaper and see themselves on TV." The adults are, however, very protective of the teens' confidentiality and individual growth patterns.

"We don't push them to be sexual or not be sexual. We let them decide who they are, whether they want to identify themselves as lesbian or bisexual or asexual. All that's okay. We place a heavy emphasis on coming out, but an equally heavy emphasis on making responsible decisions that don't get you blown out of the water."

He has found that if, in the excitement of finding out who she is, a girl comes out prematurely, "she stands a good chance of getting jettisoned from the family. It's hard for anyone to make it on their own at that age. Parents need to be there to be the glue."

He describes the meetings "as boring or as fun or as out of control as those of any other youth group I've ever been associated with. The first half hour is check-in time, see people you haven't seen for a week, and make life miserable for the adults." This is followed by programs such as "How to Defend Yourself From Queerbashers," or safe sex, or foreign gay/lesbian films. Occasionally a special event, such as horseback riding or an apartment warming for two group members who have moved in together, is arranged. Support time in small groups is always offered as an alternative so "that the kids can talk about what is going on."

Leo says that sometimes girls and boys show up who fit the stereotypes, such as boys coming in drag or makeup. "Part of that is testing themselves, part is testing the group, or the adults. They have an amazing tolerance and respect for each other. They are not particularly street kids, or more or less problematic than other kids. They are all over the place. Some drive in from small towns, some have been on their own for a while—some boys have had to hustle in order to survive. We have the stars on the athletic teams, cheerleading squad. One girl came every week not only with a different hairstyle but with a different hair color."

Leo, who prior to this job with the Wingspan Ministry had worked in crisis intervention, believes that being drawn to alcohol and drugs, being self-destructive, having to go into therapy, has "little to do with their innately being lesbian. It has more to do with the context in which they find themselves. They are at risk, not because they are lesbian but because they are trying to survive in an incredibly homophobic and violent society."

There are, according to Leo, "less than a dozen on-their-feet and stable organizations for teenagers" in the country.

A. Damien Martin, of the Institute for the Protection of Lesbian and Gay Youth in Manhattan, was quoted in the 1986 *Advocate*: "Gay youth are the most neglected members of our community, although they have the most need. The reason is that gay adults are scared to death of adolescents. They are afraid to be labeled child molesters or recruiters."

Steve Oster, a member of the board of directors for the Los Angles Triangle Project, spoke about homeless teenagers. "County foster care is not a pretty picture. Gay and lesbian youths are often unplaceable. The few who find placement are often sent back."

Greg Day, of the Larkin Street Youth Center in San Francisco, reported, "There are more than one million runaways in the country and between one thousand and two thousand youth living in the streets of San Francisco each night. A disproportionate number of these are gay and lesbian youth. We get more of these than any other city because of San Francisco's reputation as a gay mecca. There is a very high rate of medical problems among these youths. They also have a high suicide rate."

Leo spoke of boys and girls telling their stories at meetings. "Coming-out stories are part of the ritual of being gay or lesbian. Sharing the 'God, wasn't it awful.' Those stories are important in the same way it is important for the Jewish people to celebrate Passover, to remember how terrible it was. And it is important for other people to hear how tough it was, but that you survived."

Of course some don't survive.

It is Leo's belief that "the kids who kill themselves have no other resources for dealing with it and don't even know that there might be resources out there. It's like they are boxed into a corner and there is nothing else for them, and that is an incredible tragedy. They need to see something beyond where they are now. A vision for what it means to be an adult gay man or lesbian, what life can be for them. When you feel overwhelmed, you do the best you can with what you have. And sometimes that means you become chemically dependent, sometimes sexually addicted, sometimes so anxious that you get diagnosed as mentally ill. That's why it is so important for kids to know that there is a group called Gay and Lesbian Youth Together."

In September 1988 Senator Gordon J. Humphrey of New Hampshire almost succeeded in having the United States Senate pass a law stating that federal funding would be withheld from any organization that viewed homosexuality as normal and healthy.

13. RESPECTED AND HATED: CHOICES ON CAMPUS

MANY women have their first sexual experiences during their late teens and early twenties—the college years. Women-loving women are no exception. In the days when administrators acted in loco parentis and the dean of women was the final arbitrator of female morals, there were no locks on dorm room doors, and some house mothers measured to see that beds were no less than three feet apart. In many colleges residential overseers lived on each floor, "tendencies" were reported, and if a letter to the student's home from the dean requesting a psychiatric examination did not bring an acceptable response, the student was dismissed.

Julie, the teacher who in high school had intimate relationships with a boyfriend and a teammate, Kay, remembers those years. "I was excited about college because I knew there would be lots of athletes, someone with whom I could share emotional intensity in a physical way. At the end of my freshman year I was attracted to a transfer student, a junior. She had never had relations with a woman before, so again I found myself the pursuer, designing experiences that would bring her closer to me. One night I hung around her room after she had gotten into bed—her roommate was gone for the weekend. I sat down on the edge of the bed and resumed our conversation of the night before about how strongly women could feel for each other. After a while I stretched out on top of the bedspread beside her and eventually reached over and touched her hair. Finally I let my fingers caress her cheeks, her mouth. We talked for probably a half hour more with my hand resting on her shoulder. It was all very slow and gentle, and if she had not responded, I would have gone back to my room. But she did, and I stayed the night. Loving a woman's body is familiar, nonthreatening, and to me a beautiful expression of affection."

Their relationship lasted three years—the equivalent of what a heterosexual would experience with "my college boyfriend." Julie fell seriously in love with a woman when she was a senior; her college lover later married a man, a doctor, and settled into the moneyed life-style to which she was accustomed.

"In the sixties," Julie says, "it was very difficult for college students to be alone together. We took risks behind doors that would not lock. Students we knew were expelled. I was a very serious person and did have my times of agony. Usually adults—instructors with whom I felt a kinship and were probably lesbians themselves —ignored what I was trying to grapple with. Except one, who immediately set up an appointment with a psychiatrist. He turned out to be a good old boy, and I felt badly that I had degraded the feelings I knew were right. I never went back to him.

"I don't mean to imply that all college women don't do a lot of painful searching, but we who had strong feelings for women had no role models, no books, no conversation among others of like mind. We had to find everything out for ourselves."

On most campuses today the fear of disciplinary action by the administration is gone, but the woman who loves women still may experience shunning by her classmates, or hurled epithets from fraternity boys, or like Julie she may have a problem finding an adult to talk to.

The University of New Hampshire is in many ways a typical university. Old brick and ivy-covered buildings coexist with the massive dorms built in the 1960s; fraternity and sorority houses abound. Of the ten thousand students, 60 percent come from New Hampshire; less than 5 percent are minority, and the average family income is between $40,000 and $50,000.

"UNH has a homogenous environment of students," says Cathryn Adamsky, coordinator of the women's studies program. "They are not sophisticated like small liberal arts colleges, which have active gay and lesbian groups on campus. There everyone has contact with lesbians. I've heard that at some schools there are mixed dances where girls dance with girls, boys with boys, and boys with girls. Personal contact makes the difference in attitude."

Even within the university diverse student communities exist. One wing of a dormitory might be filled with bright, sensitive students to whom difference in sexual preference is not a threat, while in another wing the open lesbian would be shunned. She would not, however, be reported and dismissed from the university. According to Jan Harrow, who was once a residence director and is now the coordinator to the President's Commission on the Status of Women, "The hall directors would be fine with it because the issue is not sexual orientation, but who has been living here for four days and not paying rent. They don't care who is in bed with whom."

Jan, a lively, articulate woman who has had a long connection with UNH, describes what happened following a dorm rape in the spring of 1987. "There was widespread disapproval of the way in which punishment of the men involved was handled." In protest a number of students took over the dean's office. Other students reacted by calling them dykes and faggots. "Both men and women were screaming, 'Man-hating dykes! You're going to be next!' To be raped, they meant. It comes from fear. It's no different from the late sixties and seventies, when ROTC students yelled at protestors, 'I'll shoot your head off.' "

The following autumn two senior students, call them Sarah and Tracey, declared themselves openly lesbian in order to challenge the assumptions of other students. Sarah is an exceptionally beautiful woman in both face and carriage; Tracey is tall, warm, and wholesome. Jan describes their actions: "When they hear a slur against gays, they say, 'I'm one, do you have a problem with that?' Surprising conversations result. They are not being hassled like the gay men." Jan attributes that to the lack of a male support group equivalent to the feminist movement. "These women are feared because they challenge people. They will turn on anyone who yells, 'dyke.' Also they are very sure of who they are."

Sarah and Tracey differ from the average UNH student due to their early politicization in high school by trips to Central America. Sarah says that she came out earlier than most women because she had constantly to battle the ideas of her air force father. "The two of them," Jan says, "have declared themselves as political beings in a most blatant way. They talk about lesbianism in terms of their politics, as bisexual being the best of all worlds. But when one of them, along with four other gay men and lesbians, was fired from her job in a local restaurant, she didn't fight it because New Hampshire has no protective laws.

"When I asked them how they are viewed by the students, they replied, 'Respected and hated.' They have had fraternity men come up to them and say, 'I really respect what you are doing, but don't tell my brothers that.' "

Most college women who are discovering themselves as lesbians are hidden. Among those visible Jan sees "two groups—the out and politically active and those in athletics. The latter have parties, relationships, and boyfriends. They are into beer drinking, pickups, bars. They are not politicized and are very protective of the group. They do not want to be associated with anything that says lesbian. When I was talking to these two open lesbian students in the restaurant, I was ignored by a PE student with whom I had just talked the day before."

Cathryn Adamsky says, "A girl told me 'Just being on a team brings a charge of lesbian.' She had a homophobic male coach who was very strict about dress code, demanded the girls wear skirts, wanted 'ladylike' behavior. The girl quit the team."

In the early 1960s Julie had found no faculty member to whom she could turn. Today at UNH, Jan says, "The students are aware of lesbian faculty. They would like them to be more out in class so that gay students would not feel invisible, but they understand why they are not.

"When I was an instructor, a student decided she and I were in love. It took some time to straighten—pardon the expression—that out. There is a hunger for someone who is older and has experience, the same as with feminism. Some students come out to me now, but mainly we share political information about events, policy. There is this line they don't cross over. Other people—hall staff, counseling and testing people—deal with those issues. I never talked specifically with high school students I taught, although I emphasized, 'Be who you are.' If I run into students in bars when neither of us has been out to the other, we don't apologize. We just say, 'Hi, how you doing?' "

The vast majority of college lesbians remain invisible. They are more self-absorbed than angry and have not been introduced to concerns of political justice as have Tracey and Sarah. "People become politicized when oppression becomes personal," Jan says. "Nobody has said to them yet, 'I'm going to rip your tits off,' or denied them access, or said, 'You can't have that relationship.' They will come face to face with it when they fall in love and their family denies that relationship, when their identity as lesbian denies them employment." Jan, who is a political person herself, says, "But I don't feel helpless. These two radical students believe the mood of the late sixties is returning to campus."

The UNH Women's Student Center has always, according to both Jan and Cathryn Adamsky, been known as a lesbian hangout. "Anytime," Jan observes, "there is a collection of women without men, they are seen as man-haters or dykes 'talking about those women's things.' The way you deflate issues is to ascribe to them a label. The Women's Center has been very small the last few years, five to ten members. Students don't want to be identified as radical in these conservative times." She adds, "What would be considered radical today would have been average in '67 to '71."

Cathryn, a tenured professor whose doctorate is in clinical psychology, once met with the group, who were concerned about changing the lesbian image of the Women's Center. Cathryn told them, "When you attempt to change the image, you are complying with the stereotype." That is, if they all started wearing lipstick to prove they weren't lesbian, they would be accepting the stereotype that lesbians don't wear lipstick. Their behavior would confirm the notion that lesbians are identifiable by certain visible differences in mannerisms, behavior, and dress.

It is Cathryn's belief that "the overlap of the terms *feminism* and *lesbianism* arises spontaneously in students. Students at UNH reflect the attitudes of the general public. Because no learning occurs in the general culture, I always try to deal with the lesbian issue in class."

UNH is a conservative campus in a conservative state. However, in the fall of 1987, the Student Senate unanimously passed a resolution to add sexual orientation to the antidiscrimination clause in the student policy statement. The same rights have not been extended to staff and faculty. Jan believes that the stumbling block is the old excuse that approval of such a policy change "would stop at the board of trustees because they fear financial cuts by a conservative legislature." This attitude will be strengthened by the success of the state and federal governments in prohibiting the distribution of the teaching manual that assumes same-sex intimacies to be healthy and normal.

Of the faculty Cathryn says, "There are no out gays or lesbians except those on nontenure track," that is, those whose futures are not tied to being approved for the tenured position of professor or those who have already achieved that status. "Even though they might think they are open, at the same time nothing is open. There is a typical conspiracy of silence, tolerance for people as long as they keep quiet. No discussion. No protection. Requests for affirmative action to cover sexual preference have been ignored. There is a lot of realistic fear. Even a full professor could lose power." She explains that there are many ways a professor may be undercut while nominally retaining her position.

A double standard of awareness exists at UNH. Within the feminist community, according to Cathryn, "You know who the lesbians are—people tell you, you figure it out." But information is not passed along to those who might be hostile. This is why, even though Jan told those who interviewed her for her present position that she is a lesbian, she has heard that it is a topic at cocktail parties. "Is she or isn't she?"

"They need to try to figure it out," Jan says. "I was married so . . . The problem is feeling invisible even with people who know. They will try to set me up with dates or invite me to dinner and not include my partner.

"Students who want to know do. I read my poetry during Gay Awareness Week. I've talked [about being a lesbian] in women's studies classes. There is power in stating who you are when you're in a visible position. It would not be a wise political move to fire me on grounds of being a lesbian—I'd have the strength of the whole community of women behind me. The UNH unofficial community is a wonderful network of women who work to make things better for women on many levels. We're there for each other."

She believes, however, that her present open position is due more to her own self-confidence than to recent changes in the university environment. "Actually, not much has changed in the last ten years. There are statements about inclusion of diversity with no action behind them. The only change I can see is that now a good liberal can say *gay, lesbian, homophobia* without choking. Occasionally one can even say, 'Some of my best friends are lesbian.' " Although she had been a strong feminist for years, Jan believes her acceptance of her own lesbianism at age thirty was not a political choice. "It wasn't a choice at all, except not to be a coward anymore—that was a choice."

"I get no hassles for what I teach," Cathryn says. "A grown woman's sexuality is her own business. I have complete academic freedom and take advantage of it. I don't feel threatened. People may be more homophobic at Smith than UNH because there are more lesbian students, and to protect the school's image is very important."

Cathryn explains that in her introduction to women's studies classes "we creep up on them. For issues like race, class, lesbianism we use material by lesbians, blacks, ethnics throughout the course, then we deal with it as an issue." She will invite a half dozen lesbians to come and talk to her classes. "It totally blows away the students' stereotypes. Such an attitude change, it's unbelievable! They see real people talking about real-life experiences and hear so powerfully that it is okay for women to love women that it opens them up to combat misogyny in the culture. Not only as regards sexual preference, but the ability to love women in many ways. It frees up their boundaries. I'm always impressed how effective it is."

In the spring of 1988 such a panel was assembled by Carol Keyes, a nontenure track instructor. The two radical seniors, an English instructor, Leaf Seligman, and Jan Harrow told of their lives as lesbians. Carol, an attractive, stylish woman of thirty-eight, made sure that lesbianism was not "sanitized." She emphasized that not all lesbians are good and kind and she encouraged mention of butch/femme roles, problems in coupling, and lesbian partner battering. She says of her classes, "They know I'm a lesbian," but one of the students, in addressing the guest panel, said, "I never talked to a lesbian before." Her stereotype had proved stronger than all the signals Carol had given.

The students' concerns were revealed in their written questions to the panel. "Why is there such prejudice against bisexuals?" "I see that there is a type of 'us/them' mentality among lesbian and straight women. How do we begin to understand one another?" "Before you 'came out' and finally came to terms with the fact that you were 'different,' did you feel that you were in some way denying a large part of your identity? Did you ever 'pretend' or live a 'double life'?"

About the question "Is *dyke* a positive or a negative word?" Sarah said she loved "taking it back," that is, claiming it and making it positive. Jan said she hates it, and any correspondence that uses *dyke* lands in her wastebasket.

In reply to "What was it about being with men that you didn't like?" the panel members stated firmly that what men did or didn't do had no effect on their lesbianism. Sarah said, "Men think it is something about their sexual techniques that they can fix up, change. That has nothing to do with it. It's just that I love women."

One class member wanted to know "When you decided that you were a lesbian, how did you go about meeting other lesbians?" Jan replied, "I can't describe to you how I can tell who is a lesbian. It's just a feeling. Look at these women on the panel—you couldn't pick them out. Even we have to have some signals like short hair."

Another student questioner wrote, "Is it possible to be unsure? One of you talked about how you just knew something was wrong with your relationship with your boyfriend." Thirty-nine-year-old Jan passed around a picture of herself in her wedding gown and spoke of her years of turmoil. "I look around and see that my generation is worn out. We were raised with Doris Day and flipped hair, then came all the deaths—John Kennedy, Martin Luther King, Bobby Kennedy—then Vietnam, Watergate. We got married, we got divorced, we went through every kind of therapy available including consciousness-raising. We didn't shave our legs, we gave up lipstick, makeup. It wasn't until the mid seventies that people talked about lesbianism. We tried to make conscious choices about our lives, we got tired and we're still out there." Jan now looks very much the eighties woman in a high-necked black sweater, pinstripe slacks, big silver earrings; the short curly haircut she adopted when she came out as a lesbian is now every woman's style.

A question was addressed to one of the lesbian students: "Do you feel that the many broken relationships of your parents has influenced your decision?" The woman replied that almost everyone in the room had experienced broken relationships among parents and relatives, and they were not all lesbians.

"In my psychology class," a student wrote, "we studied Freud and Erikson and how they say children grow up. Has there been a study done that shows a child's development with gay parents as being different from a child's with heterosexual parents?" Part of Jan's answer was the observation that almost all gay children have heterosexual parents. "So how does one account for that?" she asked.

Due perhaps to the recent passage by the New Hampshire legislature of a law—the first in the nation—preventing gay men and lesbians from becoming foster parents, much of the follow-up discussion centered on the issue of children. Carol said one student commented that the panel members "would make good parents."

Another said, "Looking at those women, who wouldn't want to know them?"

Cathryn Adamsky refers to a campus survey students took about AIDS. "They found much ignorance, but that people who knew one gay were better informed. Their conclusion was a need for more education. My conclusion is: Change the atmosphere so that gays feel free to talk about who they are.

"Am I optimistic? How can you afford not to be? The positive thing is that you can teach students. They learn fast. The few who don't come to the classes where lesbians are present hear the others talk about it and are very sorry they didn't."

She paused, then summarized her philosophy. "It is so important for people to have choices."

14. JOCKS AND DYKES

MANY girls are adventurous and love running, jumping, climbing trees, exploring. They daydream of lives of challenge as pilots, cowboys, tennis stars. They would rather be delivering newspapers or mowing lawns than doing housework or baby-sitting. Sometimes these longings for physical action, encouraged in their brothers, are met with a parental list of "little girls don't." These don'ts are based on traditional assumptions. A girl may injure herself and never be able to "fulfill a woman's most satisfying role," that of mother; unsupervised girls are the sexual prey of men and boys; rough-and-tumble girls are not asked out on dates. For these girls the school gym often provides the only socially acceptable outlet.

The attitude that dainty is perfect and muscles horrifying has abated during the last decade, but the gym is still the place were girls can test their physical skills, enjoy like-minded companions, and find role models in their teachers. In high school the athlete frequently takes more pleasure in sports than in "fixing herself up" with clothes and makeup and playing subordinate to boys she feels are boorish or physically inept. She is happiest—that is, the most fully alive, the most fully herself—when she is on the playing field or having hamburgers after the game with her teammates, but she quickly learns that, unlike the male athlete, her sporting honors are basically nontransferable. They do not win her dates, or the adulation of the less skilled of her own sex, or pure parental ecstasy; they do not provide a foundation for self-esteem that bridges the gap from girlhood to womanhood, as athletics do between boyhood and manhood.

If she enrolls in college as a physical-education major, she may find classes, practices, and team schedules send her down a different track from her peers who inhabit the library, sorority houses, and weekend football parties. What they learn there she does not. Society's superficial stereotyping continues from tom-girl (*tom* in England is a substitute for *man*, as in *tom-turkey, tom-cat*), to jock (the Scottish equivalent of *man*, e.g., *jockey*—"little man"—and *jockstrap*), to dyke (mannish woman, lesbian).

Physical strength in women was not always maligned, and, for example, in rural seacoast areas the women who dig clams alongside their husbands are still proud of this fact. They split kindling and shear sheep as a matter of course, and their men are not embarrassed by this contribution to family survival. In lands where agriculture is still the economic mainstay, a strong woman is valued.

With the urbanization and suburbanization of America a woman's physical strength—even though she might perform arduous tasks—was depreciated, and after World War II her prime role became that of consumer—a spender of *his* money. She was channeled into roles that reflected dependence on men, who had in many cases been deprived of their own pride in physical prowess. The men almost en masse turned to spectator sports, vicariously embracing the traits fostered by athletics—leadership, teamwork, competitiveness, aggression, camaraderie, and physical competence. These same traits in women were viewed as not only unnecessary in the modern world but threatening.

Most women who are now in charge of America's gyms, at all levels of education, were in college in an era when to be better than a man in anything, from Ping-Pong to driving a car, was considered unwomanly. Since they were women and they were more skilled than men in many areas, this presented the dilemma of denying either their skills or their sex. Many simply withdrew to the company of like women.

Female athletes are often assumed to possess a more streamlined body, usually identified with the male, and indeed, some stars—Babe Didrikson, Martina Navratilova—are pointed out as proof of this. The remark, "Yeah, but what man would want to get into bed with them?" frequently made by both men and women, is another culturally induced reaction intended to devalue the woman unattractive by male criteria. The fact that Martina openly prefers that no man get into bed with her originally sent shock waves throughout the sporting world.

Linda, a professor at a major university in the New York metropolitan area, believes there is some correlation between body type and success in sports. "In basketball, height, broad shoulders, and small hips enable a woman to excel in this sport, which is based on a male model of skill."

Julie, a high school coach and teacher who was at one time an international-level athlete herself, thinks that the small percentage of women who have what are considered "male-type" bodies were always accepted in physical education, but they were not necessarily the most successful athletes. "Girls' schools with active athletic programs encouraged all girls in all sports, as did the women's colleges, so you found the ordinary garden-variety kid who liked to be active was on teams. It was a question of training, fitness, and coordination."

In her opinion, "The masculine image of women in physical education comes more from mannerisms than body type. Women mimic NBA male players who have refined their basketball moves, and therefore these women look 'masculine.' They adopt little-boy mannerisms, even to haircut and dress." In order to counteract this tendency, she said, her college physical education teachers "went ass over teakettle trying to make ladies of us. There was a strict dress code—only skirts in town."

Alice, the retired professor in Massachusetts, said she believed she may have gone into theater because of the freedom to wear slacks. On the playing fields, where freedom of movement is necessary, women have always been allowed more comfortable footwear and clothing. Off the field, although "only skirts in town" was the rule, the physical-education major might retain the larger, more relaxed body movements she had acquired while playing and in the field-hockey clubhouse after the games. Taylor from Spokane told of Montana women who, after a victorious softball game, came into the lesbian bar riding on each other's shoulders. This example of physical exuberance, when performed by females, sends shudders through a society that even though it no longer dotes on demure and dainty, still has its list of "women don't."

Much of the heterosexual concept of "I can spot one every time" relates to these ideas of masculine strength, masculine bodies, masculine mannerisms, and masculine clothing. A simple cultural switch—a Russian peasant woman in the fields—or a time displacement—an eighteenth-century man in silks and ruffles—shows the fallacy of this thinking.

But, of course, there are lesbian athletes and teachers. Twenty-five years after graduation four or five out of Julie's class of twenty have had an uninterrupted career in physical education. "Three of those still in the field are gay. The ones who married had other options for work—or raising families."

That it is frequently the unmarried woman who makes a career in the field of physical education further contributes to the stereotype that "all jocks are dykes and all dykes are jocks."

But what about the woman herself? What happens to a girl in the athletic environment?

Linda, who is small, neatly built, with dark hair and olive skin, by any standard an attractive woman of forty, says, "If you were aggressive on the ball field, it was fine. The other women around you were aggressive, were capable physically. In phys ed that kind of woman could be herself and be rewarded." The girl who dreamed of physical challenge and found other avenues blocked by societal expectations or male egos could do and be her best in women's sports.

Until very recently women involved in sports were isolated from men. Their teachers, coaches, teammates were all women, and because they went away on weekends and tours with teams, much of their free time was spent with women. "Male jocks and female jocks," Julie says, "have nothing in common."

Linda comments, "In teaching, if you do have contact with a man, it is a hostile one, because that man is your athletic director and he is the one telling you what to do."

"You form emotional ties with women," Julie says, "then physical ones, and if you have a positive experience, why change?"

"When I was younger," Linda says, "I played Long Island field hockey and lacrosse, and it was all women. We'd play and go out together afterward. A lot of these women are not secure in who they are because they are not the model society wants. It is much more secure for them to be with people who like them and accept them. They are not comfortable in other social situations. They don't fit. I think they are just afraid to venture out. They function safely in a very protected environment.

"At Penn State grad school, all the PE women socialized together, but it was not sexual, ever. No one wanted to admit that there were any sexual interactions. There were some, but no one ever knew about them."

Isolation from men and isolation from nonathletic women resulted in a closed-circuit life-style. And those who were lesbians were even isolated from recognizing it within their own group.

Pat Griffen, a forty-three-year-old associate professor of physical education at the University of Massachusetts, views the PE woman's insular behavior as the result of four factors. "One, they start off with a 'dumb jock' complex, even though they are not. Two, they are already breaking role expectations and are seen as masculine, therefore taking on the label of feminist/lesbian would result in stigma overload. Three, in classes they don't get the opportunity to challenge who they are. PE teachers are conservative, but even if they are feminists, they tend to focus on sport issues. The courses are oriented to telling the student 'how to do it,' so they don't get their thinking shaken up. Four, their role models maintain separate lives and tend to see incurable repression against lesbians. In college I felt I was the only lesbian at the University of Maryland."

Linda says, "It's still that way among the older women. If you don't talk about it, it doesn't exist, and you don't have to deal with it. I feel sorry because a lot of women have decided to leave out a whole part of their life because they're so fearful of loving women. The same thing existed at the University of Georgia. There's a whole group of women that doesn't want to deal with being sexual.

"In trying so hard to deny the stereotype they deny themselves. They learned how to compromise who they were with society's standards. That did not necessarily mean being 'ladies,' although that's the tack some women took, but it meant being asexual."

Linda's partner believes that "by being asexual they classify themselves as gay. It's so ironic. Everybody assumes they are gay, but it gives them peace of mind because they can deny it."

"It is," Linda says, "a double loss. I do think there are women who have experimented with being gay who are really bisexual and are intimidated to go with men. There are women who may be closeted heterosexuals. They have tried the gay life and are really not gay, but are—I've seen this—ostracized by the gay society for stepping across the boundaries. When you are gay, you want everyone else to be gay. I think it has to do with how secure you are in your sexuality, and there are a lot of women who are not, they're still torn. So, to prove that they are okay, it's better if everyone is gay." Even if they are not.

Julie, however, believes that if a woman is heterosexual, her instincts would take her that way. She tells of PE majors who had sexual experiences with women and then went on to marry and have children—"for whatever reason." She does, however, agree that asexuality is prevalent. "Education lays it on a teacher to be a prime example of society's morals. Women especially. So they tend to put sex aside." There is also the assumption that if a teacher were lesbian, she would be seducing her students.

Both Julie and Linda agree that women's sports have changed a lot since the 1950s. Title IX has given the girls in public school the same encouragement that once was enjoyed only by the students in private schools. More emphasis on fitness and dance brings a greater variety of girls into the expanding field. And high school boys, according to Julie, now accept the more athletic girls.

Among the physical-education teachers and coaches, however, there has been little change. "I think," Linda says, "a lot of women are fearful and appear fearful of having the gay issue used against them. And it has been used. The men use it to control women's sports. How do you stop a woman coach? You just throw out a rumor that she's gay and she's got to spend the rest of her energy denying it. The worst fear of a woman coach is to be accused of being gay or that her athletes are gay. Then, all of a sudden the issue shifts from women's sports and who should get the money, or this is a winning coach and should she be promoted to athletic director; it now becomes, 'Is she gay?' "

The increasing number of men who coach women's teams may also be affected by fears of their athletes being perceived as lesbians; they may impose dress codes and develop homophobic attitudes. And lesbians themselves are part of the problem.

It is Linda's belief that "gay women can be their own worst enemies. This getting other women who are gay came out of the older culture, when everyone thought they were sick. When women get scorned, when they think they are bad because they are gay, they strike back. I know of a woman in my undergraduate college who was asexual—and should have been gay. She felt she was holier than another woman who she knew was gay, so she ratted on her and got her thrown out of school. This was 1965."

In many places across the country lesbians note that they have no contact with the local college PE women, and in contrast to NOW and women's-studies conferences, where there is open and active involvement of lesbians, the world of PE has remained that of the "highly developed false front." For the past few years Pat Griffen, an attractive, tailored woman with red-blond hair and keen blue eyes, has been trying to peel away some of the fear and hypocrisy.

In 1983 she attended a sports conference and sat on a panel entitled "How Can a Woman Athlete Deflect Threats to Femininity?" At one point during the discussion she said flatly, "It's the wrong question." That was the first time she had spoken out on lesbianism and sports. Subsequently she planned how to bring the subject openly to the annual conference of the American Alliance for Health, Physical Education, Recreation, and Dance, which attracts men and women from all grade levels and all fields.

According to Pat, "Some individual courageous women have

made statements there, but there had never been a whole program devoted to lesbianism." Her proposal for a workshop was accepted for the 1987 conference. "It was the first time the words *lesbian, gay, homophobia* have ever appeared in the conference program." The panel of two men and two women was scheduled for the last day, the last time slot. "We thought no one would come. There was standing room only—almost entirely women. When Sherry and I came out as we talked, it was empowering for some, very scary for others."

At the 1988 conference, when she and a straight man who has a gay son did a homophobia workshop, more people wanted to attend than could be accommodated. "I do have a sense," Pat says, "of breaking ground and am thrilled and proud about it. Other times I hear someone say *lesbian* and feel vulnerable. I go back and forth between those powerful feelings. I have a real identification with women who are scared. I feel sad for the cost of who they might have been."

Linda is excited about what Pat Griffen is doing. She herself has been trying to bridge the traditional gap between the lesbian professor and her students. "Most of my students," she says, "have no problem at all—they just come out. It's okay to be gay. They don't go through this feeling of being 'sick,' having trouble—some of them do—but a lot of them just say, 'I'm gay, so what.' It's not real open, but it seems to be okay among their classmates.

"I wear a lambda." Linda motions to her ear, which is pierced twice. The second earring is a small silver λ, a Greek letter that is an ancient symbol of homosexuality. "I want the gay students to see me as their professor, not hiding. Most of the kids who come to me know they are gay and just need to talk about other things. Because I'm so comfortable, I tend to threaten someone who is in the middle of deciding. I don't know if they have anywhere to go. Some women would try to convince them to be straight because they have had uncomfortable experiences with being gay. 'Don't do this life-style because you are going to be unhappy.' But the kid may not be unhappy—it's just because the other person couldn't accept their life-style.

"One woman came to talk to me about her parents treating her differently than her brother, and in order to explain the problem she had to tell me she was gay. Now, because she knew I was gay, she could tell me her other story. Whereas if she had gone to somebody else, it would have been an admission of being gay, and then that would have been the issue. But her concern was that her parents were mistreating her. She could feel comfortable that I was not going to make her being gay the focus."

Linda handles a student crush by not acknowledging it. "It's a professional distance. Even if I walk into a bar, I let them know that 'Yes, I'll say hello, but I'll go off with my friends and you go off with your friends. Just because we're both gay doesn't mean I have to be your friend.' I really don't want to socialize with my students. Most of them respect that. Only once did I walk in where one of my students was drunk and she stood up on top of the table and shouted, 'My teacher's here! My professor's here! Look at that!' "

Before meeting the activist women at the University of Georgia, Linda was not aware of the political issues of being a lesbian. One of them gave her the lambda. "I think I never knew who I was. I thought I was always so wimpy, and then when I realized that 'I'm a strong woman,' I just continued wearing it. If someone at the university asked me if I were gay, I would say, 'Is this relevant to something I do?' If you want to ask me about my sexuality, you don't ask me if I'm gay or not, you ask me, 'Do I go out with my students? Do I take advantage of my students if they are physically attracted?' This is a question they have a right to ask anybody. But to ask me if I'm gay or straight has no relevance.

"I know there are some gay women who, when asked if they are gay, would love to turn it around and ask, 'Does your wife swallow your semen?' That's about as personal. Ask the same question of the men who intimidate the women students, ask whether they get sexual favors or not. There are men who go out with their students. They're straight, they don't have to account for it. So I think if someone whom I didn't want to know my private life asked me, I would say, 'You can ask me a relevant question.' Nobody really has.

"I feel very differently from the women who have to be in the closet. I got past that phase—they never got through it."

Linda and Pat are young, but hold established positions in respected universities. Perhaps they and women like them will, by disassembling the facade, also disassemble the fears and fictions that surround and permeate the subject of jocks and dykes.

PART 5

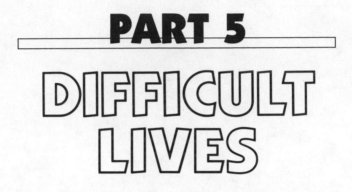

DIFFICULT LIVES

15. SOME SAFE PLACE

"PEOPLE go through life and try to purchase security. You can't do it. Pick any area—there's no safety."

Mary Morell is forty-two, but ageless in the way of heavy, round-faced women; a smile belies her blunt words. "My father raped me at three. Mother will be pissed to see that in print, but that's the breaks. [The sexual abuse] lasted from three until twelve. When I was thirty-five and my father was dying, he apologized. I was terrified when he told me, but it was better than the nothing. I had had no memory of it happening. No childhood memories at all. I thought remembering things like your first day at school was a talent—like having perfect pitch. From thirteen to thirty-five I was clinically depressed. Yes, clinically depressed means suicidal."

Many people have difficult lives. Their problems are usually stated in terms of individual acts, but cultural permission—however unexamined and overtly denied—provides the milieu. The victims are forced to make sense out of a senseless culture. They must take the givens and move them around in order to survive.

"At one point gender confusion would have been a stated cause of suicide for me. But in reality the cause would have been incest. I had no hooks for my feelings because of it. A teenager might say lesbianism was the reason for suicidal thoughts, but some giant black hole had happened before puberty.

"I certainly wasn't safe at home. Then in high school a close friend of mine was raped and murdered on Easter Sunday. She was perfect in everything, and what did she get for it? There is no purpose to living thinking there isn't some safe place."

Mary was raised in a small town in Texas in a "heavily Catholic" family; two uncles and a brother were priests. "I came out my freshman year in college, and I had a priest who refused to forgive my sins in confession because of lesbianism. That is devastating. Played loony tunes in my head."

Humor is Mary's buffer. "My college honey and I decided that since what we were doing was sinful, we would put gold stars on days we didn't have sex. We ran out of all other stars in the box before we ran out of gold."

After graduation Mary was a teacher and then an administrator. At twenty-five she reported a man who was violating university rules in order to get his doctorate; he in turn attacked her as a lesbian. "The boss called me in and said, 'I want you to know that you are the best person we've ever had in this position and you will want to resign.'

"It is my belief that the most dangerous enemy is a short, closeted male. It makes them very defensive, and he was obviously homophobic. It was a vicious case. A hate campaign that was very effective. I found out later that my boss was gay and terrified of the attention—he wanted me gone. He told me I could go alone or take my lesbian friends with me. There was no protection for an administrator, no union, no faculty backing."

At thirty-seven, two years after her father had told her about the years of incest, Mary went to a feminist therapist. "She seduced me. She swears it's the other way around, but in any case she just didn't have good boundaries. Pick any area—there's no safety."

Mary, who has lived in New Mexico for twenty years, enjoys talking about Albuquerque—"in the seventies this town had romping, stomping, no T-shirt, ball-busting dykes." She and her partner, Anne, have owned the Full Circle Bookstore for three years. She loves the work, but jokes, "In another couple years we'll be up to the salaries of first-year elementary school teachers. It's exhausting work. We are a resource center for all questions from AI [artificial insemination] to AIDS."

The power structures that define our culture—the patriarchical family, the Church, the workplace, even the new religion of therapy—violated Mary sexually, spiritually, economically, and emotionally. Men and heterosexual woman are not immune from these assaults, but lesbians carry the added weight of being "not normal." Whether this is a cause of, a result of, or irrelevant to other traumas has been much debated.

Frances Selden is very different from laugh-a-minute Mary. Her gaze is intense; white scars mark her arms and a strange smooth depression in the middle of her forehead; she speaks slowly, carefully. "I was admitted to a state hospital at seventeen." She describes the therapist to whom she was assigned as "Freudian—old school. He encouraged unhealthy behavior, encouraged me not to socialize, to stay by myself. He blamed my mother for my problems. I have always been very close to my parents, and that put a communication barrier between us."

Frances, who is now thirty-seven, had her first sexual experience at seventeen in the state hospital. "With a woman. It was very positive. I told a priest, and he said, 'That's natural for these conditions.' "

If she and her therapist ever discussed the possibility of her being a lesbian, Frances can't remember it; many memories are hazy because of drugs, her illness, and shock treatments. Of the latter she says, "They were abused and no good. Only if a person was in really bad shape were they good. There are many abuses going on in the system. Psychosurgery [lobotomy] is really bad."

At twenty-one Frances, out of the hospital and a student at the university, met a woman in group therapy "to whom I wanted to relate. I wanted to save her from all her bad heterosexual experiences. We had a good, loving relationship."

She told one of her male professors about the affair. "I didn't know this would be dangerous for me." She pauses, then continues, dragging the words up from deep inside. "Our relationship began with sexual assault. Then more sex to 'straighten' me out. I took a steam iron to my leg. I was hospitalized and given shock.

"The whole thing with him made me feel like a nonsexual being. Delayed my coming-out process. I couldn't see myself as a sexual being at all—too painful. I thought that if I ever decided to be sexual, I would be a lesbian, but I had no place to work things out. To work through the shame of that heterosexual experience."

Frances was never "committed"; she always signed herself in and out of the hospital. "For nine years my whole life was directed by that same therapist." When in the state hospital she saw the therapist, to whom she had been assigned at seventeen, every day and when outside, once a week. "He guessed I was in a relationship [with a married man, her professor] and he encouraged it. The last time I saw him, we had a nasty argument, and he threw out many things like, 'By the way, I've had lesbian clients.' But he had kept me closeted all those years.

"Society's rules were very bad in that I felt I couldn't tell my mother. Was not allowed to say certain things. I was so blocked." Frances's mother died eight years ago. "When she died, I got in touch with my abuse and got angry. I think my mother would have accepted [my lesbianism]. I told my father last Christmas, and he said, 'You're still my daughter, and I love you.'

"But I had never really talked to anyone. Traditional therapy gave no leeway for choices. I didn't have the courage to have it affirmed." At twenty-nine Frances "checked out many therapists until I found this feminist one. When I came out as a lesbian, I was aware of myself as a person for the first time."

Since then Frances has not been hospitalized. Many factors or combinations of them might account for this: her mother's death, finding her own identity, the right balance of drugs to keep her stable, her new therapist, or simply aging. The drugs make a perceptible difference in the slowness of Frances's movements and speech; in high school it had been worse. "They used to have to wake me up to finish taking a test." Now she views these medications "the way a diabetic would."

Frances has an IQ of 136; her dyslexia was never diagnosed until a few years ago when she entered the University of Minnesota. After graduation she plans to study for a master's degree in psychology. "I have a lot of goals. I would like to do something for the homeless who have been turned out of state hospitals, or in feminist therapy for women in a college setting."

Dyslexia, mental instability, lesbianism were all considered shameful and deviant during the years Frances was growing up. The suffering imposed by these attitudes cannot be undone, and to specify their varying effects on Frances is probably impossible. There is, however, a direct correlation between society's view of same-sex attraction as abnormal and the "sexual therapy" administered by her professor and the years of repression encouraged by her therapist. When a group is seen as not fully human, as has been documented in instances of war, slavery, and prison camps, license is given to the dominant group to commit what would be in other circumstances unthinkable cruelty. That Frances survived is evidence of her stubborn courage.

Freud believed trauma caused lesbianism. His followers might point to Mary and Frances to indicate the correctness of his theory. Others, however, might postulate that wariness of males after ten years of abuse by one's father or after sexual assault by a professor is a prudent and healthy response and that behaving otherwise would indicate an unhealthy capacity for masochism.

Sarah Pearlman, the Boston therapist, says, "In clinical practice you see a higher incidence of abuse and incest among lesbians. It may be that because becoming gay has prompted such a high degree of introspection that they recall early memories better than heterosexual women. Or it may be that more lesbians seek help. We don't know.

"If you have a bisexual potential and you've had a pretty lousy experience with a man, it's enough to tip you toward the sex that's safer. And to tell the truth, that's healthy and smart, better than the compulsive heterosexual who just repeats and repeats and repeats getting abused by men. I don't look at a higher incidence of lesbianism among abused women as pathology, I think it's very adaptive. Incest is just an awful thing, and worse for lesbians because it makes them feel even more 'not normal.' "

Abuse may well be a factor in determining the gender of the person with whom the woman feels safe in intimate, vulnerable situations, but not all lesbians have been abused, nor, as is well documented, have all heterosexual women escaped abuse.

In the summer of 1988 a study based on extensive questionnaires from two thousand lesbians was released. Judith Bradford, a co-author and clinical psychologist at Virginia Commonwealth University, said, "Our data challenge some stereotypes, such as the belief that some women 'escape to lesbianism' because of early sexual trauma with men." The numbers of lesbians reporting sexual abuse did not, the authors say, "seem to diverge significantly from heterosexual women."

Taylor in Spokane said, "I could drive myself crazy trying to figure out if I would be with men if I had not been raped." Rather than concentrating on examining the aftereffects of abuse, it would benefit society more if researchers studied the question of why certain men have a propensity for attacking their own female children, nieces, neighbors, and/or children placed under their protection. And what to do about it.

Mary's and Taylor's childhood abuse was not initiated by their lesbianism but by their being born female. Frances was assaulted by a man because she revealed her attraction for women; Taylor was propositioned by her college roommate's father for the same reason. Clearly in all these examples, unless one assumes that males have no control over their sexual behavior, it is they, not their victims, who should be "cured." To regard male heterosexual desires as *ipso facto* a standard to which others must adjust is a cultural norm in need of examination.

Incest and rape are not, however, at the core of all difficult lives.

"My parents told me that someday on my way home from elementary school the path would be lined with soldiers. That was how I would know the revolution had begun. We had a plan—

where to meet, what to do. I was sworn to secrecy. At twelve I was taught to shoot a 33-gauge shotgun, which I was told I might have to use on the neighbors. The John Birch Society was big-time garbage—involvement with the KKK, machine guns, you name it, they had it."

Diane, an open-faced women with a genuine smile, was raised in rural Ohio, the land of tall, stark houses framed by fields of corn.

"My father was a violent man—his father had gone into the coal mines at age nine—and hitting a child who happened to be in his way seemed normal to him. He had been the youngest in a very poor family and was raised with a rigid German work ethic. He trusted no one, certainly not churches and schools, although he was an engineer himself. He felt that there was a great conspiracy— communists everywhere making things go wrong for him.

"I got back at my parents' strictness—no music on the radio, no cards—by being promiscuous, starting in junior high. I was a popular bad girl and thought I was having a good time. My parents only caught me once. I cut school, and my father—he had been fired again—was home when the office called. My punishment was that when I came home the next day, my dog, to whom I had told everything, was gone. I thought about suicide all the time.

"As a teenager I was involved with a conservative political group and, like my father, believed that English and social studies teachers were suspect—my grades, except science, were not good. My guidance counselor told me to take a secretarial course in the community college, said I'd be lucky to make it through that."

Diane survived her mother's mental breakdown, an extremely dependent relationship with her best girlfriend and her poverty-stricken family, a wild sexual affair with that friend and her woman lover, and a boyfriend who had had his hand cut off in an accident and who kept hassling her to marry him and have babies.

When she switched from the community college to Kent State as a business student, she discovered sociology and changed her major. Her family disowned her, her father shouting, "I won't have any Commie-Pinkos in this family!" Since then the money for Diane's schooling has come out of her own pocket. At thirty-six she is completing her medical residency and plans on specializing in psychiatry.

"I'm choosing psychiatry because I feel most psychiatrists can't relate well to women patients."

And to provide at least one safe place.

16. COPING WITH RELIGION

MORAL attitudes about sexuality have long been the province of churches. They have governed, in either specific detail (how many Hail Mary's for what) or in lofty abstraction ("That's an "abomination in the sight of the Lord!"), what is acceptable or unacceptable behavior, what is praiseworthy and what is sinful, what brings heaven or hell.

How does the young lesbian, raised to love her family and obey God—the omnipresent, omnipotent arbitrator of life—cope with the conflict between these forces and who she believes she is?

Lil Cardwell is thirty-three, self-employed, and head of Common Knowledge, a Santa Fe women's resource center. She was raised in a Mormon family in Salt Lake City and describes her growing-up years as "very well protected, very innocent." At eighteen she received her patrimonial blessing from the church fathers. "They tell you your heritage and where your life will go, your trials and tribulations. They put oil on your head and have a vision for you. They said I would have problems with drugs, sex, and rock and roll, but eventually be married, have children, and be sealed to the family forever."

At twenty Lil left to do missionary work for the Mormons. "I didn't know I had any feelings for women until I came back and met a sweet young thing. I lived with her for a year and a half." This secret for which Lil had no name separated her from intimacy with her church and family, the two most important elements in her life. So in 1976, when she was twenty-two and the affair was over, Lil went to the church leaders and told them. "They said, 'It's called lesbianism!' " The Quorum of Men, twelve in number, reviewed the circumstances, and Lil was not merely disfellowed but excommunicated. She felt enormous guilt.

"They call excommunication a form of repentance. You have to forgive yourself, which is the first step in repentance, which will eventually lead you back to the Church. They were very brutal to me. Asked very specific physical details of what I had done, how many fingers I had used to penetrate her. I said, 'None of your business.' They said it has everything to do with your repentance. They would type it all up so that I could see it later and know how awful I had been.

"I was sincere about changing, so they put me into therapy. If you want to be cured, you go through shock treatment. They show you film clips. They monitor your brain waves, and when you react to lesbian and gay scenes, they shock you through your fingertips and armpits. It's enough of a shock to make you think!

"A month was all I stayed in therapy. I decided I needed to make a decision for myself. Was I a Mormon or what? When I decided I was not, a peace came over me. Not riding the fence anymore. I came out to myself, and there was no more guilt. I just boxed the rest up and threw it out the window to be forever done with it.

"My second relationship lasted five years—she left me. Moved out, then came back three months later. I said, 'I'm gone.' My family came and took me home, set ground rules, thought they had a second chance to reform me. They think it's a disease that can be cured. After three months I said, 'I'm thirty. I'm old enough to do what I want to do.' I moved to New Mexico."

Lil, a short, heavy, blond woman, spoke about her work with Common Knowledge in a brisk, businesslike manner. And although telling the story of the Mormon church fathers aroused her emotions, her chin stayed stubborn and firm until she came to December of 1984.

"My family was going to the mountains skiing over Christmas. They said they would stop and pick me up Christmas Eve. I bought presents and wrapped them, got my bags packed, and had my skis standing in the hallway. I waited and waited. They never came."

Lil's partner, Marcia Martimatz, sitting silently on the couch beside her, gradually moves closer until her shoulder and arm form a support for Lil to lean against.

"Ten days after Christmas—when they had gotten back—I finally had the guts to call. 'Well,' my mother said, 'I decided not to go, and the others just forgot.' Two brothers and a sister and a father were in the car. Mother had stayed home. She said, 'They *forgot* to stop.' I boxed up the Christmas presents and basically told them to have a nice life. I've never heard another word. It's like I don't exist anymore." Her voice breaks.

Marcia squeezes Lil's hands and says, "It was very hard on her."

Lil explained: "Mormons believe the mother, father, and children are all bonded. There are three kingdoms after death, and the top is Celestial Union, with all the family together." She believes that in one sense her family's anger with her is due to their belief that she has hindered their chances of attaining this top kingdom.

Maria Martimatz is Mexican American, and her face with its rectangular eyes, broad cheeks, and flat nose remained impassive while Lil talked. Now she speaks quietly in carefully considered, precisely grammatical sentences. Raised in Santa Fe by Catholic blue-collar parents who strongly believed in education and were willing to make great financial sacrifices for their daughters, Maria and her two sisters achieved the high grades required for admission to Loretto Academy. Maria graduated from the Academy in the top academic group and joined the Sisters of Loretto, an order of teachers, therapists, professors, psychiatrists, and other professionals.

"I wanted to go into the convent, wanted to be a teacher, but I had a terrible time with my own identity. I had all these feelings for these women there." She laughs, and the image of a happy woman emerges.

"Sexuality became an either/or thing. It was very, very hard to accept church rulings *and* my own feelings. If I hadn't taken the time to investigate my own life at that time, I might have gone insane. My mind was blurry. I couldn't think straight. It was an individual guilt trip. Until you are taught differently it is hard to change ideas that you have grown up with. I couldn't find anyone to support me."

Maria was in the convent during the late 1960s. "The whole world was changing direction. The Sisters of Loretto were active— but not in lesbian rights." Again the hearty laugh. "Closeness was called 'particular friendship,' and the nuns in charge were against them because they wanted you to go from state to state in a community spirit."

Maria is not merely guessing that the "particular friendships" were sexual. "I *know* that some nuns were lesbians. We had encounter groups. All secret. We weren't supposed to talk after ten P.M. We'd put a towel under the door and open the window for smoke. Only a few very special young people were invited. The nuns told of lesbian experiences. Imagine a protected young person coming out of high school hearing this! I was so innocent, had no knowledge of worldly things. The very open discussions were a shock to me. We had to protect each other. No one ever knew."

Maria loved being with the Sisters of Loretto, but she could not accept being a lesbian within the context of the convent, nor could she reject her own sexuality. "The more experienced could deal with it because they had lived as women. I hadn't gotten to that point yet. I was not flexible. They could do it without guilt, believing that God would understand. I couldn't." Unable to compromise, she left for San Francisco with lesbian friends. She did not even tell her parents she was going.

At thirty-eight Maria is a very successful professional who wishes society would "just accept us as friendly little people with smiley faces. We just happen to love women. They see us as separate from their norm. That is not necessarily their fault, they have been raised to believe that way. We should just move forward and educate as many of them as we can and ignore the others."

All the time Maria talked, her hands held Lil's. "But," she says, "I don't think our quest will end for a long time." Lil nods.

"When I woke up in the morning, the Christian radio stations were playing, and I never heard any other kind of music except outside the house." Glasses give Vanessa's pleasant chocolate-colored face a shy, studious appearance, but her movements flow with an athlete's grace. Her smile is wide when she calls herself an upwardly mobile child living on the west side of a city among "the blacks who had grown up on the east side, who were educated and wanted to move a little way toward suburbia."

Although Vanessa, now thirty-one, was an only child, foster children, day care children, and relatives from the east side filled the house. Her father, twenty years older than her mother, retired when she was in junior high. "He did side jobs, different in the different seasons. He also had a pension."

In high school Vanessa—not her real name—concentrated on sports and religion; she didn't date much. "I had always heard negative things about boys. There was always that fear that you might become pregnant."

Her parents, both born-again Christians, didn't agree on ministers, so her father went to one black church and she and her mother went to another. At thirteen a summer camp introduced her to the white people's type of religion: "Not being so emotional, being more intellectual, studying things." When she returned home, she went to an interracial Presbyterian church, and her mother joined her.

Vanessa followed her high school patterns at Messiah, a white church college, and stayed away from the non-Christians, who partied and drank. "I figured all that other stuff [boyfriends] would come later. People studied the Bible and they were in church and they started dating each other and they got married and had this nice family unit and brought their kids up in the Church, and maybe I was going to marry a minister or a missionary and we were going to serve the Lord for the rest of our lives." She pauses.

"Then my senior year I met this woman. At college. At Messiah. We spent a lot of time together, became physical with each other, but never said we were lesbians or said that we were branching out into something. The one time we discussed it, we just decided that neither one of us had ever had a close friend, so this must be how best friends behave with each other. No one had come right out and said it was wrong, because no one talked about it. We knew homosexuality was an abomination before the Lord, but what we were doing was not homosexual. We were just best friends, although we planned a life together just like a marriage." Their closeness lasted through Vanessa's senior year and beyond because she had taken a position at a nearby Christian center for high school students.

When Vanessa's father died, she came home to live with her mother and to see how she could manage in "the real world." She went to work for the YWCA believing it was a fundamentalist Christian organization, and when she discovered differently, she thought she "had this mission to save these people, enlighten them, witness to them. It impressed me that they didn't put me down for believing differently than they did." Vanessa channeled her energy into working out and racketball; she became state champion.

"I began to question my sexuality. Whoever I was going to be, I was not going to find that out if I stayed at home." She moved in with friends, a lesbian couple. She had no serious relationships —"a few couple-weekers here and there"—before she met the woman, call her Ruth, who sits beside her. Vanessa has been with Ruth "in some kind of relationship" for six years. For the first two years they did not have a primary relationship with each other, but rather "a nonmonogamous affair." Next they lived together in a sexually exclusive relationship for three years, but never made a marriage-type commitment. Then the issue of monogamy arose. They agreed to live apart, to have their own homes, but the twenty-minute drive between their houses "became a real pain," Vanessa explains. "And we had joint custody of a dog. But we weren't ready to make some sort of commitment, so . . ." For a year they have rented separate houses on the same block.

Vanessa told her mother she was lesbian several years ago. "She was devastated. She said, 'You're my daughter. I love you no matter what. But what you're doing is wrong. It's against Scripture. I can never condone it.' It's a constant war, in the sense that my mother is still around. Whenever I see her, or am with her, she always throws something in there.

"I know it's a sin. I've chosen not to deal with it. I've chosen this life-style knowing what I grew up with."

Ruth, thin and white beside Vanessa's firm brownness, adds, "And knowing what that means for your soul. Not really integrating it. Sometimes I think people are never able to square it with their original values and yet make a decision to do it regardless."

When the barriers between the compartments of Vanessa's mind slip and she feels guilt, she withdraws for a while. "I become quiet, very isolated. Work it out, think. Then decide, 'This is my life. This is what I've chosen. Basically I'm a good person.' Basically the values I learned from the Church I believe in, respecting people for who they are, what they are. Being able to understand, be flexible. A lot of fundamentalists aren't." She talks about Jerry Falwell and the others who base everything on Scripture; she, however, has not searched the Bible to see whether it condemns her life-style or not, because "I was indoctrinated really well. You have to allow the Holy Spirit to interpret Scripture for you. So I can't read it and come to a different conclusion, because that's man's conclusion and that's wrong. So I can't even do that."

Sometimes she wishes she had never heard of the Church, and Ruth mutters, "Or the reverse, that you'd never left."

Vanessa's voice is very soft when she says that it is the secrecy that hurts the most. "The lack of being able to be honest about your life."

"It's not that simple," Ruth interjects. "It's the way you have to integrate that internally. The way it makes you think about yourself."

Vanessa, who works for a construction company, says her life can never be totally open. "God, I wouldn't be able to work! I'm the only woman out in the field supervising men. People can be very cruel. I don't want to deal with it in a male-dominated sphere. I think that's part of choosing the life-style. You choose that part of it also."

Ruth, who is a closeted lawyer, says, "I think about the days going into work just feeling rotten because of things that are going on at home, and you can't even say to somebody, 'I'm upset because Vanessa moved out last night.' "

"Or 'Ruth and I had a fight and we weren't speaking to each

other this morning.' There's none of that. You come in and you feel terrible and you look terrible, but you go on. You act like there's nothing wrong."

"It's the way it is. It's probably one of the bad parts of our personalities—whatever comes, comes. We could probably spend fifteen years in psychotherapy trying to figure out our anger."

"Being lesbian I can control, I can't hide being black. Whatever they do, I have to put up with it. I've paid my dues to racial prejudice. People can be very cruel. There are enough other things I have to deal with without lesbianism."

Ruth will not excuse people on the grounds of ignorance. "It's hostility! People hate black people just because they're black. There's *nothing* to hate them for, but they do. I think it's the same thing for gay people. I think that's the nature of real prejudice. Real prejudice isn't just ignorance."

Lil tried very hard to remain within her Church and family, but finally boxed those feelings up and "threw them out the window." Vanessa coexists with diametrically opposed beliefs. Another young woman, Elizabeth Conner, chose a different path.

Elizabeth is a cheerful, blue-eyed Norwegian blonde from Minnesota. Her family was deeply involved with the Lutheran church, and her father constantly searched for spiritual connections; at one point he had the entire family attending Silva Mind Control sessions.

As the oldest daughter Elizabeth felt pressure to be perfect from what she believed was the perfect family. In high school she was not invited to the parties of her theater group because "I was too square, although they all loved me and I ended up with lead roles. The spoof award they gave me was Miss Perfect—spelled wrong." She went on to major in theater at Augsburg and St. Olaf's. "Theater and music, feeling centered things, especially the piano, were what I loved."

As soon as Elizabeth realized she was attracted to women—she had at eighteen fallen in love with a girl she met at a summer Lutheran retreat—she told her parents. Then at nineteen, disturbed over the death of a gay man at college, she attempted to talk to them about the politics of being gay. "My father told me point-blank that it was not appropriate to talk about this part of myself, that they did not want to hear it. 'We don't want to know about it and we don't want anyone else to know about it either.' He had friends who were gay, and they never talked about it, and that was how you were supposed to deal with it." He threatened to cut off Elizabeth's college funds. "I said, 'No way, you can keep your money,' and I left.

"I was freaked out because it was not what I had expected. This big illusion—the bubble had burst. So I was very scared. I moved and I didn't tell them where. I really didn't know what to expect from them now. I had had friends whose parents had tried to deprogram them. Cult deprogrammers, who used some pretty bizarre tactics. It was kidnapping, keeping them awake; and that kind of thing just terrified me. This was '78 to '79.

"Almost all of my religion had come from my parents, so when I came out and my parents rejected that part of me, I threw out the baby with the bath water. All the religion, all the Silva, everything got thrown out—for years. They did end up funding my college education and not pushing their rules, but never again did I try to talk to them. Occasionally they'd refer to my lover, but it was never discussed point-blank ever again.

"I was very isolated when I lived in Northfield, Minnesota, but somehow I began to hear about feminist spirituality in 1980. I realized that I had experienced a real loss and needed to do something about the spiritual part of my life. I kept trying to throw God out, but it wasn't easy. The concept kept coming back to me."

Feminist literature revolutionized Elizabeth's thinking. "The ideas of hierarchy and of giving my power away were new concepts, and suddenly almost everything I learned religiously was not going to work for me anymore. I had trouble with saying even 'Goddess,' trouble deifying anything because that implied giving power to something outside of myself. I found I had the option of using 'the goddess within.'"

Overwhelmed by lesbianism, feminism, and spirituality, she left college and bought Dino's, a Northfield eatery famous for its fried onion rings. As her father had done, Elizabeth began to cast about for a satisfying context in which to relate to forces beyond the human. His search was an intellectual one and he became a respected theological thinker, but Elizabeth's journey was based more on emotion, what she felt. She had, for example, never believed in hell, because of her strong emotional connotation of God as a force of love.

Most churches blend the intellectual and emotional, with some, like the Catholic, leaning more toward mysteries—chants and chalices, saints and scents—while the Quakers, for example, seek God in people and in silence. Just as her father left the Lutheran church to explore new possibilities, so Elizabeth looked beyond organized religion.

"In the Amazon bookstore in Minneapolis I got Z. Budapest's *Holy Book of Women's Mysteries,* which is like a recipe book of rituals, chants, holy days, different ideas women have had. I loved the idea of spell work and ritual. The steps you go through. You cast the circle, call the four corners of the earth, raise the cone of energy. You do your work, you ground it, and then you party."

It has taken Elizabeth ten years to go from organized religion to one harking back to ancient beliefs. "As a feminist and lesbian I had had to learn to reclaim and reinterpret women-based things and lesbian-based things." She found it was the same with the concept of witchcraft, but there were times when certain aspects "felt silly, sounded stupid. That's probably the reason I never joined a group. Too scary to do with other people. I've been practicing solo all these years. It's also very hard to find a group you can build trust with, that are all on the same wavelength. So it was me and my books and the candles.

"Ten years ago it wasn't 'New Age,' it was still 'occult,' and some pretty strange people get into this stuff. I'd look around and think, 'I'm in an occult bookstore. I can't believe I'm doing this.' Gradually there was more feminist stuff there, women-made crafts. The little bags to carry your herbs really attracted me, they were such pretty things." Elizabeth was also attracted by the secrecy. "I liked that, but it has also hindered me because it reinforces the 'being silly' part."

Being a witch is a very personal religion, and Elizabeth thinks it probably means something slightly different to everyone involved. "It feels positive for me as a lesbian feminist to identify myself as a witch because a lot of the witches who were burned were wise women healers, powerful women. I like reclaiming those old traditions that were completely trampled by the patriarchical church. A reclaiming of common wisdom, not wisdom that's held only by somebody who can read Latin."

For Elizabeth, a good child, a dutiful oldest daughter, to take control of her spiritual life was a long experience in personal growth. "But I really did learn to validate it for myself. Now, eight years later, I am just beginning to feel totally comfortable talking about it with people, starting to feel at home within myself.

"Over the years I have focused on what has been useful and helpful at the time. The old spells and rituals basically create an environment—in my opinion—a vehicle for you to focus your mind. You can make or draw or build some physical things to help you focus, to draw the energy toward the end result you wish.

"It is my personal belief that we all do that all the time anyway. We end up creating our own reality constantly. That's pretty well accepted psychologically these days, but I believe that to be true down to the wire. The skill that has caught my attention is creative visualization, which is not just a Wiccan skill. It can be a New

Age—the clean name that everyone feels more comfortable with—skill or an occult skill." To Elizabeth the term *witch* means "craft of the wise"; *Wicca* is the name of the religion.

Elizabeth is preparing to teach a class on creative visualization. "It involves relaxing, meditating, being able to image and feel the end result of what you want. Athletes use this all the time—you imagine yourself performing exactly, perfectly, the entire thing you want to do. The biggest problem is clearing up whether or not you really want it." It being anything from a parking space to a new job. "If you take care of all the blocks, you'll get what you want." She agrees that the concepts are the same as prayer or Silva Mind Control.

"What Wicca has helped me believe is that there is always enough. This is a wonderful world to be in—there is always enough. It is my responsibility to open myself up to let it in." When Elizabeth speaks about her spirituality, she rests her fingertips against her breastbone and then lets them unfold outward.

She agrees that most people associate witchcraft with evil and thinks that there are people who cast evil spells. "I've heard of people in Minneapolis who called themselves black witches. It's energy, and you can do whatever you want with it for good or for bad. The law of tenfold return—whatever you put out comes back to you ten times over—is the reason you don't use it for evil. What goes around comes around. So you need to be really careful."

The language, the naming of the belief or faith is different, but the basic concept of a power that can be evoked is similar to that of all religions.

"People form groups called covens for several reasons. One is the same as my going to the Unitarian church—to be part of a social-religious community. Secondly, to be with spiritually like-minded people, because singing, chanting together is very powerful, very moving emotionally. For me the goal would be raising power, hooking power together. Once you raise that cone of power, which can be done in a million different ways, then is a good time for casting spells, naming people you want to heal."

A prayer circle or a minister reading the names of those in the hospital is, to Elizabeth, exactly the same type of act. "This is a very focused way. In church you get kind of scattered. I love the idea of casting a circle, going through the motions, creating sacred space for me."

What Elizabeth has done is to draw all her beliefs into one system to avoid being "scattered," fragmented. The intense emotions of theater, music, spirituality, secrecy, and love of women can all be combined in the very personal philosophy of a witch. Some lesbians

152

who are in a literal or figurative sense disowned by a father or a god search for a new integrating principle, a philosophic base for their lives.

Elizabeth does not expect to have children or to have a long-term relationship "because I don't see it working for others." This outlook, which involves perhaps social concerns but not intimate, lifelong responsibility for certain individuals, is shared by many young heterosexual women of thirty. It no doubt contributes to the numbers of women drawn to witchcraft, which, as Elizabeth practices it, allows for no outside control. She is her own ritualist, lawgiver, priestess, the ultimate in responsibility. No chance, no destiny, no will of God—just Elizabeth Conner.

Louise Miller, a registered nurse and transplant to the Southwest, has as one of her primary goals "developing a sense of spirit."

Raised in a Quaker family in suburban Philadelphia, Louise attended a Quaker college in Ohio and worked in a Quaker bookstore in Philadelphia. Her family was a very accepting one, but "real issues like sexuality were not easily discussed." She knew nothing about lesbianism until her senior year in college and never acted on her feelings for women until she was a graduate student in political science at the University of Wisconsin; her first lover was her partner for seven years. Now, at thirty-five, Louise describes herself as a person who feels "it is necessary for me to be who I am. I am out to anyone who is interested. Telling people is important to me, and I'll deal with the risk."

Louise's hair is cut in a blond whiffle, her eyes are blue, and her complexion peaches-and-cream. In the heat of a desert afternoon she wears shorts and a sleeveless T-shirt. She speaks with assurance. "I come out of the Quaker background of silence, and I place a high value on nature and a nonmaterial existence." These have been reinforced by her years as a nurse on the Hopi reservation and the high, clear beauty of the Southwest.

Her name is listed as a contact in a lesbian magazine, and during the time people are making vacation plans she receives one or two letters a week from lesbians planning to visit New Mexico—half of whom are investigating settling there. Spirituality is an important factor in that decision.

"Albuquerque is the best place I've ever lived," Louise says. "I feel good about myself and it."

Louise, drawing from components of her Quaker background and the Indian ceremonies with which she has been involved, is "assuming an eclectic approach" in her search for a spirituality that is compatible with her lesbian life.

* * *

All four of these woman are in their early thirties, but coping with loving women and church doctrine is not a new struggle. Before organizations like Dignity (Catholic) and Affirmation (Methodist), women who wished to retain their ties with a church had even more difficult lives.

Rose Mary Denman said, "There is the sinner who can be there in church and say, 'Father, I've sinned.' Then there is the lesbian or gay who has the audacity to sit there and say, 'I haven't sinned.' There are the repentant sinners and the ones who can't even see they're wrong. You can run around on your wife, but if you're ready to be forgiven—fine! You can still be in the Church. This is the place to be, we're the hospital for sinners. But you've got to admit you're sick. No one goes to the hospital unless they know they're sick. But if you won't admit you're sick, you won't take the medication, what can we do?"

A seventy-three-year-old woman writes from a small town in Iowa. "I think the thing that has hurt most about people's view that gay is not okay is the refusal of the Catholic church to include us in her membership. Because I was raised Catholic, the knowledge that a social institution representing so much of what I believe has no room for me has been the great rejection. As I began to understand what being lesbian meant, this conflict precipitated alcoholism and mental illness. For twenty-five years I was celibate and trying to understand the Church.

"Finally I accepted me and rejected the Church. Until fairly recently I went to church on my own terms, now I sit home Sunday mornings and watch mass on TV with my ninety-seven-year-old mother. I'm happy to say last Sunday my lover and I fell asleep watching the service, so it can't mean much anymore.

"Since weaning myself away from a traditional church, I have had significant experiences with the Goddess. So I know there is someone ready to welcome us."

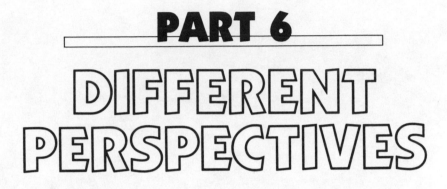

PART 6
DIFFERENT
PERSPECTIVES

17. MAGNOLIA TREES IN EVERY YARD

PAM was raised in Montgomery, Alabama. She writes, "You might well wonder why I would choose to remain in the South, where I am not allowed to openly practice my lesbianism, where women in general are still suppressed, where the mayor of Montgomery totes a gun and the words *queer* and *nigger* are thrown around quite casually. First off, I love the South. It's in my blood. I couldn't survive in the crowded cities with the anonymous, uncaring populace. With all their faults, southerners are warm and friendly, unless you cross them, and they go out of their way to be helpful." Three years ago she and her lover moved to a small rural town thirty miles outside Montgomery. "There's a guy that lives down the road from us who flies a Confederate flag over his house, and although I have no doubts he knows we're a couple, I think he would do anything to help us if we asked.

"Secondly, I feel strongly that lesbians should stay in the South to help bring about change. Sure, it would be great to move to P-town [Provincetown, Massachusetts] and surround myself with a wall of security and cut myself off from the real world, but that won't change things."

Pam, a highly specialized skilled craftsperson, works in a shop with twenty-five men. "So, I am not out at work for fear of getting gang-raped to teach me a lesson. It honestly has been hell working with all these redneck 'good ole boys,' who never wanted me here in the first place, but I would not let them harass me out of this job." She adds, "I think the vast majority of lesbians in Montgomery are not in a position to be out in their workplaces."

Pam is thirty-four; her Southern Baptist parents came from an "Appalachian-type background, but raised themselves up to a solid middle-class level." Pam herself has "about seven years of college, but no degree—too many interests." Of her lesbianism she writes, "I think genes determined my sexuality, but I'm not positive. I was sexually abused as a child, but other women have been abused and are heterosexual. I just always knew. I knew as a child, though I didn't know its name." She has had erotic relations with men, however.

"The heterosexual population here doesn't even acknowledge the existence of lesbians. When we are, on rare occasions, it's with a great deal of snide superiority. My theory is that since the South is still a conservative, male-oriented society, southern men can't comprehend a woman choosing another woman over a man. But on the other hand, many heterosexual women have been labeled lesbians for the simple reason of refusing sex—you know, the old 'if you don't want to go to bed with me, you must be gay' syndrome. But as a group, lesbians are ignored.

" 'Outsiders' have never been well received with the group of lesbians I am familiar with in Montgomery. My lover, Dotti, is a prime example. Although she, too, was born and raised in Montgomery, she went north and got some 'strange and radical ideas' while there, so that upon her return she was snubbed."

Dotti writes, "Montgomery is very cliquish, very much the social-conscious southern town. Its gay society is just as cliquish and snobby. The lesbians here couldn't figure me out because I didn't fit either butch or femme, but they thought I was 'supposed' to be femme—I think the wallet in my back pocket really threw them off! I gradually softened my appearance (almost unconsciously), but still wasn't accepted until after I joined with my current 'home-grown' partner. I still don't compromise by wearing makeup or those hideous heels!"

Dotti grew up in a happy home with five siblings and nurturing parents. Her mother she describes as a "natural feminist before her time. I was not taught prejudice toward gays, blacks, or other groups. I think this was atypical for my socioeconomic status." Dotti was a "good" girl, and during high school, family and the Southern Baptist church were her most important concerns. At the University of Alabama she got a degree in social work and later an MSW.

She describes Tuscaloosa, where she lived for eleven years, as "a liberal southern college town with a small but very feminist and very close lesbian community." Dotti was politically active in that community and also in Dayton, "a large, open, 'together' lesbian community" into which she "withdrew" for three years.

Dotti was married from nineteen to twenty-six, but had erotic relations with women from age twenty-one on. "I don't believe [loving women] is due to choice or environment, it's something 'inherent' in me. I'm simply being myself." She had two two-year "committed relationships" after her divorce and has been with Pam three and a half years.

"I'm tired of fighting (doing activist stuff) and I try to make the minimum number of compromises to mainstream myself. The result? *A lot of isolation*, a small circle of friends and family, fortunately fairly open-minded colleagues, no social activities outside of these folks. But isolation is not bad, and I enjoy our privacy.

"No matter how 'open' Dayton, Boston, and other places I've been were to lesbians, those places never filled my other needs. My home [in Elmore] is cleaner, more beautiful, and more laid back. Crime is lower, and there's a sense of neighborliness that doesn't exist anywhere else I've been. I guess it's called southern hospitality. And then there's the magnolia trees in every yard, and the azaleas blooming in spring and camellias, and the fields so ripe with cotton that it looks like a layer of snow. And I'll be damned if any amount of prejudice is going to keep me from where I belong."

"I thought all lesbians were feminists." Mary Vogel lived in Chicago until age thirty; she has been in Atlanta three years.

"Southern women don't look like the lesbians I was used to. I've been shocked a few times to find out a particular woman was lesbian. They look like suburbanites with frosted, sprayed hair, and makeup—blazer dykes. In Chicago there was a uniform—boots, jeans, and flannel shirts, and a variety of bohemian dress. Lesbians there *tried* to look different."

Mary, an RN, a supervisor in surgery, has a direct, intense gaze; her face is expressionless. "I'm oriented toward being comfortable. Lots of lesbians, feminists who will not buy into the patriarchy, are downwardly mobile. They are making just enough to survive, but who will take care of them? They can't dig ditches when they are old." Her partner, whose fifteen-year-old son they are raising, is a biomedical engineer. When the boy finishes high school, they plan on leaving the South—maybe for San Francisco.

"What is most damaging to me is the Christian bigotry. The news media are dominated by it, and I get real angry. I know a lesbian who is my stereotype of a southern woman. She goes to church three times a week, wears dresses to work, and says, 'I keep reading my Bible. I can't find anything in the Bible that says it's okay.' She has a lot of guilt. Things won't change here for a long, long time."

Sabrina Sojourner—she had her name changed legally—is a small, pretty black woman, dressed in a wraparound jean skirt and a yellow halter. "Those of us born outside the white middle class have to make sure we are clean, neat, presentable. We don't want to be categorized. Some young lesbians believe they have to dress in drab clothes, or jeans, or leather so as not to attract men, but I needed to reclaim my femininity. I got real tired of people thinking I wasn't a real lesbian, or was into roles, or just not knowing what to do with me. I attempted a relationship with someone into roles. It didn't work. There are some women who would never identify themselves as butch, yet talk of me as femme by saying, 'Too much makeup.' 'Why dresses?' That's really butch/femme talk.

"At first I felt guilty for turning men on. Now I realize it's totally their problem, and since then I've felt fine. It's my reclaiming my sexuality. My right to be who I am."

Both communities, lesbian and straight, catagorize people by clothes and mannerisms. Although the South seems to be the place where differences come to the fore, they are prevalent everywhere. A woman in New Hampshire said, "My partner and I were moving up from Connecticut and kept seeing all these women driving pickups, and we were so excited! Look! They're everywhere! Of course, we eventually found out that all women in New Hampshire drive pickups."

A young woman who was part of a lesbian community in Pittsburgh for three years and is now married to a Maine man, says, "I like to get all dressed up—earrings, skirt, heels—and then drive the *big* pickup into Kennebunkport. The look on people's faces when I step out!"

Lesbians at a party of both gay and straight people thought a married woman who roared in on a motorcycle and put another woman in a headlock was surely a lesbian.

A Michigan woman said, "Dress is the longest-running argument within the gay community. Do we wear hobnail boots, overalls, and black T-shirts and then get angry when we're not accepted by mainline society, saying, 'That's their problem'? Or is it our problem?"

"Some days," Julie says, "I feel femme. Other times like a real she-woman." Dress, for both lesbians and heterosexuals, reflects those moods, except when community approval dominates choice. Custom, region, politics, race, economic status all influence that approval, but gender is the baseline. A blurring of the strict dichotomy of masculine/feminine has taken place over the last thirty years, but a sliding scale of clothing and behavior from birth onward would hasten the acceptance of diverse sexuality.

Sabrina, now thirty-six, lived in the San Francisco Bay Area from ages two to twenty-eight and taught at San Francisco State College. She is the oldest of five girls, an incest survivor who married a physically abusive white man at eighteen. The marriage lasted two and a half years; her fifteen-year-old son lives with her mother.

When she moved with a lover to Kansas City, "It was like stepping back five to ten years. It's one of the gayest cities I've ever lived in and one of the most homophobic, racist, and sexist. Everyone seemed to have a stake in the system staying as it was." She believes that in the rural areas "there are a lot of lesbian high school sweethearts who just go on and on."

After six years in Kansas Sabrina moved to Atlanta. "I love Atlanta. It's more like either coast in the exchange of ideas and creativity. Being an artist is okay here." Sabrina works as a food server at a local restaurant while she completes a novel of lesbian erotica. "We need to tell our stories. Our lovemaking is missing from our literature. We need to be the ones talking about it, saying it, but none of us should say we speak for all. We can't forget that we cut across all lines."

Sabrina is a member of the existentialist church and is very involved with the Afro-American Lesbian/Gay Alliance. "It's wonderful working with gay men. I really care about them. I differ from the lesbian separatists, who are almost all white."

She believes that irrespective of cultural expectations or personal experiences, she would have loved women. "If the world were less sexist, I would have been able to love men too. I believe that we are equally capable of loving all people, but we are driven by society to seek opposite-sex love objects. Eventually we will have a world where bisexual is the norm and homosexual and heterosexual are the extremes."

Charis Books and More in the Decatur City section of Atlanta is a center for feminists and lesbians. One of the owners believes that this community has been overlooked by women in other parts of the country because of "general prejudice against southerners. We've been in existence thirteen years. The Atlanta Lesbian Feminist Alliance is the oldest ongoing organization in the United States that actually has a building. On Memorial Day a festival of music and comedy was attended by twenty-one hundred."

For whatever reasons, the southern lesbian has been more invisible than most.

18. OKLAHOMA

SEVEN members of Herland Sister Resources, a women's support group, are crowded into Jean and Karen's living room on a hot summer afternoon. Jean, Karen, Cindy, and Zona are Oklahoma natives; Cathy grew up in Minnesota; and Rhonda Smith came from California. A young journalist, raised in Asia by Baptist missionary parents, is also present. In soft, twanging accents they describe Oklahoma City as "the buckle of the Bible Belt," "ten years behind the rest of the world," a place where a classroom of English teachers resent aspersions cast on Jerry Falwell and Oral Roberts. Cowboy mentality, economic changes that conflict with old value systems, fundamentalist gender expectations, are some of the reasons why they say, "There's fear here. Fear for one's job."

Jean, the director of an agency that serves low-income people, and Karen Lewis, who is studying for her master's in counseling, have recently rented this attractive ranch house on the outer edge of the city. The lawns are broad and well watered; dogs and children abound. A knock on the door precedes an invitation from a neighbor to attend Vacation Bible School. After she leaves, someone jokes, "Maybe we should go en masse," and Jean replies, "You want me to have to start looking for another house already, huh?"

The women respond to the idea of eviction by saying,

"I think it's a possibility."

"I think it's a distinct possibility."

"I think it's a definite possibility."

It is Jean's belief that "no matter who we were renting from or what part of Oklahoma City or Norman we lived in, that threat is always there. We're behind in economic development, in attitudes. Which is one reason I stay here—it's a challenge." Jean's wry tone carries through the laughter. "People's attitudes are not accepting of homosexuality in the state of Oklahoma. I try to help a little bit."

The journalist, a tall strawberry blonde, remarks that the daily paper parrots the ideas of its very conservative owner and adds, "There are jokes about Oklahoma. Like, there are no lesbians in Oklahoma City—it's too dangerous. I think of myself as a subversive, sneaking gender-neutral language into the editorial page."

Cathy, who joined the army to escape a life in the factory, leans forward, elbows on her knees. "One reason we get away with a lot is that people just don't believe there could be lesbians in Oklahoma City. Out of sight, out of mind. Out of mind, out of sight."

The women talk about the flip side of invisibility—the isolation. "In a work setting," Zona, not her real name, says, "it would be very surprising for a woman to admit she was gay, even if she knew the woman she was talking to was one too. There's a lot of paranoia about being out at the workplace."

Rhonda tells of a witch-hunt at United Parcel Service in 1986. "One woman was discovered to be gay by the higher-ups, and she revealed the names of others."

Cindy, whose father is a colonel, says, "Same thing as in the army. We'll give you an honorable discharge if you reveal three names."

She contrasts this with the attitude of her employer, a large corporation. "I'd say eighty-five percent of the women who get promoted at my plant are lesbians—and most of them are pretty out. They know that so-and-so's been living with someone for five years, but she'll get promoted. They know we're good workers, get along well with people, are good management material. I had a discussion with the plant manager about it."

"It's not a readily used weapon," Cathy says, "but it's an available weapon. It's accessible if someone wants to get rid of you. If you beat up on a gay person, it's okay. People would be shocked at the person [who was fired] fighting back. They think that we're asking for trouble by being gay. We don't choose to be gay, but they think we have an option—that we do not have to live this lifestyle. Some might be shocked at a blatant firing practice—the majority would be shocked at the futile attempt of fighting it."

Karen Lewis is slight, with a long, slender neck, sandy hair, and a gracious, delicate demeanor. In the late sixties, as a sophomore at Oklahoma State University, she fell madly in love with a girlfriend, and one night "when I was good and drunk, I told her. She backed up against the wall of her room and yelled at me to get out of there, so I did—dutifully. First thing I did was call my parents and told them all about it. 'Stay where you are—we'll be up in the morning!' "

Home was a small Oklahoma town, and her parents set up an appointment for Karen with the local psychiatrist, who referred her to a psychiatrist at OSU. "I saw him for about three months, and he went through all this Freudian garbage. I went on to have my first 'real' heterosexual experience. All therapy did was to inhibit my coming out for a few years.

"A couple months before I graduated, in 1971, I was on a plane coming back from my brother's wedding in New York. I was sitting next to someone who had this *Village Voice* and I said, 'Am I seeing what I'm seeing?' It was Jill Johnston on the front page kissing another woman. I just knew that New York was the place for me —my feelings had been validated by that picture." Six months later Karen, who describes herself as a basically shy person, was in New York; she stayed for seven years.

She believes environment determined her sexual attraction toward women. In a household of three brothers and no sisters, "I always got to do the household chores; my brothers got to play," and she had to endure behavior from them that was "less than 'loving,' " including "some brotherly incest." She had "no kind and loving men around to pique my interest," and "male attitudes toward women were/are a real turnoff."

At thirty-eight Karen is of the opinion that it is not any more okay to be gay in New York than it is in Oklahoma City, although her attitude then made it seem as though it was. "I was young, ignorant, and the world was beautiful. I came back here because crime entered in my front door." She returned with a New York lover who had an unfavorable opinion of Oklahoma, and the two had great difficulty meeting lesbians in Oklahoma City.

"Every time we went out—which was rare, maybe once or twice a year—we'd have a negative experience, and then we'd fight, and it just wasn't worth it. Basically I was a hermit for the first eight years I was back in Oklahoma. It just kept on going downhill. The isolation gets deeper and deeper." Although Karen had lived as a lesbian in Manhattan, eight years of Oklahoma isolation made her "too scared to go into the bookstore."

The women present agree that partners living in isolation become fearful that if they do go out to a bar, their lover might meet somebody, and then they, because they know no other lesbians, would be left totally alone. Karen thinks that if lesbians were open everywhere, if they were a part of everyday existence, there would not be this debilitating fear. She left her position as a computer programmer/analyst to obtain a degree in community counseling in order to help young lesbian women for whom "religion and societal influences have such devastating consequences."

Zona's skin, in contrast to her brown ten-year-old daughter's, is fair, her face pretty, and her mind quick and competent. She grew up "fourteen miles from the nearest paved road. If you asked me, I could name every family who lived ten miles in any direction. My people were Trail of Tears Indians—Cherokees." She says that Baptists, in contrast to members of the Assembly of God and Church of the True Followers of Jesus Christ, "were the liberals of my neighborhood." Zona's family was Baptist, but she "went to Indian spirit dances as a kid.

"There was isolation, a lot of intermarriage. I'm my own fifth cousin. There were no visible homosexuals in the neighborhood— I didn't know about gay people until I was about seventeen. My cultural background is a lot Indian, but my dad was adamant that I not date Indian boys—there was still that much prejudice. However, his best friend was a full-blooded Indian who could only speak English when he was drunk, while my dad could only speak Cherokee when he was drunk."

Zona was born in 1951; her father owned a grocery store; her mother was frequently "locked up in an insane asylum. My family came apart when I was a teenager. My dad became an alcoholic."

On the basis of her test scores, Zona was offered full scholarships to five universities. "One of my problems growing up—beside being a gay kid and not knowing it—was that I was a lot brighter than my peer group." Her parents refused to sign the scholarship papers because "they just didn't want me to get too far away. They always perceived themselves as very loving parents, but their best was a pretty hard brand of medicine. I was whipped—I suppose every day of my life—with a stick or belt. It's considered normal child raising in Oklahoma to whip your children."

Zona left school and home and did odd jobs in Tahlequah in nurseries, canneries, and greasy spoons until she was offered an opportunity in the Job Corps. "I said, 'What's that?' He said, 'We'll teach you a trade.' 'How much does it cost?' 'We'll pay you to go.' I said, 'I'll take it.' So I ended up in the Guthrie Job Corps in '68. That was my first experience with girls coming up to me and saying, 'Gee, I think you're pretty' and my saying, 'Well, thank you very much.' "

Zona was interested in their attentions, but she was "too busy surviving. When you come out of an alcoholic household with a crazy mother, you're real interested in finding out how other people live. What good manners are. That was my staying-out-of-trouble phase." At eighteen she took a job as a draftsperson with the state and moved to Oklahoma City. She knew no one, and in addition was given guardianship of her sixteen-year-old sister.

"I found a nice guy who seemed stable and safe. I was twenty years old. I figured, 'Well, the normal, average person gets married at this age,' and I was living a normal, average life, not knowing exactly what that was. It presented itself as an opportunity, and I thought, 'Well, this will work.' We were good friends. I thought all women formed deep emotional attachments to all the women in their lives." Zona's family of some fifty people consisted of almost all women. "We were real short of men. And I never noticed.

"I was going to school and working a forty-hour week, so my husband and I didn't have much home life, but we were buddies. We went places—fishing." She motions to her daughter, call her Betty. "Then Betty came along, and I decided to stay home with her." Zona did La Leche League work with nursing mothers for four years. At twenty-nine she "fell head over heels in love. It was the first time I had ever been in love, and it was pretty stormy." The person was her best woman friend.

Her husband, an oil field geologist, was seldom home. His income was over $200,000 a year, but although Zona "enjoyed having lots of money," the marriage had disintegrated. She started what were to be lengthy, painful divorce proceedings. "He was trying to run me out of money." Zona, as a take-charge person, had organized her husband and his business, set up his offices, managed his people. "So he was very angry, because his life didn't go well when I wasn't there. I'm working now on just letting people alone to run their own lives. That's given me time to work on my novel, finish my poetry, and get my degree."

Zona, who had originally gone to engineering school, then decided, "I wasn't temperamentally suited to living my life with logarithms," has now completed studies for her master's degree in English, her first step toward a doctorate. About her novel she says, "I fell in love with a woman I found in a footnote, an Indian woman who lived about the time of the Revolutionary War, so I decided to do a book about her." Red Dirt Press has published her book of poetry.

"I am pretty pleased with life. I've had some bad things happen, and my earliest memories are sad, but my mother spent her life being angry and look where it got her.

"Around the time of the Trail of Tears, when the Indians found out about Christianity, they also found out about patriarchy. But it's new, they aren't used to it yet. I had an aunt, my dad's sister, who still tries to run the family by long-distance phone from California. As a young child she was a very active presence, in charge and cheerful—she lived across the field. She was a great role model, because every time I did something stubborn, the family would say, 'Oh, you're just like your aunt!' So I grew up knowing that my life didn't have to be the way it was. Very early I began to plot how to make it different—which is one of the reasons I left home."

Finding out she was gay did not depress Zona. "In a way it gave me a good excuse to do some things I needed to do, like get a divorce and correct some things I'd been putting up with. Because, my God, if I'm a *lesbian*, I really can't be bothered with this. It was a freeing experience."

In Oklahoma lesbianism cannot be brought up in divorce court. "It's okay unless the child knows about it. Then they feel that community pressure et cetera would be too hard on the child. So, Betty and I have a pact. She knows, but she knows she's not to tell. She was eight when all this happened, and she advised me not to take my interest in women too seriously, that it was probably a stage." Betty, who has sat silently pressed against her mother's knee, joins in the laughter.

Cindy, a lean, dark-haired, cocky woman of twenty-three, says, "I have been a nondrinker now for twenty-one months and four days. I started going to bars when I was sixteen. We're talking about every night from the time it opens until the time it closes. I was really aggressive too. Had a lot of anger. Got in a lot of fights, caused a lot of problems. My life has done a drastic turnaround since then, and it has to do with a lot of different things. A lot of different people that gave a damn about me and gave some time.

"Because my life was centered around the bars, I thought that's what gay was about. See, I didn't know about politics, and if I had, I wouldn't have given a damn about it anyway. Bars were the places we could be together. That's where I could be open, where I could totally be who I was.

"When I first discovered I was an alcoholic, I thought, 'Well, I can't be a reformed alcoholic because then I can't be gay.' " Cindy, who had tried quitting drinking several times and failed, knew abstinence was the only answer for her. But because she equated gay with drinking, she thought she would then have to give up life as a lesbian.

"I think alcoholism has to do with upbringing and environment. I don't say lesbianism isn't somehow related, I just don't think that's the primary reason."

Louise Miller, the RN from New Mexico who worked with alcoholics in gay/lesbian groups, on the Hopi reservation and in the Albuquerque Indian Hospital, believes genes, oppression, and environment are all components of alcoholism. "Lesbians are in a particularly vulnerable situation due to oppression. The genetic predisposition may come to the fore more readily as a means of dealing with the pain. The pain comes from all angles. I think it would be similar to heterosexual pain, but with added features. The message is that what you are doing is not okay. How can you feel good about yourself when others around you are saying, 'We do not condone that'?"

She believes lesbians are also vulnerable to codependency. "The term came out of the addictive-drug field. It means somebody who becomes obsessed with another's behavior. For example, the partner of an alcoholic becomes obsessed with finding the bottle. Her consciousness focuses on her." She spoke of an ex-lover. "I wasn't paying enough attention to myself. I lived vicariously through her. I didn't know my direction; she did. Her addiction was alcohol; my addiction was her."

Cindy does not view oppression as the reason for her drinking, and she questions studies that claim that a higher percentage of lesbian than heterosexual women are alcoholics.

"Where did the researchers find the people to interview? In the bars where the lesbians are? I'm serious. That's the stereotype, that's the visible dyke. Well, of course you're going to find more alcoholics in bars. People who do studies do it where they can find the people they want to study."

Cindy's partner, Rhonda, who is ten years older than she, says that she knew a lot of lesbian alcoholics in Berkeley. "There is incredible pressure in being lesbian in this country, in this world. One of the ways of coping with pressure is drinking. There are also a tremendous number of reformed alcoholics in the lesbian community."

Cindy adds, "For most of the women I know, recovery in the lesbian community is a lot harder than it is in the straight community. Oklahoma City is an easier place to be a recovering alcoholic, because it is the only city in Oklahoma that has gay/lesbian AA meetings. That had a big part to do with me deciding to get sober. I had tried not to drink many times before, and it didn't work. That goes back to what I said about 'I can't be a reformed alcoholic because then I can't be gay.' Well, here [at the AA meetings] I found other lesbians and gay men who were not drinking, and so then it was okay for me not to."

Cindy also believes, from conversations held at her AA group, that more female alcoholics, including, of course, lesbians, are being identified today. Formerly it was the males who were confronted at work, but "since there are more women employed, more women are becoming involved with recovery. I went through a treatment program through the corporation I work for. I went and asked for help. I wasn't threatened with loss of my job, because I was a good worker, I had a perfect attendance record. The first Herland retreat was the last weekend I drank.

"I thought when I went there that everyone drank the way I did—as much and as frequently as I did. But that wasn't true. And at the July retreat I didn't see anyone there who was acting drunk. And we had eighty-five to ninety women there, and not a high percentage of the women were into recovery. There were just a few of us there."

"I can speak not as an alcoholic," Zona says, "but as one who sure has the potential. I eat instead of drink." Zona is a woman of some size. "I think alcoholism has more to do with childhood, home life, and background. I think of lesbianism as more like one of those accidents—like having brown hair.

"If your programming is to be alcoholic, it starts around infancy somewhere and is a problem before puberty. If you have this pre-disposition, when you go out and begin a social life and you do it in a bar, you are going to end up an alcoholic. I think it has a lot to do with your community. In my community, being Indian and rural and Baptist, it was really taboo to drink. They preached sermons about it every week, so it was always on everybody's mind, and when you did get hold of a bottle, you drank it until it was gone. And there were a tremendous number of alcoholics. Maybe it is a problem of Indian metabolism, but I think it has more to do with the social circumstances of how they drank.

"I think in the lesbian community what I have observed is that to have a good time, you go to the bar and drink. My cousin in Houston and I—we were both raised Baptist—were talking about this. She told me she went to the [lesbian] bars until she found someone nice and made some friends and then she quit going to the bars because they're not terribly interesting. Not much fun, boring. A lot of women who don't drink won't go to the bars very long, so that if the surveys did take place in the bars, it's like those women are not there."

Zona's point of placing the focus less on genetic predisposition or oppression and more on community behavior seems to apply in Cindy's case. At sixteen she, rather like a young man entering a fraternity, perceived drinking as the way lesbians behaved. It is difficult, perhaps impossible, to gauge the strength of the connection, if any, between women-loving women and alcohol addiction, but certainly the two are not linked chromosomes; one does not predetermine the other. Self-image, however, is linked to the mirror of society—lesbian/shame/alcohol—or to a particular society—lesbian/fun/bar.

Herland Sister Resources is holding up a new mirror—lesbian/joy/community.

Herland is a nonprofit corporation, a collective of women who rotate organizational responsibilites among Sister One, Sister Two, and so on. The collective, as opposed to a hierarchy that has a permanent director, operates on consensus and utilizes a wide range of each individual's skills. A volunteer organization like Herland demands an enormous amount of time and energy from the Sisters, and without a reserve pool of willing talent or funds to pay a coordinator, many such organizations collapse. Herland, which began as a bookstore, still has its founding mother as a rallying point.

On this Sunday evening she sits, surrounded by friends, at a table in DJ's bar. Barbara Wahru is the name she is known by among these friends. A commanding black woman dressed in black and flashing gold, Barbara is theater, very effective theater. Her stated reason for starting the bookstore is "I was lonely," an old, but apt joke in Oklahoma.

Five years ago she went to Nashville and saw her first women's bookstore, heard women's music playing. "I felt a sense of peace, like I'd never felt before. There were black women heroes on the shelves. On the way home I thought about it. I knew what I wanted, but I didn't know how to get there. I called women's bookstores in other parts of the country, and people told me what to do. I took over an abandoned project and bought two hundred dollars' worth of books." She spreads her hands a foot apart—"This much. And opened up. I was so excited. August 14, 1982. Now Herland is a lending library, resource center, produces concerts, a newsletter . . ." She smiles hugely. "It just got away from me.

"We're still building here. You can make mistakes and recover. Everything is new here. For every musician it's the first time in Oklahoma City. It really started grassroots with a woman selling women's music out of her home.

"Make friends—that is the core of it. We're all friends. I go to see a woman's football team play, and then after the game I tell them about a concert. They look at me sort of blank, and I say"—Barbara swivels her head at her imaginary audience—" 'You guys gonna come, right?' " She nods as though including each one of a circle of players. "And they say, 'Right, Barbara, we're gonna come.' "

Barbara was raised in poverty, then received a scholarship to go to college, where she was an athlete, playing on varsity badminton and fencing teams. "In 1962 Oklahoma U was very homophobic. It was very traumatic coming out and learning to play field hockey at the same time." Humor is Barbara's style. "The people who reached out to help me were white lesbians on sport teams. They'd lend me their meal tickets—literally kept food in my mouth. Now some black sisters challenge me. I tell them I can't deny those who helped me. They didn't pity me, they understood—and they were all white."

She reminisces about the racial tensions of those times. During one game emotions between black and white field hockey players reached the boiling point. "I just dove for a freshly limed line, rolled over and over, and started screaming, 'Help! Help! I got white on me! Help!' Laughter helped."

The bookstore—still the only women's bookstore in Oklahoma—is operated by volunteers working four-hour shifts on Saturdays and Sundays. There are fourteen on their board of directors, designated Sister One, Sister Two, Sister Three, for decision-making purposes. They hold weekend retreats, which also serve as fundraisers, for 75 to 100 women at state parks. Their newsletter has a mailing list of 650. What began with Barbara's original idea of bringing some literacy into the community and making it more cohesive has resulted in an energetic, expanding group dedicated to feminist ideals and lessening the burden of loneliness for Oklahoma women-loving women. "Some who come into the bookstore," Zona says, "admit that they have driven around the block five or six times—maybe for several weekends—trying to get up the nerve to come in."

Barbara Wahru, now a college chemistry teacher, says, "I respect the fears of Oklahoma women."

DJ, a woman in her sixties, has for twelve years run—with an iron hand—this Oklahoma City lesbian bar. She says, "In the old days two hundred women used to eat Sunday brunch here." DJ came out in the forties, when "the police would spot a license plate outside a gay place, call your employer, and have you fired." Now, she says, "if I had any trouble I'd go straight to the police."

Her long-time partner, Pam, is a fashionable, attractive woman, while DJ's appearance is gray and formidable—until she smiles. The "girls" are in awe of her. She charges for water because she doesn't want people going outside to smoke dope, then coming in thirsty. "I'm in the liquor business," she says and adds that it has been very profitable. She allows no straight women in, but occasionally admits a gay man from the bar next door. She charges a dollar entrance fee on Friday and Saturday nights.

The dance floor is big, the music country/western—a lot of two-stepping goes on—and at the pool tables a few young women with male-style haircuts self-consciously line up their shots.

Michelle, a friend of Cindy's, is a skinny young woman with short, curly brown hair. "I had a crew cut last year and I really liked the way it felt." She rides a motorcycle, "because of the feeling of freedom it gives me. Close to nature, not like in a car. It expresses something of me." As a college prank she had a tattoo done on her stomach, but had it removed when it got infected. She wears leather sometimes.

Cindy says, "I used to wear leather because I didn't want anyone to mess with me. Leather says, 'Back off.'" It was a statement to both men and women. "Now that I have self-confidence, I wear it for fun. Rhonda likes it. I like the feel." She laughs. "I never grew out of the tomboy phase."

Rhonda, a woman with a steady gaze and bright pixie air, laughs with her, then is off to the dance floor, moving with the grace of one who has studied modern and classical ballet. She has started her own apparel design business—Dyke Town—in an attempt to give some brightness and style to the traditionally drab lesbian dress code.

The singer, Peggy Johnson, is playing pool. "I want to sing about life as it is. Not doll it all up with moon and June." As a teenager she "couldn't find any live lesbians in Oklahoma City, so I read." But she no longer believes the Jill Johnston literature she came out on.

When Peggy was in the navy, a woman on her ship was accused of being a lesbian. "She was scared, had just come out. She told on others. When they asked me, I said, 'Yes.' I got an honorable discharge, but it says 'Lesbian' on it." Her utopian ideas are gone. "Lesbians can be just as shitty to each other as anybody else can." Peggy writes her own music, sings locally, hopes for the big break.

A woman—call her April—with her kinky blond hair and wide baby-blue eyes, looks like a woman who must have had a hard time convincing DJ to allow her in on her first visit. She lives far out of town and seldom gets into the bar. "This," she says, "is the only place I can come and be me."

Her drawl is very pronounced. "I tried as hard as I could to change. But I can't change. I'm just me." April has had three hus-bands. "I would marry because I was lonely. So awful lonely."

She is getting her degree in elementary teaching and has two little girls. "I hope they grow up and get married and have children. It's just too hard this way. But I know what I am. I just didn't want to be in bed with a man. I won't marry again. Everyone wants to fix me up with dates, and I have to lie and say I'm not over my bad divorce yet. I don't see any hope for things changing." Against a backdrop of doleful country-music lyrics, she adds, "I'll just have to go on and on living a double life."

The very thought of coming out straightens April's back and jerks up her head. "If anyone found out, I'd lose everything I love! My children—my kids are everything to me. My standing in the community. I'd never get a job as an elementary school teacher. Why, I'd be shot right out of the saddle!"

The statement seems very fitting, very Oklahoma.

19. NEW YORK CITY

"**PEOPLE** think that New York is the liberal hub. It's not."

Emily, the young woman who wants to talk without marbles in her mouth, calls from the kitchen end of her apartment to her friend, Trish, who sits on the sofa bed. "Is there one bar now? Two? Two bars for women in the city. Two that are seven-days-a-week gay women. Now, there are some in the Village that have one-night-a-week gay women before the men come in. It's very strange. We can't figure it out.

"There was a wonderful women's restaurant. The bar downstairs was a little too tough for me, but upstairs was this beautiful restaurant. It was always packed. I used to take my mother there. I mean, it was gorgeous, good food. And it closed down. Somebody told me they hadn't made the right Mafia connections. I don't know. But it's amazing to me. I don't know if women don't like to go to bars, or they don't have as much money as men. But still—I know enough women who would like to go to a neighborhood bar and hang out.

"There are gay men's restaurants. I mean, women can go in, but they are predominantly men, owned by gay men. It's shocking. All the bars closing. The bookstore." The 92nd Street Bookstore had closed that week. She says you cannot walk down a street and see gay women the way you can see gay men on Christopher Street, that you can't find them unless you join an organization. The number of organizations is, however, legion.

Trish has mixed feelings about staying in Manhattan. "You are ruled by the city. You don't have the city by the balls—pardon the expression. The city plays with you, controls you."

Emily argues, "The city is what you make it. I've met some of the warmest, most concerned people in my life in New York City. Look at this apartment building." Everyone in the building knows that she and Raja, who is there four or more nights a week, are lovers.

"For a while I didn't want to go out of the house." Trish says. "I feel like I'm taking a risk by just living in the city. It's a love/hate, but you get it in your blood. You get used to having all of the world right here. This is it. It's a microcosm. It's hard to remove yourself from all these opportunities."

December's early darkness coats the apartment buildings of Greenwich Village; two teenage girls blend with the sidewalk shadows as they close-dance. The Village, the haven that beckoned lesbians for half a century.

The Gay and Lesbian Community Center is an old school building that looms massively ugly in this upscale residential neighborhood. Faded notices curl behind the window grills, and the inside is cavernous, bare, enlivened only by attractive young men, one of whom sits at a table behind the sign AIDS Legal Counsel. A dozen women with short hair and dark clothing are hunched in a semicircle gazing at a video about women in prison. The drab dress seems protective, a hand-me-down custom from women coming from bars in bad neighborhoods who needed to be able to fade into the night for protection from both dyke-baiters and police.

Through swinging doors and up a stairwell brightened only by photos of women musicians is the Women's Coffee House. People drift in. A woman past forty-five with a plain, honest face and clothes to match comments, "New York is a bleak place for lesbians. Bleak. And I don't know why. But it is." Laughing at the notion that Park Slope in Brooklyn has the most lesbians per square inch, she says that the Upper West Side might make that claim too. "We are all arrogant about our turf." She is interrupted by the arrival of a beautiful younger woman in a dress-for-success business outfit. They brush lips and move off together.

The women, congregating for a reading, are from different areas, different life-styles, different ages; Connie is a member of SAGE (Senior Action in a Gay Environment), a Manhattan organization for men and women over fifty. "SAGE saved my life," she says, but does not elaborate. Members of the sponsoring organization, Herstory Archives, set out refreshments of tea, coffee, pretzels, and seltzer water at the back of the room. Spyke, the twenty-one-year-old University of California student, agrees to a tour of the Archives in the morning, a Saturday.

The Lesbian Herstory Archives, located on the Upper West Side, is, according to their newsletter, "a concrete expression of a people's refusal to lose their memory. For thirteen years we have been nurturing and sharing a collection alive with voices that the larger society has judged obscene, or sick, or inconsequential. For thirteen years the apartment of Deb and Joan, and now Judith and Joan, has been home to the collection and to the thousands of visitors who have come to see and to touch.

"We have outgrown the apartment, just as in the past we outgrew rooms. The collection now spills over into another apartment and into storage vaults."

Spyke is in New York doing an independent-study project on how small organizations operate; Herstory Archives is her model. She stands against a backdrop of floor-to-ceiling material by and about lesbians—paperbacks of the forties, a biker jacket of the sixties. She says, "We keep all copies of all newsletters. Anything anyone wants to contribute by way of letters, diaries, unpublished manuscripts. Both the famous and the ordinary. There is no government funding—all personal contributions. Here's a collection of paperbacks written by men for men as sex teasers—but that's all gay women had to read then." Photographs, sketches of women touching each other with love, memorabilia crowd the corners between the shelves; a huge photograph of a beautiful black woman with marceled hair reclining on a couch fills one wall.

The door opens, and Mabel Hampton, the lover of the woman in the photograph, hobbles in carrying a plastic basket full of clothes from the laundromat. She is, with Joan Nestle, a founder of the Archives. "That's all I lived for," she told an interviewer for Boston's *Sojourner* magazine, "to see that something comes to generations that I had been longing to see. And when the gay movement really came out, I said, 'Here it comes! Here it comes! Whoopie!' "

Spyke says Santa Cruz is "a university town, full of liberals, hippies, and homosexuals. You can really be blatant there. I had a wild hairstyle—a mohawk with a long braid. But no one in town even looks twice—only the tourists.

"Everyone there is weird. Everyone in New York is rigid." She hunches her shoulders and stands stiffly. "But in Santa Cruz everyone is politically correct. No lesbian bars, only one mixed with men. Pickups are not acceptable. It's a small community with an army of ex-lovers.

"The anonymity here is a plus. I can flirt and be flirted with. There are two bars in the Village where I go to dance, and the clubs—both straight and gay men's—have women's nights." She explains that they are advertised and run from eight to eleven, when the men start to drift in. The cover is five to ten dollars.

"My girlfriend came for nine days in October and she was scared to hold hands. I couldn't say, 'No problem.' I'm more afraid here than in Santa Cruz."

She waves a thin arm at the bulging walls. "I'm nothing in courage compared with them, the women who came out in the fifties."

Both Alice and Beverly, the Massachusetts women, had come to the Village in the 1940s and 1950s; Karen Lewis had fled here from Oklahoma in the 1970s. By their early thirties they had all returned "home," but there are those who stay. Women like Emily, who cannot imagine living anywhere else.

Another native, who now lives in Park Slope in Brooklyn, says, "Young out-of-town gay women are moving into the neighborhood." And she agrees with Spyke about the value of anonymity. "There is freedom in being one of so many—you can get lost around here."

But a woman with two decades of working in a New York publishing house says, "I know lots of gay men, but not a single gay woman."

Anonymous often means invisible.

PART 7

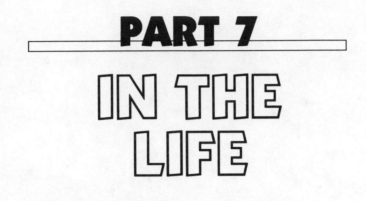

IN THE
LIFE

20. MUSIC, BOOKS, AND THE MEDIA

HETEROSEXISM, *heterocentric assumptions, the bias of compulsory heterosexuality* are the words and phrases Adrienne Rich uses in her essay "Compulsory Heterosexuality and Lesbian Existence." Defined in terms of daily living, they mean radios that bleat songs of he/she romance and lust; television that assumes male plus female indicates sexual involvement; books in which, as Rich said, "lesbian experience is perceived on a scale ranging from deviant to abhorrent, or simply rendered invisible." A person who does not find herself reflected anywhere—in music or books, on a TV screen or a movie screen—soon begins to doubt her own existence.

From the time the pink birth announcement trills, "It's a Girl!" the assumption is that this infant has an innate desire to make males the object of her passion, to choose them as lovers, as life partners. That this is a destiny toward which society must mold and condition her is not considered; if she is "normal," she will "naturally" date, take male lovers, and marry. The media are not seen as instruments of propaganda for a certain type of sexual expression but as a reflection of the way things are—and it is all-pervasive.

The same pressures that are part of every girl's growing-up years persist for the self-acknowledged lesbian. Not only do lesbians walk the streets of heterocentric assumptions outside their homes, but the media bring them inside. When the media—which have willynilly become a standard of behavior—validate their own women-loving feelings, their own experiences, they are, as one woman put it, "blown right out of the water." What the heterosexual woman takes for granted can be for a lesbian a tremendously moving, even life-altering experience.

"I came out to Cris Williamson," a Detroit woman said, and it is a statement echoed by many. Just as wives and mothers were birthed to feminism by Helen Reddy belting out the lyrics to "I Am Woman," lesbians were, and continue to be, overwhelmed by the folk-rock music of Cris Williamson, Meg Christian, Margie Adam, and Holly Near.

Julie, now almost fifty, was in her thirties when she borrowed Cris Williamson's album *The Changer and the Changed* from a friend. For the first time in her life she could connect with lyrics without changing the pronouns. She bought her own album and sang before work, after work, and in the evenings. Then she discovered Meg Christian: "I Know You Know." To know at last that others she could respect—talented, professional singers—not only shared her view on loving women but had strong enough convictions to sell music on the theme proved to Julie that "lesbianism was more universal than I had ever imagined." Once women pass that barrier, attitudes of heterocentricism appear more as a mechanism of domination than simply an expression of the "normal."

For the enormous number of lesbians now past fifty, *The Well of Loneliness* was the only concrete evidence that women-loving women existed. In silence and secrecy they read Radclyffe Hall's plea to the heterosexual world to have pity on the poor monster Stephen, who was "born an invert." The vague references they heard of literary figures like Gertrude Stein being "masculine" seemed more connected to her reputation as a genius than a sexual being.

The women's music of the seventies was, however, not sad, not secret, not pleading, not connected with incomprehensible expatriate poets. It was here and now, rocking and rhythmic and impelling Julie and thousands of other women to dance, to weep, to joyously shout lyrics that portrayed the world as they knew it. The conveyors of the message were not strange and tragic types; they were handsome, stylish people on album covers in the music store at the mall. They were not untrained voices changing the pronouns in heterosexual songs as they sang in dim bars in bad neighborhoods but first-class professionals who loved women and were proud of it. They took slices of lesbians' lives that were held in uneasy secrecy and rocketed them into a common humorous bond.

"So go to any gym class . . . And you'll be sure to see/One girl who sticks to teacher/Like a leaf sticks to a tree/ One girl who runs the errands/ And who chases all the balls/ One girl who may grow up to be the gayest of all."

Other lyrics, like those to "Sweet Woman," are gently erotic; "The Changer and the Changed" symbolizes the political struggle for identity. Julie said of "Beautiful Soul," "During a very painful breakup I would play it, tears running down my face as I drove. It told me that sadness can be part of a lovely lady's life, but shouldn't threaten the idea that you are a good person, have a good soul, and that your feelings are in place."

Margie Adam's lyrics—"Could it be that you ask too much, loveable lady, from a world that's out of touch, beautiful woman?"—were extremely comforting and uplifting to a person who had had to spend her adolescent and adult life shoring up her belief in her own goodness while the world continued to define her as perverted and evil. "So you're hammering at a door that will not open and your beautiful soul is weeping. Do you hate yourself, loveable lady, can I be of help, beautiful woman?"

Meg Christian, as the cover to her second album, *Face the Music*, explains, "writes and speaks in concerts about issues which are vital to the women's movement—especially lesbianism, class and the commonality of women's struggles everywhere." The chorus of "The Rock Will Wear Away" has become symbolic of that message. "Can we be like drops of water falling on the stone/Splashing, breaking, dispersing in air / Weaker than the stone by far / But be aware that as time goes by / The rock will wear away / And the water comes again."

In Minneapolis Liz Pierce said, "I came out to 'Lavender Jane,' " and then immediately burst into song. Her first time at the Michigan Music Festival "Blew my mind! All those women! All that music!" While records often ended isolation inside the home and brought a woman to acceptance of her erotic feelings for women, concerts breached the outside world and carried her into contact with other lesbians, often for the first time.

An older woman isolated in a coastal village remembered a Cris Williamson concert at the University of Maine. "I had never seen so many gay women. I suppose I knew they existed, but it was overwhelming to be a part of them. I tried to hold hands with the woman I was with, but even there she was too frightened."

The fascination and the fear connected with a live concert is that lesbians in huge numbers "come out of the woodwork" for that one night. In flannel shirts or down vests or army pants or whatever is in style for gay women in that area, they flood the hall or gym or auditorium. "Ninety-two percent were 'members of the church,'" is the way one woman described a 1987 Cris Williamson Boston concert. For this reason attending a concert can be a public coming out to one's self, an acknowledgment of: "I am one of them—one of these women who surround me. A woman who loves women. I'm not just in a special friendship with a special woman, or experiencing an immature crush, or curious. I am a lesbian." It is learning to acknowledge "the *L* word" by seeing and being seen—at least by the women's community.

Concerts can bring to the forefront conflict between self-perception and social acceptance. In the early eighties Julie vacillated about going to a Cris Williamson concert in the town where she lived and taught. "My friends gave me a potted palm. The idea was that I could sit behind it and not be seen."

On a dark, snow-threatening night deep in the North Country of New Hampshire, a small college blazes with car lights, and inside the entranceway to the auditorium are three hundred women—92 percent lesbian. The women, mostly under forty, hug old friends, ex-loves, and women they have just met. Cris Williamson is late—almost two hours late—but there is no anger among these people, who have literally driven out of the forests to be here; they talk, and finally sit on the floor and sing.

Cris is greeted with a roar that seems to last the full two hours of the concert. They sing the old favorites—"Waterfall," "Sweet Woman"—with her and stand and sway, arms around each other, as they shout, "The Song of the Soul."

Julie describes the feeling of singing about the light that will heal you and banish sadness. "When they play 'Song of the Soul,' it's like Friday afternoon when you've endured so much and you just let go. And you know the women next to you have endured so much too."

In a basement dressing room after the concert Cris explains why she ended with two songs no one knew. "They are so hungry. I could feel their hunger reaching up on the stage. If I had ended with a popular song like 'Waterfall,' they would have stormed it. So I cooled them down." She looks small, exhausted, emotionally drained from trying in two hours to replenish women who live for days and months on end in an atmosphere of compulsory heterosexuality. But she beams when she says that next fall, 1982, she and Meg Christian will perform—in tuxes—in Carnegie Hall.

Tickets for both performances were sold out months in advance. Julie describes the scene: "Outside the hall the streets were filled with gay women. Some came in horse-drawn carriages. Some stepped from limousines in evening dress. There were lots of tuxes, slacks, blazers. My eyes were wide. It was being more than legitimate, it was as though there was room for acceptance.

"When the first show got out, I looked to see if I knew anyone. Anyone with years as a lesbian behind them was doing the same. It was a nationwide reunion."

Another woman who attended the October 1987 Washington March for Gay and Lesbian Rights remarked on the same phenomenon. "Streets were filled with friendly faces. All kinds of people, and you knew they were gay. We got on a bus, and people cheered our lesbian T-shirts. It was wonderful!"

These moments at concerts or marches or the vacations in Provincetown or San Francisco are treasured for that feeling of acceptance. Six years later lesbians across the country still glow as they speak of that night in Carnegie Hall—"the night we arrived."

Inside the hall the air was electric with pride and excitement and thunderous gratitude to the women who had dared to write the songs, to move out of the bars to public stages and form a record company of their own. Most straight nonfeminist women did not —and, fifteen years after the founding of Olivia Records, still do not—know that this folk rock called women's music exists.

There is a moment in all, or almost all, women's concerts that is hushed, sacred. At Carnegie Hall it was Meg Christian, who gave the long guitar introduction, then softly sang: "I'm thinking about the ones who are not here. And won't be coming in late . . . won't be coming out tonight. Wish I could know all the lovers and friends kept from gathering . . . we're all of us refugees.

"Telling myself and the family, my friends and the folks on the job, one by one . . . Some never speak again. Every pot off the wheel can't bear the kiln, and every love can't bear the pain. So let's pass a kiss and a happy, sad tear and a hug the whole circle round for the ones who aren't here, for the hate and the fear, for laughter, for struggle, for life. Let's have a song here for me and for you and the love that we cannot hide. And let's have a song for the ones who aren't here and won't be coming out tonight."

Two thousand women—symbols of probably ten million—rose, wet-eyed, applauding, sharing a moment of the sisterhood of loneliness that is peculiarly their own.

Gay women ache at hearing this song, but their twenty million parents and eighty million relatives and ten million of their own children have probably never heard it, do not even know of its existence. They are part of this pain—they have inflicted it, perpetuated it, and also borne it, but because heterosexism demands that lesbianism go unacknowledged, very few ever participate in any events of lesbian culture. Cris Williamson's mother did attend her daughter's concert, and she received a standing ovation for it. The word *hungry* seems fitting.

At a 1987 Boston women's music festival, where the audience was evenly divided between women whose "dates" were men and those with women, not one performer in words or song gave any recognition to the latter. The closest was the word *sister* but the context was strictly heterosexual feminist, not lesbian.

The women-loving women conceded their turf without a murmur. They did not demand—probably did not even expect—the slightest recognition that their loved ones were of the same sex.

If the lyrics of "Sweet Woman" had filled the hall, would all the men and straight women have left? Were the singers heterosexual and afraid to be identified as lesbian, were they closet lesbians themselves, or had it been a political decision of the performers, Buffy Sainte-Marie and Sweet Honey in the Rock? Lesbian singers expect to dub masculine pronouns when they sing in a straight club, but here no one could—or would—make the slightest effort to recognize the sexual preference of half their audience. Perhaps the situation is analogous to a person whose blood is one-thirty-second black being "legally black." One pronoun might have labeled the concert lesbian, might have "tainted," "polluted," its heterosexual purity.

Julie barely noticed the exclusion. "You get to expect it," she said. The majority rules even when it is not a majority.

Being ignored is not the worst lesbians can expect. Many still describe women-loving women as "abnormal." For this reason women's bookstores and restaurants, gay-pride marches, concerts and festivals, are the few public places where, as Sissela Bok writes of those who hold secrets, "their own sense of privacy blends with an enlarged private space of the group," and at least briefly lesbians can enjoy the feeling of being not only legitimate but accepted.

Some minority groups are sustained by oral family traditions, which provide a refuge for members being ignored or mistreated by the dominant group. As a Chicago public high school teacher pointed out, a black child taunted for her color can find solace at home. This is rarely true for the lesbian. Because families have been so secretive about their gay members, there has been, as Ann Muller wrote in *Parents Matter*, "no healthy cumulative oral history." Of course, families have also been secretive about members who are mentally ill, retarded, or have spent time in prison, but because most lesbians have the option of remaining silent and cooperating in this conspiracy, there is even less pressure for families to explore and understand.

Even if a lesbian does have the courage to tell her parents, rarely do her parents have the courage to share the information. Because that part of the person's life, or even the total person, is erased by silence and denial, the next generation—having had no other example of how to cope with a member inwardly viewed as a failure, disgrace, or aberration—repeats the pattern. It is extraordinary when a woman can say to her sister-in-law, "Tell me what it's like to have a gay daughter. I'm pretty sure my Anne is too."

Girls growing up with a great admiration for a maiden aunt are told not that she is a lesbian but that she never married because of the possibility of tuberculosis, or young love gone wrong, or too intense a commitment to her career. The girl either accepts this and denies what she senses is true or represses her curiosity about what is obviously a forbidden subject, as most sexual topics are. Or, because "never marrying" is a condition her aunt must view as a great tragedy, she avoids hurting her with questions. The young girl is thereby cut off from the person to whom she could turn for information and support. It is the private equivalent of censorship; it preserves the illusion that heterosexuality and celibacy are the only life-styles in existence.

Books have traditionally been the source for children to learn what their parents or other adults are unwilling to discuss. But until very recently there have been literally no books in which a girl might discover anything about her erotic feelings for women. Today she might sneak a look at her mother's copy of *The New Our Bodies Ourselves*; she might even try to follow up on some of the resource suggestions. Unfortunately, the books and magazines listed would almost surely not be available in a local library, and university libraries, if available, are restricted to tuition-paying students. Writing to women's bookstores in order to make purchases from their lists would be a costly hit-or-miss experiment. It would be a challenge for even a confident, educated woman of some means to acquire a bookshelf of lesbian fiction and nonfiction, a near impossibility for the adolescent.

Because women's bookstores are geographically inaccessible to most women in the country, those who are curious—or desperate for information—cannot go and browse and choose what they would like to buy. Even with a specific title in mind the road is not easy. For example; a woman in northern New England who called New Words in Boston would be told, "We do not fill mail orders," and be given the name of only one other possibility—a place in Maine. But that store does not carry the book, and the clerk sounds hostile at the mention of an overtly lesbian title. Even in New York City a call to the Gay and Lesbian Community Center in the fall of 1987 netted one bookstore just closed, another that "has some lesbian books in the back," and one that was called "good."

In addition to these physical barriers are the psychological ones. Even if a woman found titles in her local library or bookstore, it would be traumatic to check out or buy them. The power of a heterocentric society is such that the belief persists that no "normal" person would be interested in such subjects.

Books with lesbian themes are published by small presses known only to insiders. For the general public who buys from B. Dalton or Waldenbooks their chances of running across a book in which a lesbian is realistically portrayed are very slim. Notable exceptions are the books of Rita Mae Brown, Lisa Alther's *Other Women*, Margaret Erhart's *Unusual Company*, and the rash of biographies about notables who loved women—Vita Sackville-West, Virginia Woolf, Willa Cather, Sara Orne Jewett, Amy Lowell, Margaret Mead, Eleanor Roosevelt—although sometimes the references are veiled and disapproving in tone.

Sometimes it is a book review that provokes frustration. A *New York Times* (May 1988) reviewer labeled *After Delores* "a rare, insightful look into the lesbian mind." He justified this by quoting a character in the book who feels that "lesbianism is so well accepted these days that it's almost not worth the trouble: 'It's too easy to be gay today in New York City. I come from those times when sexual excitement could only be in hidden places. Sweet women had to put themselves in constant danger to make love to me. All my erotic life is concerned with intrigue and secrets.' " By stating that this is a look into *the*—not *a*—lesbian mind, the reviewer perpetuates the misleading assumption that lesbians prefer a secret, adolescent life.

Books about homosexuality concentrate on men which has probably led the public to conclude that lesbian behavior is identical. Ironically in many ways—sexual activity for one—the opposite is generally true. The AIDS crisis has exacerbated the situation to the point where newspapers using the word *homosexual* are referring only to men.

Even feminist books, as Adrienne Rich points out in her essay "Compulsory Heterosexuality and Lesbian Experience," treat lesbian existence as "a marginal or less 'natural' phenomenon, as mere 'sexual preference' or the mirror image of either heterosexual or male homosexual relations." General-title books, such as *The Third*

Sex, which deals with women executives, is written as though lesbians do not exist. Occasionally, however, there is an unadvertised surprise, as in Florence King's *Confessions of a Failed Southern Lady*.

But as with women's music, many lesbians did manage to acquire books like Del Martin and Phyllis Lyon's *Lesbian/Woman*, which they read with startled exclamations of, "Yes! Wow! That's me!"

Phone lines between lesbians buzz when they hear that Oprah Winfrey is going to interview gay women, or that *Golden Girls* featured a lesbian, or that *Heartbeat* has a real, honest-to-God lesbian character, or that *Waiting for the Moon*, will be rebroadcast.

Good reviews in big newspapers of the frankly lesbian movie *Desert Hearts* were treasured like private victories. But one step forward sometimes means two steps back. When scenes of women loving women occur in movies, they are not ordinary women snuggling into bed with their partner but rather titillating bits of evil intrigue. The 1987 movie *The Last Emperor* continued this tradition with the toe-nibbling seduction of a good woman by an opium-toting spy. Audiences accepted this portrayal, but the tender, erotic scene between two women in *The Color Purple* brought murmurs of "disgusting," and "no wonder it's rated R."

The hunger persists.

21. JUST FOR FUN

"WE don't just sit around wondering how we got this way." Julie's eyes twinkle, but she is adamant about dispelling the image of the sad lesbian.

Sarah Pearlman, the Boston therapist, speaks gleefully of "an outrageous subculture," outrageous because it exists under the noses of heterosexuals who remain blind to its existence.

They are oblivious, not only because lesbians don't talk about their parties at work but because most of them have never stepped in the door of a known lesbian's house. An invitation might bring an intellectual response of "Oh, sure," and a gut-level response of "Oh, no." A lesbian who speaks to women's studies classes acknowledges this by taking the students on a field trip to her home.

As they crowd into the kitchen, she will say, "This is a lesbian refrigerator. These are lesbian dishes. This is the table where a lesbian eats." She proceeds through the apartment pointing out the lesbian TV, the lesbian chairs, lesbian shower, lesbian comb, and finally "the lesbian bed!" By this time the students' nervous giggles have turned to roars of laughter.

Just as an older Baltimore lesbian was flummoxed by a heterosexual neighbor's invitation to a Christmas party, a sudden invitation to a lesbian party would produce anxiety in many straight women. Murky pictures of seduction, drink, and drugs might arise. Would she be insulted if someone put the moves on her? Or insulted if they didn't? If she imagined, as Julie suggested, women "sitting around wondering how we got this way," she would surely feel out of place.

Julie admits that she loves hearing stories of lesbian lives, especially romantic ones, because they fill the gap left by TV, movies, and books, but she adds, "I want to be where the fun is. I like events that make my calendar sparkle."

Julie is not referring to public-space occasions like concerts, or a drink with acquaintances after fundraisers or sporting events. Not comfortable "old shoe" evenings, such as another couple in for dinner or partners alone reading or watching a video, but private lesbian gatherings.

Potlucks in La Crosse, Wisconsin; cross-country ski weekends in Ashland, Massachusetts; New Year's Eve parties in Bar Harbor, Maine; informal get-togethers in Spokane, Washington; poker parties in Epping, New Hampshire; and Memorial Day farm weekends in western Pennsylvania.

In Akron, Ohio, Chrisse France says, "We used to have gatherings of two hundred in the Union Hall over the holidays." Her partner, Diane, adds, "Every Sunday the woman I lived with and I used to have open house. Ten to twenty would come and eat, some would play cards, others read the paper, some talk. Just like a family Sunday."

In Manhattan women hold afternoon "teas" in a Village loft apartment, where champagne is served, the food is catered, and the entrance fee is twenty-five dollars.

Halloween is a holiday made to order for lesbians. That is the night they can mock the masquerades they live and the stereotypes others believe. As one woman remarks, "A lot of us have a dramatic streak." As at any party nine-thirty finds the hostesses fidgety as only a half dozen people drift about in the wildly decorated three-room apartment. But by midnight a woman in a tree costume stands rooted in the kitchen, a living room emptied of furniture shakes with dancing feet—including two women in one football uniform—and where-do-you-live? conversation takes place among pirates, pumpkins, and vamps in the chair-filled bedroom.

The 1988 Fall Herland Sister Resources retreat in Oklahoma was attended by seventy-five women and comedienne Karen Williams. Rhonda Smith wrote in the newsletter about funky cabins, staying up till all hours talking, groggily chowing down Mary's pancakes, skinny-dipping. "Being part of a minority in our society, if we want interaction, we have to actively seek it, and then there is always a beginning and an end to the interaction (a date, party, dinner engagement, ball game, etc.). But, in the 'village' of the HSR retreat, we get to interact in a very natural way. We can either talk or not. Play or not. Bump into someone and either smile and walk on, or hug, or wander off and take a long walk together."

Five years ago a woman living in southern Maine decided to brighten the winter holiday season by reserving the back room of a fine country inn for friends and friends of friends. One hundred women showed up to eat, drink, and socialize. In 1988 they booked the entire inn—capacity 230.

Raja, Emily's lover in Manhattan, says of this "outrageous subculture," "We have our own rules, ways of thinking. There is an enormous amount of play in the lesbian culture. Heterosexuality seems to make prisoners of us all, limits the things that you can pursue. A lesbian can be my age [fifty] or older and like to play with her life."

Many heterosexual women also question the rules that have defined what the life of a woman past forty should be. But "play," for them, beyond the occasional dinner and theater with "us gals," "my women friends," usually involves the presence of men. Lesbian play—a neighborhood social group, or a housewarming party—will include straight males, but the parties that put the twinkle in Julie's eye are the ones where women-loving women can be openly and "outrageously" themselves. Trival Pursuit parties, video parties, summer picnics, gay-pride dances, and of course birthday parties.

Acres of lawn sweep to a backdrop of woods; four tables laden with the careless aftermath of a catered picnic squat deserted. The brightly clad guests have left the pool, the volleyball net, the table of drinks, and are clustered on the gentle slope cheering a cream BMW convertible careening across the immaculate greenness. The smiling blond driver whips the car toward the group. A Fairy Queen in a white net gown who is perched on the top of the backseat clutches both her tiara and the huge bakery box balanced on her lap.

The car stops amid cheers and applause. A dark-haired woman, call her Beth, steps forward, and the Fairy Queen hands her the birthday cake. An assortment of campy gifts, including a pink plastic flamingo, follow. Beth and her partner own a consulting firm that grosses a million dollars a year; her passions are music and art. The driver is well known in political and business circles; the car belongs to a highly successful insurance agent.

Twilight melts into summer darkness, the bar table is moved up onto the patio. Beth takes her place at the baby grand piano in a room her partner, whose avocation is carpentry, has added to the house for just this purpose. Face framed by vases of fresh flowers, hands rippling over the keys, Beth leads familiar sing-alongs and then her clear soprano voice soars alone in "Jesse," "The Rose," "Andante."

Emma Hixson—Minnesota

Leo Treadway—Minnesota

Donna Keiko Ozawa—California

Left to right—Stephanie, Jacki, Eric, Deb, Kellie—New Hampshire

Randon T. Eddy—New Hampshire

Diane Jhueck—Washington State

Stasia Ruskie—Maryland

Frances Eileen Selden—Minnesota

Nancy, Sherry and Benjamin—Michigan

Louise Miller—New Mexico

Stephanie Pettey—Maryland

**Shelia Scanlon and Dorothy
Whitcomb—New Mexico**

Sarah Pearlman—Massachusetts　　　**Kass Newman—Maryland**

Rose Mary Denman and Winnie Weir—Maine

Joy Holthaus—Wisconsin

Elizabeth Conner—New Hampshire

Jan Harrow—New Hampshire

Liz Pierce—Minnesota

This is her forty-seventh birthday, and many have come from Manhattan to join her local friends in the annual celebration. Their careers are in advertising, education, law, computers; one is a writer, another a librarian, another a boutique owner. Between songs a mother chats with her son's teacher, couples find each other and sit with hands touching, others cluster around the piano.

Some of the guests have just met, some are friends dating back to grad school days, some are ex-lovers.

Everyone present, except for two gay men, is female. This is their world of just-for-fun.

PART 8

WOMEN TOGETHER

22. SHERRY AND NANCY, A COUPLE

―――――――

TO understand lesbian couples, one invariably compares them to female/male couples—about which women know a great deal. Women study relationships; their survival and that of their children often depends upon it. They think, they daydream, they read, they talk. They puzzle over the complex varieties of people mixed and matched in couples and the failed stereotypes of male and female, and over individuals who wrestle with parental legacies of domination, indifference, exaggerated expectations, abuse.

In the fifties, when women married young and ignorant, they immediately began reading "Can This Marriage Be Saved?" in *Ladies Home Journal* and studying the male/female relations of neighbors, friends, and family. In those pretherapy, pre–open-communication days, this was not an idle diversion but a dogged attempt to perform the woman's duty of holding together a marriage until the children were old enough to support themselves. Personal happiness was not a priority.

Lesbians are raised in families alongside their heterosexual sisters; they absorb the same information about how relations between people are conducted. A lesbian now in her late fifties said, "Don't expect me to become feminine in six years—I spent forty years learning how to behave like a man. We had our hair cut in men's barber shops, wore boxer shorts, bound our breasts, shaved, went out to the bars, and fought for our femmes. We learned to play pool and act angry when we lost. We walked like men, talked like men, smoked and swore like men." She grew up at a time when differences between males and females, in dress, in occupation, in the smallest and largest aspects of living, were expected, exaggerated, and honored.

During the seventies both men and women rebelled against these attitudes; androgyny was "in." Youth jettisoned old patterns of courtship, marriage, and children, which clashed with their affluent, population zero, pill-and happiness-oriented world. This astounding revolution changed deeply ingrained values in one generation. Men and women who had themselves been married as virgins were subsequently confronted with offspring who brought home lovers and expected to sleep with them, who cohabitated with members of the opposite sex for years (sometimes with men or women still legally married to someone else), who married shortly before or after their own child's birth (if at all), who divorced and remarried and raised children not their own.

The sexual revolution belonged to the lesbian too: butch/femme faded, the flower-child attitude of "form a community of friends and take lovers as they come" ruled. Now in the AIDS panic of the late eighties there are rumblings of long-term monogamy among all sexual groups.

Will monogamy mean a return to rigid sex roles for heterosexuals and butch/femme for lesbians, or will all couples strive to openly practice more fluid partnerships? Do lesbians, because it is not traditional that the taller one take out the trash, the youngest bear the children, the one with the deepest voice have the most sexual freedom, the most educated be the breadwinner, have a head start on individually designed coupledom?

Sherry, the chief marketing officer for a small computer software company in Ann Arbor, Michigan, believes they do. "I think gays, both men and women, have something to teach the straight community—how to relate on a peer-to-peer basis. How to build relationships on 'You're an individual and I'm an individual with equal rights to have our needs met and equal responsibilities to see that the relationship works.' Take my brother—he's feminist, thank God—and his wife. He's a physician and she's a minister, and they work very hard at maintaining an egalitarian stance in their marriage. They have a tough time. You know why? The entire society is arrayed against them. Those assumptions [about married roles] are very hard to work against.

"Peer-to-peer relationships are almost impossible to find with men. And if you found one, society would do it in. I paid for part of the house my second husband and I bought, but everyone said to him, 'Isn't it nice you could afford to buy such a nice house for Sherry.'"

The house Sherry now owns with Nancy is theirs. No one would automatically assume that Nancy had bought it for her. As Emily in New York pointed out, women who like structure might be uncomfortable in a relationship where everything is up for grabs. But for those who are adventuresome it is a freeing experience. Of course, two strong women may clash, each being unwilling to surrender her independence.

Trish, Emily's friend, said, "Independence is so important for lesbians. We can't hide behind a man. We have to do it ourselves." And Emily added, "Hiding behind another woman doesn't seem to be an option. Besides, combining wardrobes is a great advantage."

Economic independence has always been a factor in lesbians' relationships; except in rare instances, both women have psychologically and by training prepared themselves to be self-supporting. In college they concentrated on career goals, they took no time out to "put hubby through," no children interrupted their work life. That does not mean, however, that couples do not operate as an economic unit. Mary Kuholski and Lauren—not her real name—are an example of eleven years of cooperative living.

They grew up a mile away from each other, and Mary has moved with Lauren as she made her way through college, medical school, internship, residency, and a couple of job moves. "I need someone to care for," Mary says. "Take care of. Lauren is my job in life." Mary loves to run print shop presses, wear a denim jacket, and ride her motorcycle. "I never grew out of the tomboy stage." She is tall, rangy, and handsome; her black hair is cut short; she enjoys "yukking it up" in conversation.

Lauren is very attractive in a soft, quiet way and she basks in Mary's affection. At times during Lauren's long years of study, Mary stayed home to run the house and cook for her. Mary says, "I went back to work full-time for my mental health more than the income. I was driving Lauren crazy. We get killed in taxes because we're not married."

A Detroit woman said of her ten-year relationship, "Money was a big problem as it is for any couple. V——only worked part of the time for the last five years. She got raped at work and sued them, so she had to do 'undercover' jobs while the suit was going on. After five years it was a little much. Then she started spending a lot. Champagne tastes on a beer budget. Finally I decided I wanted someone to give *me* something for a change."

Of all the living-together details of lesbians' lives, men seem most fascinated with "What do they do in bed and how?" while long-time married women wonder about the day-to-day operations of a house. Misogyny plays a part in both questions. The male believes there is no sex without a penis, and the female imagines another woman in her house as bossy, intrusive, manipulative. Many a woman would not admit this, but instead say, "I like the men." And indeed, she has watched her mother, aunts, and neighbors "handle" men. She knows how it's done. Besides, the house is woman's territory; she runs it. Another woman would be an enemy trying to take her importance away from her. A maid or daughter would add to her importance, an equal diminish it.

Many heterosexual women under thirty have had more experience with living alone and making decisions about cars, houses, and careers than their mothers ever did. They may envision that their marriages will be free of traditional roles, more like the lesbians'; a sharing, not a set division. And it may be, if their husbands and society allow it. Marriages where he cleans and she builds bookshelves have always existed. It is only society's imposition of "henpecked" for him and "wearing the pants" for her that have made these arrangements seem "wrong."

Lesbians have no pressure from society; there are no traditions for their relationships except those that they as individuals bring to it. It can be a freeing experience; as Zona in Oklahoma said, "My God, if I'm a *lesbian*, I really can't be bothered with this." The specifics of their peer-to-peer cohabitation are dictated only by preference, compromise, and habit. Of course they, like everyone else, enter relationships with a full complement of parental legacies, life experiences, and expectations. A woman raised as Daddy's little boy will bring a different set of skills and attitudes than Mother's little cook and helper, and lesbian partnerships, just like heterosexual ones, are formed by attraction to complementary characteristics and differences.

Most women, however, are raised not to *be*, but to *be adaptable*. The male is the center, and the female builds her life around that. One lesbian when asked, "Why do two women move in together so quickly?" replied, "The rush to servitude." Two women who fall over each other making life smooth have a different set of problems. But the opportunity to individualize their relationship—without guilt imposed from within or without—is prized by most lesbians.

Sherry, forty-four, and Nancy, thirty-three, did not rush into cohabitation. Sherry says, "We date our relationship not from when we first slept together but from when we bought the house and moved in together—which was two and a half years after we met."

The old house, on a shady street in the university town of Ann

Arbor, has a sprawling, homey feel. A transient friend's boxed belongings occupy one end of the living room; in the July hot kitchen a boarder, an Asian graduate student, bustles about preparing a traditional dinner; no pristine "second bedroom" exists. The furnishings have been chosen with taste and flair; floor-to-ceiling bookcases are filled with thought-provoking reading; Sherry's fencing trophies gleam. The two women radiate a love for their home, each other, and the lives they live.

Nancy—tall, lean, and dark; a self-employed consultant to companies marketing new computer products—is the daughter of a high school principal and a teacher. She jokes, "I was alive during my high school years, but was I breathing? Get a mirror."

In the side yard the two women relax, sipping iced tea and dipping grapes into yogurt as they tell their story. Sherry, an extremely attractive woman with a warm smile and hair that is a flowing mixture of gray and brown, begins. "One of the things that is unusual about us is that we are completely out and open to everyone in our lives—both families, all family members, friends straight and gay. We spend at least as much time with straight friends as we do with gay friends. Both of us are out at work.

"People fear what they can't predict. And Nancy and I are about as predictable a couple as you can find—except that we are two women. There is nothing unusual about us."

They joined a church as a couple. "It's a Congregational church in town, not a gay church. We suspect we're the first gay people there." The religious tie, a sense of spirituality even when they were not members of a particular church, has always been important for both of them.

"We've never made an 'announcement' of our lesbianism," Nancy says, "we just live. An announcement is confrontational. I'm in sales, where you just move forward assuming the answer is going to be yes."

"We're not defensive," Sherry adds. "That makes a difference in people's attitudes toward us."

Not that all has been smooth for them. Sherry's parents' attitude is still negative, but her four siblings have been very supportive. "It's a process, like everything else," Sherry says, obviously at ease with the situation. "Acceptance of homosexuality is not along economic lines. My family is old Boston blue blood, Ivy League. They are an extremely prejudiced bunch of people, and they live in an extremely prejudiced town—Oakbrook, Illinois, a very wealthy community. They are as hidebound as any people I know." She herself is a Smith graduate.

It took Nancy's parents a year and a half to recover from the shock of their daughter's lesbianism, but they have been "just wonderful" in the decade since. Nancy explains. "I, frankly, was not as comfortable with my first partner in terms of being out. There's nothing about Sherry I would change, nothing I'm ashamed of in her. She's acceptable in all kinds of groups. She's cute, she's funny, she's smart, she dresses well."

"I do believe," Sherry says, "that how you take care of yourself reflects how you feel about yourself. And I think that's the secret to being out. You must begin with feeling good about yourself. You must look hard at how you feel about being a lesbian and the consequences of your choices. If you are comfortable with that, then I think the assumptive pose works in an amazing number of cases."

They realize, however, that Ann Arbor is not Bridgeport, Connecticut. "University communities," Sherry says, "celebrate the natural variation in people." Sherry passionately believes in that natural variation. Nancy, who also opted to move to Ann Arbor, adds, "Choosing where one lives is an economic luxury that not everyone has. Just as it is a fact that jeans cost less than suits."

Sherry and Nancy believe that by acting like a couple they will be treated as one by heterosexual neighbors and others. "We are a couple, so straight women don't have to deal with the unease of us as potential sexual partners."

They note that with their straight friends, conversational remarks like, "Well, do you guys file joint returns?—oh yeah, I forgot," are not uncommon. They are legal guardians for the children of two heterosexual couples. "They say we're the most happily married people they know." One of these children is a fifteen-year-old girl whose parents' attitude is, "We don't know if what you have is catching, but it doesn't bother us anyway."

Nancy says, "I may pull the money for dinner out of my billfold because Sherry's forgotten hers, but we've merged. We have joint checking, power of attorney, wills, and medical power of attorney, which means that if either one of us was in the hospital and unable to make a decision for herself, the other could make it. It's legal in this state. We're as legally entangled as we can be without a marriage license."

Sherry adds, "Although my company tried to get health benefits extended to Nancy, the state of Michigan licensing board says, 'Legal spouse.' " And of course they cannot file joint-income-tax statements or inherit without taxes.

"If we could get legally married to get those few benefits we're lacking now, we'd do it," Nancy says, and Sherry adds, "Including all the legal entanglements we'd have to go through to get divorced."

Nancy reasons, "We associate with the straight couples that we do because they value their marriages. The gay community is not as focused on couples. They have the attitude that this one will last until the next one comes along. And I don't feel that way with Sherry, therefore I don't want that. I want my good feelings validated."

When the idea of monogamy being related to age is discussed, Nancy interjects, "I think that it is actually a function of choke chains." The women eye each other and laugh with glee at the private joke.

"At some point," Sherry says, "you decide that the intimacy of a relationship is more important to you than experiencing, and that may be a function of age. But it may also be a choice you make early."

"It may even be," Nancy adds, "a reflection of the times. The eighties are more settled than the sixties and seventies were."

Sherry had a relationship with a woman at college and has "been married a couple of times, and gone to bed with more men than I care to think about."

"Certainly more than *I* care to think about," Nancy says. Sherry laughs and continues. "I have a male view of sexuality. With men and with women too. It can be a wonderful roll in the hay without any emotional attachment. But ask me if I believe in the monogamy of this relationship and I'll say, 'Absolutely.' "

Sherry's second marriage was to an alcoholic and "a denier like my father. I said to my father once, 'You're a denier.' 'No, I am not!' he yelled. If only I had laughed. A woman I was with was also an alcoholic and a denier. This is the first relationship where I have not had to go into counseling." Sherry's first psychiatric sessions were initiated by a college same-sex affair, but they were more successful in helping her cope with the rage she felt against her very controlling father. She had other classmates, however, to whom psychiatric "straightening" did irreparable harm.

Repetition of partners with the same fault as a parent is not confined to the lesbian world, but one therapist noted, "Lesbians are often already living with a new partner before they have found out what went wrong with the last one."

Nancy believes, "The haste with which two women move in together may be a desire to legitimize the relationship. Due to the lack of any societal recognition, sharing an address and a kitchen and pets is a way of legitimizing it."

The women believe that the two and a half years they spent "building basic communication patterns" before they moved in together have helped make their relationship successful. "People stumble over each other when they're living together," Nancy says. "Our rule is to bring up the disagreement immediately. You do not save issues until you have about fourteen little things lined up. We don't have big blowups, we have our disagreements as we go along."

Sherry adds, "So we are not filled with premonitions about blowouts."

The women lean across the table, extending their left hands; their rings are a delicate gold, similar but not identical.

"Most people," Nancy says, "don't wear rings, because it leads to questions."

"But," Sherry says, "being out is a very important way of supporting a relationship."

Nancy agrees. "That is one of the things you lose when you stay in the closet—the support of people out there who would be willing to if you'd only tell them. Half the people know anyway. We get a lot of support from being out."

She then brings up the subject of sex. "There is a lot of talk that sexual relationships for lesbians last only two years, or you do it only three times a year because you have to." Sherry blurts, "Terrifying, isn't it!" "And that's certainly not the case with us. But I think the assumption that the sex is going to end, that once the passion and excitement of getting to know each other is gone, that there will be nothing to sustain the relationship, affects the longevity of the partnership."

Sherry does not believe that it is biological or psychological differences between the female and male that keeps sexuality alive. "At one point I looked on the world as my Garden of Eden—"

Nancy's voice, quick and dry, interjects, "Fortunately we're beyond that phase now."

"—so, knowing both sides, I think it's the individual personalities that keep the excitement going. I don't think sexuality is any different from any other form of communication. It's something you pay attention to, you work at, you nurture. We value the sexual part of our relationship. People—straight or gay—who have a fear of intimacy willy-nilly lose their sex lives. I think people can be really terrific sex partners with strangers and in intimacy they freeze."

Nancy and Sherry believe that lesbians should take the wraps off their sexuality, should stop having conferences at which discussions about long-term partnerships exclude sex. Just as Sherry believes that the gay world has information to share about peer-to-peer relationships, she thinks that they in turn can learn about sexuality from the nonsexist heterosexual world. "A lot has been lost by throwing out the baby with the bathwater."

When the subject of children arises, the women suddenly beam with delight, and their words tumble over each other. "You bet!" "We're working on it!" "We'll know in about two weeks."

Sherry's grin is from ear to ear. "As we speak, Nancy may be pregnant. We went through artificial insemination this Thursday."

Nancy, though she was never interested in having children until her relationship with Sherry, agreed to be the one to carry the child because of her age. Sherry, coming from a family of five, had always wanted a family of her own. They decided on a sperm bank in California rather than the local insemination program, for several reasons. They wanted to do it openly as lesbians, choose a donor who looks like Sherry, and have information about his background and the health of all members of his family tree. Because of ovulation problems Nancy had to endure tests and take fertility drugs. Neither woman is frightened of twins, because they want at least two children anyway. The nurse who came to their house to do the insemination has assisted over five hundred woman; this was her first lesbian couple.

"It's hard," Nancy says with a smile, "to focus on anything else. In two weeks we can do one of those home tests!"

"Boy or girl," Sherry says, "it doesn't matter." The child's last name will be the two women's surnames joined by a hyphen. "We think one of the wonderful things we can do for Nancy's parents is give them a grandchild living nearby."

"They may be initially stunned," Nancy says, "but how can you turn down a baby?"

Sherry remarks that they know children are work—she was once the stepmother of teenagers. "We have been thinking hard about the adjustments we'll have to make. And jobs are one of those."

"We've been paying off debts. Thinking about what college costs will mean," Nancy adds.

"We had dinner last night with a straight couple who are thinking through having a child. She's so excited for us. Planning a baby shower . . ."

"Last night," Nancy says, "is an example of how we are really blessed with friends. It was a hot night; we were all casual. We sat at the table for hours. Darrell and Ann with their hands on each other. Sherry and I sitting like this." They are close; their bare upper arms touch.

They smile at each other, then Nancy leans across the table and says in her intense way, "We want to raise a child."

Sherry's smile envelopes her whole face. "We want to be a family."

The birth announcement read, "Our baby just arrived! Name: Benjamin————. Date: May 3, 1988. Weight: 8 pounds, 7 ½ ounces. Length: 21 inches. Proud parents: Sherry and Nancy."

23. ATLANTA PARTNERS

MARLENE Johnson is black and towering and wide in her T-shirt and skirt. She motions to a painting over the couch. "I like [R.C.] Gorman's paintings. He does substantial women. I like women who aren't about to be blown away." Her laughter is strong.

Brooke Hopkins, Marlene's partner of nine years, is first generation out of England, Florida raised, a graduate of the University of South Florida, and has never been in the North. Beside Marlene she looks smaller, older—although they are both thirty-eight—and very white.

Leni, black and lively, has been with them for all of her one and a half years; it was a private adoption. Marlene, who is physically unable to conceive, had just gone through therapy to rid herself of the desire for a baby when she was offered the soon-to-be-born infant of a relative. She called a big meeting of all her friends— prochild and antichild—weighed the evidence, and decided on motherhood. Brooke says, "I could not say no to something she wanted so badly." They are thinking of adopting a sister for Leni when she is four, probably a racially mixed child from Peru or Bangkok. "Too much hassle for a lesbian to adopt in this country," Marlene believes.

About Leni's adoption she thunders, "You don't think I would tell anyone I was a les-be-an when taking out adoption papers! They didn't ask, but hell no, I'd have lied through my teeth. They would never have given her to me. I have a client whose husband's an alcoholic and she's a state protective worker, but they took her son away from her because she's a lesbian."

Marlene is a therapist with a woman's counseling collective, which she helped to found in 1973.

"I could not," Marlene says, "have survived as a black lesbian in the straight white world. I had to create my own world—that was the price I had to pay for being out. I will never make as much money as I could because I work in an alternative environment. To get federal money or go into a big-time agency, I'd have to go into the closet. The people who come to a lesbian counselor are usually women, and women do not have a strong economic base. Ask most women for two hundred dollars a month, and they say, 'Excuse me. I got a life. I got rent. I don't need my head shrunk that bad.' It's a real economic choice for me to be out." The collective had to wage a long fight for nonprofit status because they refused to agree to tell their clients that lesbianism was a disease.

A curtained sun porch off the living room serves as Marlene's office. The house is a large bungalow, nicely furnished and comfortably cluttered with paperbacks, pets, and the lives of two working women raising a child. While Leni is bouncing naked on the bed after her bath, Brooke talks thoughtfully about her future. "We're hoping that out there somewhere there will be a good, gentle man for her to marry." Brooke works eight to five as an administrator for a small service organization and takes care of Leni while Marlene sees clients in the evening. The women's time together on weekends is jealously guarded from Marlene's political friends who are not in favor of "coupledom."

Brooke, who has settled herself behind an ironing board, talks about the influence of religion in her life. Both sets of her grandparents were Methodist ministers, Salvation Army officers. She, like Vanessa, has never fully resolved the question of sin.

"If you wanted to say being lesbian was a sin, it would be no greater a sin than, say, lying. But I guess I've never answered that question whether it *is* a sin or not. I feel that it is a sin to be something that you're not. To me being with a man would be a total fake. I think it's a sin to go against your nature. That's what they're talking about, I think. But I haven't totally convinced myself, obviously."

Brooke can talk while guiding the iron, but Marlene, even when seated, is movement and drama. "Early in our relationship Brooke needed some religious stuff, and we tried different churches." One was an existential church to which a lot of lesbians belong. Another, the Atlanta Metropolitan Community Church, which a lot of gay men attend, they found "a little extreme," and a charismatic group was annoying because of the pressure to speak in tongues.

Brooke adds, "There is also a very large church here where they love and accept homosexuals, but—here's the kicker—they also have groups to *help* the homosexual. To cure them."

Marlene was raised in a church, "as most black people are. My mother was sort of a primitive Baptist. My father was a more in-town Baptist. But I was baptized Methodist. That was because— my father was a Marine—that's the church we were near when puberty struck. They thought I had to get something going for me. I wanted to be a nun, but the Methodists didn't have any parts for nuns. I loved the idea of holding your wimple together with your brains."

Marlene's grandmother had been a teacher, but when normal-school certificates were no longer sufficient credentials, she became a laundress on a military base; she had "run off" her alcoholic husband. Marlene's mother graduated from high school at fifteen and college at nineteen; she returned to teaching when Marlene was fourteen and put her six children through school.

Her father came from a very poor family; his father had left when he was three or four months old; his mother was a maid. In the late 30s he had gotten an academic scholarship to Cornell, but he had not been able to survive—he had to work three jobs—so he had ended up in the Marine Corps. "He was in 'em all, you name 'em—Second World War, Korea, Vietnam."

Marlene describes her family: "I have five brothers and sisters, and we were all born at a different base marking my father's career—except for my twin brothers, who for my mother's sake were born in the same place. I came to Atlanta because I got a scholarship to Morris Brown." She did not feel it was a good school, and after two years she "got married to a guy and did my script. He was in the Marine Corps also.

"Well, it was a god-awful marriage, and I was used to god-awful marriages, and so I thought that's how marriage was. But I certainly didn't like it, and it certainly didn't get better. My mother would say such things as, 'Now, now, now, it'll get better. He'll get tired.' He was incredibly abusive—not physically."

Marlene stayed in the marriage primarily for the sake of her grandmother, with whom the family had always lived when the father was overseas. "Shortly after my grandmother died, I met a woman. I had been a good girl all my life. Always followed the rules. I was the oldest, with all this pressure to be a good kid. And my father was an alcoholic, so I was a real good kid.

"I fell hot in lust for Anita. I was so extreme with it that I moved her into the house with my husband. He worked nights. One morning she didn't wake up in time. After that it was pretty clear that this was not going to work, and I left him. I was in my midtwenties."

Marlene describes Anita as a "stone dyke. Really rigidly butch. She had been in the army. Kick butt and be happy to."

"My family," Marlene says, "weren't wild about her. I was separated from my husband and I was living in this one-bedroom apartment with this WOMAN. They came down. A divorce? You're crazy! My mother said, 'Sweetheart, I lived with your father all these years, surely you can.' My father said—as only a Marine DI can—'You have two choices. You can go back to your husband or you can come home with your father.' I didn't want either choice. And then he said, 'Just exactly what are you doing?" And I said, 'Pop, you really want to know?' And he changed the subject, and they never brought it up again. And he went out and got my mother and told her, 'Marie, get your things, we're leaving. We no longer have a daughter.' They tore my name out of the Bible.

"I was ill, I went crazy for about a year. I was unemployed. I had this basement apartment and I used to lie on my bed and watch feet go by. No one caught up with me—I was smart enough to stay out of the clutches of society. Then somehow I found myself back in school [in 1974] and got my degree at Georgia State as a therapist and lived happily ever after."

Brooke has always been either celibate or gay. She does not use the term *lesbian* because she doesn't like the way the word sounds. "I wasn't celibate on purpose, I just didn't like boys. I couldn't stand the thought of penises. I had some experience, and it lived right up to my expectations. Ooo—" She shudders. "I was just one of those people who didn't date. God, I didn't know I was *gay*. But, looking back, I was real possessive of my best friends. Gay was never discussed in my circle of friends."

At twenty-five Brooke got involved with a woman who used the fact that "everyone I ever loved left me" to lock Brooke into the role of unconditional mother. When Brooke tried to move away, the woman, who was involved with drugs and men, followed. In Jacksonville, Florida, Brooke got together with another woman, Gloria, who was also in a bad relationship, as a means of extracting them both from their current situations.

Brooke now knew a total of four, including herself, gay women. Not a large group from which to choose a partner. "So Gloria and I moved to Atlanta, and I met Marlene."

"Now there's five," Marlene says. The two women have developed a routine of deadpan humor. "'Course I knew there were other lesbians, cuz I'd been with A-ni-ta, who had come out in a youth detention center in D.C. at thirteen. She'd been around the old mulberry bush several times. I'd been to bars. I knew there was millions, millions of us."

"By then," Brooke said, "I'd read about it and knew there were some out there. And that it was perverted."

At that time Brooke was running programs for the Salvation Army, and Marlene applied for a job. "Of course, I was infatuated during the interview, which was why I hired her. And she was just as infatuated."

Marlene corrects her. "I was intrigued."

Brooke broke up with Gloria. "By that time I knew that Gloria was just 'better than being alone in a strange city.' She wasn't gay —she was just going along."

Marlene adds, "She'd go along with anything."

"But I liked her," Brooke insists.

"What's not to like? She'd do anything anyone wanted her to. She's married now with two kids. We go to see them sometimes. Gloria's still going with the flow."

Brooke and Marlene met in February, by May had declared their sexuality, and by August were living together. Both women brought a lot of "hangovers" from their past relationships, and they split up after a year and a half.

"I had had two bad relationships," Marlene says. "The first with my husband, which was incredibly abusive, and the second with Anita, which was incredibly dependent. She needed me, and I needed her to need me. She had come out butch, and she showed me the femme role. I was Momma and did all the work, and she was in charge. I knew I didn't want any more of that shit. So, when Brooke and I separated and she moved to another apartment in the same building—"

"You can see we cut these ties severely."

"Yeah, she moved downstairs. And almost immediately when we stopped living together, Brooke went back to being Brooke and I went back to being me—"

"And we liked each other again."

"Immediately. But we stayed 'apart' for two years."

They both believe women move in together too fast. Marlene explains, "It's so impermanent, there's no structure. I see it in my clients."

"What do you mean, 'impermanent'?" Brooke asks.

"I really believe that gay people have so much to fight against that they want to hang on to anything that good."

"I never felt that."

"Then why did you want to move in so fast?"

210

Brooke looks over the starched blouse she is ironing, lowers her voice, and says, "Oh, God, because I just loved you so much."

Marlene giggles, and Brooke adds, "I didn't want to live alone."

"Women are raised not to live alone. We're raised to take care of things."

"But gay men move in fast too."

"They're trying to be women. No, I believe they're vulnerable, that any minority clings."

"Maybe it has something to do with age," Brooke says thoughtfully. "If we broke up, I wouldn't move in with anybody else right away. I wouldn't want to go through the hassle of a relationship again. I mean, it's just a lot of work."

"When you're young, you can fool yourself into believing that impermanent things might be permanent. When you get older, you know that limerace—"

Brooke looks up quickly. "What's that mean?"

"The hots. Infatuation, sweetie."

"She comes up with all these words. I was never a bright child."

"Yes, you are. You play dumb, and it works very effectively."

Marlene talks about young women getting in and out of relationships and how even her older clients seem to be looking for youth.

Brooke asks, "Are you attracted to younger women?"

"No, but I'm wise." Marlene laughs with her whole body. "After a woman has bought two houses with lovers and had to sell them, she doesn't do that anymore. She says, 'You can move in with me, but I ain't selling my house no more.' Older women are not out on the meat rack. They are tired of doing it. And whether lesbians want to own it or not, there is ageism. It is very much a part of the culture, and therefore it's part of ours."

Marlene believes that sexuality declines in lesbian relationships. "On the hierarchy gay males have more sex than anybody, heterosexual couples come next, then poor lesbians fall on the bottom of the totem pole. Women are not raised to be sexual beings. We have to keep ourselves in check because men have NO control. Parents certainly don't encourage girls' sexuality, and with men it's, 'Go, boy! Nail that girl.'

"So, you have two women who have played up more their emotions and feelings, caring and nurturing, who have to work harder than any other people for their money, who have this script saying they have to make a nest. After you work hard, take care of a nest, nurture your partner and yourself, there ain't a lot of energy left over for sex. I find in couples who have been together for a while, sex kinda falls back, and they do more of the affection, caretaking, nurturing of each other and are not as sexually active. I think they can stay nonsexual partners for years and years or have very intermittent sex. And as long as it's okay with the two of them, they'll be happy as ticks.

"There is a song, 'Only Two Years,' about lesbian relationships. So Brooke and I find ourselves—at least among the fairly visible lesbians—the old married people. We just had our ninth year. We get a lot of shit for 'coupleism' from the lesbians in *the community*."

"They don't value it," Brooke says.

"They say it's selling out to the patriarchal system that says one must become part of a couple. One builds a community of friends and you take your lovers as they come." Marlene's voice is staccato with scorn.

Brooke says dryly, "I think it's just that they aren't in a relationship right now."

"We like each other a lot," Marlene says. "We're very different." She turns to Brooke, who, in contrast to her partner, looks plain and pale behind the ironing board. "I like you better than anyone else."

"That's why we say if we ever broke up, I'd move upstairs. We'd still be roommates."

"Our sense of humor runs on similar lines—hers is a little strange, mine is more normal. So, we like each other a lot. Like doing the same kind of things."

Brooke believes they have achieved a balance. "When any couple comes together, they have this idea that they do everything together, that they live for each other, and that they are going to provide for each other's needs—"

"Totally," Marlene interjects.

"If we concentrated on each other all the time, we wouldn't stay together a week. I have needs that Marlene is not interested in—"

"Nor am I interested in pretending that I am interested."

"And I'm not going to go to—"

"These women's concerts and poetry things."

"They're all political. I don't know what they're talking about. So, Marlene needs to get another friend to go with her. In other couples that's not the expectation."

They don't believe that because they are the same sex, they understand each other better. "That's a crock," Marlene says. "I get a lot of that in my work. Because you can SEE that men are different. . . ." She talks about the similarity of the problems her gay and straight clients face.

"Brooke and I have a commitment to see if rough spots can be resolved. If you broke up each friendship any time your friend irritates you—and they ALL do—you would not have a friendship that lasts longer than two years. Because you know your friends can really work your nerves. You learn the tolerance when it rubs. One of the reasons Brooke and I work as a couple is that we have a high tolerance for each other. We don't get tired of each other."

Their current rough spot is Leni and where they will spend Christmas. Brooke wants to follow her family tradition of "Whoever's family you spent Thanksgiving with, you go to the other's at Christmas."

Marlene insists you always go to mother's. "A husband goes to where the mother of his wife is—if he's got ANY SENSE at all. Extremely matriarchal. I'm telling you MOTHER. And someday I'm going to be MOTHER, and Leni and her little children going to come HERE."

Brooke says quietly, "You're not going to do that to her."

"I might. It's hard to break from one's roots. I'M DOING THE BEST I CAN."

"I suggested that this year for Thanksgiving we all go to Disney World, and her mother loves the idea."

"You notice she said MOTHER. She's new, but she's got it figured out."

Holidays present special problems to lesbian couples when their parents don't know the totality of their relationship. Marlene believes her family knows, but Brooke questions it. Brooke's family knows that they have bought the house together, the cars, that Marlene and Leni are her family. "There's no need to make them hear the word *gay*. Let them do whatever they need to do to feel comfortable." But Marlene does not feel comfortable around Brooke's father, and race is part of the reason.

"I feel that in this karmic life I chose a doozy—a triple minority. I'm working out something big this time." But she does not feel oppressed and attributes that to the way she has structured her world. "I work for myself within the collective, which is a racially mixed group. But I know it's a small world I've created, and when I go out of it very far, I bump into the other one. And it kinda pulls me up short, and I get indignant.

"I've felt pressure all my life, so being a lesbian was kinda a minor thing. After being a woman and black—WHAT? They're going to call me a NAME? Wow, get down! Black people know about being a minority. They may not like it, but they're familiar with it. You have some mechanism."

She believes the ratio of black lesbians is the same as for whites, but that they are even more underground. "I know very few black lesbians. And I think I'm the only black lesbian counselor in a city the size of Atlanta that's out. There's very strong, strong injunctions in the black community. Because it's a matriarchal society to some degree it's more acceptable for a black man to be gay than a black woman."

Marlene talks about isolated women who would not even acknowledge themselves as lesbian. "Every once in a while in my work, I find a couple who just wandered out. But I think there's a huge number underground. There's no way of knowing. There must be hundreds of thousands of women, but we don't know where they are or how to i-den-ti-fy them."

"When I first went to work four years ago," Brooke says, "there was a black woman who thought maybe Marlene and I were lesbians but she didn't think any black women were. She thought only white people did that, so we couldn't be."

"One of the more active political lesbian groups here is trying to process their racism—no blacks are in the group, of course. It drives me mad when minorities attack minorities. Lesbians have the same racial stuff as everyone else. They've been raised the same way. Black lesbians are very exclusive too. Even white lovers are not invited to some parties. Same stuff. It's very painful to me as a black person to see that oppression. It's incredible to me how we use all kinds of mechanisms to separate, divide, and therefore de-power ourselves. Because as we splinter smaller and smaller into specialized groups . . . ." She flings an arm in the air. "Pretty soon Brooke and I are going to form a group—black and white couples who have been together longer than seven years with a child—a black child a year and a half old, female. AND ONLY PEOPLE IN THAT GROUP CAN COME. I used to think that women were a higher evolved species—"

"That's not true," Brooke interjects.

"I know. It's so discouraging. So terribly disappointing. I see women doing heinous things, and I just can't BELIEVE." She pounds into the kitchen for more coffee.

Resettled, Marlene continues. "I have women clients who are in the closet and I'm not going to tell them to come out. 'Sweetie, you need to teach. That's all you know how to do. And you'd better wear that paper bag over your head during gay pride. The reality is, whether it's fair or unfair, you'll be walking the streets and you will not teach again anywhere.' "

Brooke asks, "Why, if I was a teacher, would I need to show other people that I was gay?"

"To show people that lesbians are normal, that we do not go around molesting children. So that people know someone. It's the same difference as a white person really knowing a black person rather than them just saying, 'Oh, I know you are really an op-pressed people and would you like to come to my house for dinner?' For people to get over their fear, they have to know someone."

"I'm not denying the need for the political element," Brooke says. "That's what it takes to make change. We have to have them. I say why is it necessary for every gay person to do that?"

"It would quicken the process." Marlene sighs. "But it's an ideal thing, I don't think it's going to happen. There are realities.

"So, you see we are not politically correct with *the community*. We smoke, we eat meat, we do not wear Birkenstocks. We're in big doo-doo. My friends say, 'Marlene, you're wearing a skirt,' and I say, 'I can march just as well in my SK-IRT, I don't have to put on boxer shorts to prove—' I know who I am."

"We've never been to a gay-pride march," Brooke says. "I don't want my face on TV. That's just not where I am. I move slowly, one step at a time, and I can change attitudes. We have friends, staunch separatists, who can't understand why we want men in Leni's life."

Marlene observes, "She will probably grow up in a world where there are a lot of them, so she'd better learn how to deal with them."

"She will probably marry one."

"She might even be heterosexual." Their explosive laughter does not wake Leni, asleep in the next room.

"Because women are, as a whole, nonentities," Marlene says, "that's why we're not harassed [like gay men are]. We're one step down from general women, and general women are not even ac-knowledged, so why would they waste their time on LES-BE-ANS? And it's so hard for them to image a woman being interested in anything other than a penis—it doesn't compute. So they think of us as old maids, if they think of us at all."

Marlene and Brooke believe things have gotten better for lesbians in Atlanta, but they fear the combination of fervent, primitive re-ligious believers and AIDS. Marlene says, "I think lesbians are going to get caught in the fallout. We won't be the target, because women are insignificant. I think women will watch it come and watch it go. Those few of us who stand up are going to get blown a-way. And then the rest of us will sit down."

Brooke says, "I—we're not going to stand up, we'd lose Leni."

"I'd like to think I'd stand up, but I don't know." Marlene's face sags in thought. "Women have been taught to survive."

"I don't think," Brooke says, "racism has gone anywhere but into the closet. In the last two years it's become okay to say that word. It's upsetting. They shout, "Nigger lover," across the lot at a major mall. What makes them think they can say that?"

"Except when they see two women, they don't say it. They think I'm her maid."

"I think about moving a lot. But then I think I might be disappointed. But it would certainly be outside the state. Marlene and I have to be very aware when we travel outside Atlanta. We are careful."

"You have to travel from pocket to pocket—from New Orleans to Atlanta to Miami. There's not much in between. Brooke and I get some looks because of racial stuff. But, honey, it would never cross their minds that we were lesbians, were lovers. I mean, if they could ever get to the fact that two women might be having sex, they'd NEVER suspect we'd cross RACE!"

24. WITH THREE CHILDREN

THE question of children—if, when, how many—is one that concerns many young women today. Lesbians are no exception. In addition they, as did the unmarried mother of thirty years ago, carefully weigh the possibility that their child will be stigmatized by their actions. Divorce, single parenthood, two-job families, have eliminated the Mommy-at-home/Daddy-at-work stereotype, but even the most liberal of people often assume that children and lesbians do not belong together. The more outspoken say, "It's selfish. Let them live that way if they feel they have to, but leave children out of it."

Knowing these attitudes exist, lesbians wonder if it is fair to subject a child to possible prejudicial treatment from teachers, classmates, and neighbors. And will they themselves, under that kind of pressure, be able to provide a good, stable home for the child. They sort through scenarios of moving to an urban setting where differences are commonplace, of lying about their sexual preference to outsiders and the child, of living alone until the child is out of the house.

For Marlene motherhood, a child of her own, was the deciding factor in the adoption. Sherry and Nancy's desire to be a family impelled them toward artificial insemination. Some women already have children.

A narrow road overhung with wet autumn leaves runs parallel to an old stone wall as it winds away from a small town in New Hampshire. On a cul-de-sac sit several houses. The newest, a comfortable, two-story house, was purchased while it was still in the building stage by Deb L——and Jacki P——, women who divorced their husbands six years ago and merged their three children into a family. The upper level is for adults, although in what would be a second bedroom—no fake separate bedrooms in this house—a child kneels in front of book-lined shelves. Stephen King occupies the place of honor; lesbian books are just below. Kellie L——is ten, a wispy child with blond hair and large brown eyes. Her smile is shy and curious.

Downstairs in the utility room two covered kitty litter boxes and four food dishes stand neatly in a row; four cats and one dog are part of the household. Eric P——a thoughtful, alert ten-year-old, and his sister, Stephanie, a vivacious brunette of eight, are playing a board game in his room; the girls share another large bedroom. On alternate weekends the children are with their fathers and fathers' parents who live nearby.

In the spacious living room, the decor of which includes arty naked women, Jacki and Deb, nicknamed "the twins" because they are both four feet eleven and one-half inches tall, settle on the couch with their legs tucked up. Jacki says that before she had her hair cut, they looked even more alike—hers is dark and straight around her lean face, Deb's is curly and pulled back away from her soft, fair skin. Both women are thirty-one.

Before they moved to this house, they lived in a small city a few miles distant, and they both still work there—Jacki, who has an associate degree from a community college, as secretary to the branch manager of a bank, and Deb, who goes to school twenty hours a week for emergency medical training, as secretary for an ob/gyn. Their combined income is $26,000 and their husbands contribute $125 a week in child support. Four thousand five hundred dollars, Jacki's share of the equity from the house she and her husband, Bob—not his real name—owned, helped with the down payment on this one; the monthly payments are $476. Each summer the women rent, for $500, a lakeside site in a nearby adult campground and park their camper there.

Jacki graduated from high school in June 1974 and married her boyfriend that October. She worked four years in a factory, which enabled them to buy a house two years after Eric was born. "When Eric was two, we had Stephanie. I did everything just right, then sat at home and said, 'I have the perfect life. I have a husband who loves me dearly—no problems there. Two great kids—no problems. Own my own home. Twenty-two years old. This is wonderful.' Then I got restless." Jacki's voice is low with the broad *a* and long *o* accent of a born-and-bred New Hampshirite.

She had been interested in women since she was a teenager but had never acted on it. At twenty-three she had an affair with another curious married woman ten years older than she. "I didn't feel guilty at all. There was no competition. She was no threat to my husband. She was giving me a whole different side of the coin. The affair lasted six months, and then she decided that she was perfectly happy being married and thanks a lot, but . . .

"I was more sexually attracted to her than I had ever been to my husband, but the fulfillment wasn't there. Neither one of us knew—it was like putting two virgins together. There was never enough time. We were always on pins and needles—husbands were going to come home, kids were going to wake up. I realized it was infatuation, all sexual. But I liked it. After it was over, I felt like a teenager who has experimented, but it had hurt too much, and I had taken a lot of affection away from the kids." They were one and three at the time.

"I felt there was a good chance I was homosexual because since being with her, I had had much less interest in my husband. Not that there was a lot there to begin with, but I did my wifely duties. He was very good to me, and I felt obligated to sleep with him, I felt obligated to make supper for him, I felt obligated to clean for him. I wasn't happy, but I thought you were supposed to feel that way. That every wife felt that way."

Both women agree that that was the image of marriage they got from their parents: "He comes home, asks, 'What's for supper?' and sits down with the paper." Jacki's mother was forty-two when Jacki was born; her father retired the year she graduated from high school; she has four siblings, ten to twenty years older. In contrast, Deb's parents are only twenty years older than she, the firstborn.

Jacki's husband, two years her senior, didn't know about her affair. "He's kinda numb. He's not stupid. Naive. He was a virgin when we married, and so was I. But he tried to do all the right things." Because Bob worked second-shift in a machine factory, Jacki could escape the house to teach exercise classes to kids and work part-time at Papa Gino's. "Bob's always been a great father. He did get up in the middle of the night with the kids. He changed many diapers."

Deb has a high-pitched voice; her New Hampshire accent is even thicker than Jacki's, and her story is similar. A few months after graduation from high school she married the boy who had been a lifetime summer neighbor on a Maine lake. "It was just accepted that we'd get married. I don't think I ever loved him. We had had premarital sex, and I had thought, 'This is it?' I wasn't overly thrilled with it. He was a very demanding, selfish lover and at eighteen always horny. But he didn't satisfy me. He'd roll over and go to sleep, and I'd be all wound up.

"I had started experimenting with girls in grade school. Playing doctor. Some of the things we did we'd be arrested for as adults! Fifth grade stands out in my mind. I wasn't interested in playing doctor with little boys at all, and in high school I had crushes on all the female jocks. You bet! Very emotional. My grandmother would catch me wrestling with another little girl on her bed in seventh grade. 'Now, Debbie, that's not nice. Young ladies don't wrestle with each other.' We weren't just wrestling, but my grandmother didn't know that. But then doing things with little girls ended, and after that it was just emotional."

Her husband was in the army, and abuse and drinking began early in the marriage. "Peter is very intelligent, but he's always been a little crazy. But at eighteen my ego was this big, and I had to stay and see if I could make it work. I wasn't going to go running home to Mom and Dad." Because he wanted a baby, she stopped using birth control pills. "Taking them was ridiculous anyway because we hardly ever made love. I'd go to bed before him and fake sleep or wait until he was asleep. I had plane tickets to fly home when I found out I was pregnant."

They moved back to New Hampshire, and Deb decided that she was "not going to stay with this jerk just because of the baby. Kellie would get all upset and crying. 'Don't hurt my mommy, don't hurt my mommy.' I got a job to save my money and buy a car. I went out with other people—a gay man, sort of on the right track! Lots of crushes on women. When I finally met Jacki, I said, 'I've got to act on this one.' I took a big chance, and it worked."

The women met in the summer at the exercise class Jacki helped teach. "I was always the eager beaver," Deb says. "Helping the instructor put the equipment away after class. I would have had a wicked crush on her if we'd been in the same high school."

Deb came to see Jacki when she was in the hospital for a knee operation, and a close friendship began. They saw each on a daily basis, talked for hours on the phone; the emotional and physical feelings became intense. "I had never really had a best friend," Deb says. "Someone I could tell anything to. My husband felt really threatened by that because I had never been friends with him."

"We just spent time together," Jacki says. "Grab a sub and go sit in the park. I had the kind of husband that if I said, 'Let's do this,' he'd say, 'Oh, all right.' 'Couldn't you get a little more excited?' 'What do you want me to do—get up on the table?' 'No, forget it.' He'd always say, 'You've changed. I liked you better when you were eighteen.' Because then I was madly in love with him and extremely jealous and all my waking hours were just to please him. Listening to him tell his stories from work over and over again . . .

"When Deb and I became friends, I wasn't going to let it go any further. I had been hurt very badly and I wasn't going to ruin another friendship. But I felt absolutely no guilt about loving a woman—it was just the wrong woman, and this was also the wrong woman because she was married with a kid."

Deb says, "I would try to imagine myself with her. What would we do? How would we do it? I never knew any other lesbians, so I thought I was the only person in the world who felt this way. I lived in a very straight community. You think of a lesbian as a big, masculine-looking woman with a cigar hanging out of her mouth."

"And they lived in Boston, anyway," Jacki says with a laugh.

The two women tell the day-by-day, almost hour-by-hour details leading up to their physical expression of love. "We were," as Jacki put it, "in lust at that point."

Although they both had experimented with other men, they had never known passion before. "Twenty-five years old and brand new," Jacki says. "Fireworks and everything," Deb adds. They grin.

Both women feel the attraction was a combination of gender and person. Deb says, "I liked Jacki, but I also liked the way she felt and the way she made me feel."

"The physical was the frosting on the cake," Jacki adds. "It was almost too good to be true. Sexually it was amazing the things that were happening. After six months of lust we began to stabilize in the real world again."

"My feeling right from the beginning," Deb says, "was—this is it. I wanted a lifelong commitment. Jacki was saying, 'Well, what about the kids? Maybe we should wait until they're eighteen.' "

"I was very, very kid oriented, and I still am," Jacki says forcefully. "As it turns out, I'm a real Mom. Those are my kids, Kellie included. I want to do what's best for them. Then and even now I will sacrifice some of my own happiness or some things that I think are right for me. There was a lot to take into consideration."

Jacki, who had taken fertility drugs in order to get pregnant, had been surprised when her mother said, " 'I didn't think you'd ever have kids.' I couldn't understand why she thought that. 'Of course, I'm going to have kids. I've always wanted kids. Two as a matter of fact.'

"To this day, looking back on everything, I don't have any

regrets. Even if I had recognized my preference earlier on, I still would have had to have my two kids. Even if the method had been different."

Deb had never wanted children and would not have had any if her husband had not been so insistent; certainly she did not bargain for three. "It was a package deal. I was madly in love with Jacki. The kids were two and four and they were adorable, and then they started to get older and mouthy and bratty. Now at eight and ten they are good again. So, we've got a few good years before thirteen."

Deb's husband had suspicions about the women and was drinking a lot. After a scene involving the police, an officer asked Debbie, "Do you have someplace you can go for a few days?" " 'I sure do,' I said. I had already been to see an attorney the day before. This was March. Yeah, it was fast, real fast. I was at Jacki's about two weeks, and sometimes she'd stay out in the living room all night with me."

Jacki's husband was working sixteen-hour shifts, so, in order to give him quiet time to sleep, Jacki moved to Deb's house after a restraining order was issued on Deb's husband.

The women were not afraid of losing custody of the children because Bob would, Jacki knew, not contest it, and Deb felt that her husband would not stand a chance of getting Kellie. "I had a good attorney," Deb says. "Real good."

Jacki told Bob she wanted a divorce. "He cried a lot. Eric was four going on thirty, as he is now. Stephanie was two. We sat down and told the kids. Told them we'd been fighting a lot, but they'd still get to see their daddy. Eric threw a fit, yelled, 'We can't do this!' That broke my heart. I was seeing a psychologist, and there was a lot of stress because of the kids."

She agrees that it would have been better for Bob if she had known her sexual preference earlier, but she likes the idea that "the kids have a father that is a real person they can see. Having that male in their life is very important to them." When Bob and the woman he is about to marry come to pick up Eric and Stephanie for the weekend, the couples always sit and visit awhile. "Deb and I have our cake and eat it too, so to speak, in spite of everything that happened. We have every other weekend off, we have half of summer vacations, so we have our own single life. Actually it's a very ideal situation."

Deb agrees. "Women I work with say, 'God, I envy you and Jacki so much.' I say, 'Hey, you're just in the wrong kind of situation, and they go, 'Oh, no, no, no. We'll keep it just the way it is.' " Laughter runs through her words.

In the beginning, however, both men tried to undercut the children's feelings for their mothers because of the lesbian relationship. Deb's husband would say to Kellie, "Your mother doesn't really love you." Deb has since explained the whole situation of his alcoholism to her daughter. When word got around among Jacki's in-laws, one aunt commented, "The kids aren't happy living in that situation." Jacki confronted her ex-husband, who admitted the kids were fine. The gossip stopped. Neither woman has downgraded the men to the children, and they believe their relationships with their fathers are healthy.

Although Deb and Jacki did not announce, "We are lesbians," to their families, they did not rationalize away or soft-pedal their total commitment. Jacki says, "I got my divorce in July, hers was in August. We moved in together on Labor Day weekend. We had a three-bedroom apartment—Eric had one room, the girls another, and we had a room with a double bed. Nothing was said. Deb was accepted into the family. I had known my husband and his family for ten years, and when his brother was married in September, both Deb and I got invitations to the wedding. It was odd being back at my in-laws' house, but we have never made any bones about our being together."

Jacki's father, who had no high school education, had been a lobsterman; her mother had worked for years in a shoe shop. "My father has always thought I was just wonderful. When Deb and I first got together, I didn't have a job, and he'd come over and slip me money. My mother was sixty-eight then, but she's really sharp. Both of my parents had been married before and divorced. My brother is on his third marriage. They have always said, 'You make your own mistakes. It doesn't matter. You're still my kids and you're okay in my book.'

"My feeling was that my mother was well aware of what was going on and 'if she wants to know, she can ask.' When we brought her up to see the house under construction and took her to McDonald's, her favorite place to eat, she said, 'Now I have something to ask you girls. And I hope that this doesn't make you angry.' And she said, 'Are you girls lesbians?' And we said, 'Yes.' And then she started asking questions. She was real good. She did say, 'And you knew back in high school, didn't you, Jacki? What about that friend of yours?' I guess that's why she was so crying happy when I got pregnant."

Deb's family has always been financially comfortable. "My parents were divorced after twenty-five years—just before Jacki and I got together. My dad was just waiting for the kids to grow up and move out. He is remarried, and we get along wicked good with them, but we don't get along with my mother. She went off the deep end with the divorce and never got over it. My younger sister graduated from Katie Gibbs and thinks she's the cat's meow and says, 'What are you guys, queer or something?' At first my mother would come up and visit, but my sister wouldn't. My mother does everything my sister tells her to do, and she would really rag on her after she came back from visiting here. It's been two years since we've seen her."

Their social life includes many types of people, and they are thinking of making a church connection for the children's sake. For several years they served on the board of a woman's club in Portsmouth, which, in addition to being a bar and restaurant, brought in speakers, did charity projects, and held activities for lesbians with children. They socialize with heterosexual couples who are openly comfortable with their relationship, and with family. Jacki's ex-husband, one of eight children, has two brothers who are gay. One lives with a man and his child, and the two couples and their children get together on the weekends. Occasionally Deb and Jacki go dancing with the gay men at Fantasy in Boston.

From the beginning the confidence the two women had in their relationship allayed their fears of pressures on the children. "They still," Jacki says, "had two parents in the house. It didn't matter that we were both female. Kids are very adaptable to growing up in a gay household. Deb and I have openly shown our affection toward each other since they were little. We don't hide anything. We sleep together, they know that. We sleep nude, they know that. We hug, we kiss. We'll dance in the living room. They know our favorite songs.

"At a family campground Eric said, 'Are you going to the dance tonight, Mom?' I said, 'You have to understand that you think it's okay. We think it's okay. But there are a lot of other people who would be offended because they don't like to see anybody but men and women dancing together.' He still insisted, 'But I don't see anything wrong with it.' Actually, I'm hoping that if someone approached one of the kids and said, 'Hey, your mother wears army boots,' that he'd say, 'Yeah, so what?' "

The children decided on their own to call both women mother, and Jacki affirms that "they consider each other as brother and sister and protect each other. When my husband protested that Stephanie didn't have a 'sister,' I said, 'Well, honey, you find somebody who's willing to marry us. . . .' "

As dual parents they find that the children give Deb a hard time, and she has little patience with them, while Jacki is more in tune with children's priorities and enjoys time spent playing with them. Disagreements revolve around issues of obedience: Jacki sees Deb as too strict, Deb sees Jacki as lenient. Because both mothers work, the children lock themselves in the house after school, tell phone callers their mother is in the shower, and let no one in. In the summer they go to a baby-sitter. As is the case with most parents, the women find that the children interfere with their sex lives and that time alone is precious.

At school there are "no problems," according to Deb. "All the teachers know us. We go in and introduce ourselves. I say, 'I'm Kellie's mother, and she's her other mother. And she's Eric and Stephanie's mother, and I'm their other mother.' Teachers deal with both of us. They treat us as a family. 'Okay, two parents, three kids.' That first year when Jacki wasn't working, we got the reduced-cost lunches for all of them."

"You have to be concerned about education," Jacki says. "We have three very different kids as far as schooling goes. Eric is leading the way and makes things easier for all of us because he is very bright. Then we have an eight-year-old for whom 'Hey, everything's a breeze.' We have a ten-year-old, Kellie, who has hated school since kindergarten."

Jacki is firm in her belief that attitude makes the difference in how they are accepted. "We don't feel anything wrong with it. We're not going in and lowering our voices and saying, 'By the way . . .' We're saying in effect, 'This is the way it is, and you still have to teach my kid.'"

Deb adds, "And no one has ever taken it out on the kids. All of the teachers have been great. They'll call either one of us and talk about any of the kids."

The change from a large school where they were well known to a new rural one caused some adjustments. Deb says, "I think people here took a little step back, because it's a small town, and said, 'Whoa.' But they seem to accept us. One of the teachers did say, 'You've got three very bright children. They're all well adjusted.'"

Jacki interrupts. "Why the hell are they so surprised? Maybe they are surprised to see that they act like normal kids. Kellie and Stephie don't attack the other little girls. They play Barbie dolls. They play mommy and daddy. They're getting into beads and painting their nails now. Kellie will write a story, however, and use *she, she, she* all the way through. You can't get a much more male boy than Eric. The way he struts around. He's a go-getter. He's a leader."

Sex is a very open subject around the house. Everyone was part of the discussion when Kellie's breasts started to grow. "I feel as they get older," Jacki says, "there will be problems. Somewhere along the line something real bad is going to happen when they are teenagers and they are going to blame the fact that we're gay—say that's why this is happening to them. But we know that whoever they were living with, this is inevitable. If they use that against us, it will be just a cop-out.

"The chances are real good that they will be heterosexual. Number one, I think that's fine because life is going to be a lot easier for them. Number two, if they are heterosexual, it is not because they don't know the difference. Not because they don't know that there is something else out there and it is perfectly okay to go for it if they want. On the other hand, if they are gay, they will have an easier time than most gays and hopefully be able to live what we consider a normal life.

"We have pajama parties on the kids' birthdays. They all invite a friend over. Now, where we lived before, it was common knowledge of who we were, and their parents had no problem with letting their kids come over. See, they know me from the bank." Jacki has a picture of her family—her and Deb and the kids—on her desk. "I'm the normal person who sits out front and works with the public and I haven't spread any germs and they still let me work there. And Deb works in an ob/gyn office, so a lot of people know her. And we've done work in the community." For thirteen months they were volunteers at the alcohol and abuse center of a local hospital; neither Deb nor Jacki, however, drink more than a couple glasses of wine a week.

"When we moved here, parents would come to the door with their kids, looking for something different," Jacki says. "Making a point to scope out the place. And we'd let them walk in. Yeah, we do have a living room—couch, chair, TV, just like everybody. 'Would you like to see the rest of the house?' And we'd take them through." She mimics the women's thoughts. " 'Look, the girls have their own bedroom, don't sleep with their mothers. Look, the little boy has a room by himself. Oh, look, they have a kitchen table, they eat. Oh, Jesus! there was a double bed in that room—where does the other one sleep?' We get these feelings, but we've always handled it very casually.

"We had a housewarming and we invited people I work with, people she works with, our gay friends, and our relatives. We couldn't afford three parties."

Deb smiles widely as she says, "Bob's brother was the perfect little hostess. He greeted people at the door. He swished around, and everyone thought he was just adorable. He'd clean the ashtrays, show people the house. We have some real dykey friends, and they said, 'Sure, we'll come.' It worked out wonderful. The people we work with were amazed and thrilled to meet our friends. And our relatives were amazed to meet the women couples we talk about all the time."

Jacki adds, "My ninety-four-year-old grandmother thought E——was 'just handsome.' "

"And Jacki's father has such a crush on E——. He always asks about her."

"He'll ask, "Is she married yet?' And my mother goes, "Floyd, no.' "

Deb chimes in, "He says, 'Well, I don't understand. She's a good-lookin' woman, she should get married.' Same thing about R——. 'He's a nice boy, why doesn't he get married?' "

"And my mother goes, 'Shut up, Floyd.' "

At the party someone showed the grandmother a card one of the gay women sent: "The nicest thing about a new house is it's a new place to have sex." The grandmother laughed. "Who needs a new house to do that?"

Jacki and Deb tell with glee about a couple who brought their thirteen-year-old daughter and introduced her as "my boy with a bra."

"And all our gay friends in the kitchen go—'Whoaaaa'—and say, 'She'll grow up to be an adorable dyke.' "

Jacki leans back and smiles. "Everyone ate out of the same dishes. Nobody caught anything. There have been no outbreaks reported."

The girls, who have been inching their way up the stairs, rush to show their mothers the results of an afternoon spent with scissors, tape, and colored paper. The mothers beam with pride.

PART 9

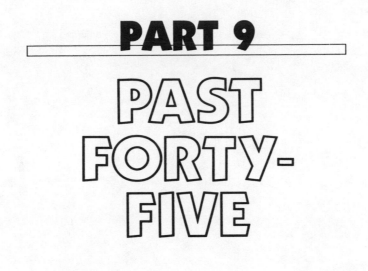

PAST FORTY-FIVE

25. SOLITARY WOMAN

THE ultimate dream of many—including women who love women—is to trade the clocks and pressures of the city for the wooded silence and pristine glory of the coast of Maine. They feel if they could just get a little business going, something they enjoyed, they could live simply and love solitude.

Twenty years ago a commercial artist, loner, and sexual innocent, Claire Wallis—not her real name because she has "this gut feeling that if people here knew about me, they'd just not talk to me again"—followed this dream.

Maine was not foreign territory to Claire. During her preschool days in the 1930s her father had been a minister there, handling seven churches and doing three to four services a Sunday. Although she shudders as she remembers the poverty and "rummage sale" clothes of her growing-up years, she was never "prim and proper like my older sister. I played cowboys and Indians and did all the wrong things at the wrong time. My dress didn't stay clean for more than three minutes."

Claire attended a small private university and spent four years at the Boston School of the Museum of Fine Arts. During the years she worked in Boston, Pittsburgh, and Philadelphia, she retained close ties to her parents and her brother, who plays with a midwestern symphony orchestra, and her married sister. Claire's high school boyfriend had been killed by a drunk driver on Christmas Eve, and she never had much to do with men after that. When her mother would ask, "Haven't you met anybody nice?" she would reply, "If God intends me to marry, he will put a man in front of me and I'll be smart enough to catch him." In Pittsburgh she was harassed on the job by a mentally disturbed man; in Philadelphia she worked with all men where "I could hear them talking about 'the old lady at home.' If I were married and thought my husband talked like that about me, I would die. I became conscious of the male attitude toward women, and it turned me off."

She had already been turned off toward women. At twenty, Claire's first year in the Boston Students House, her roommate, who "smelled unclean and of pancake makeup," told her she was " 'studying lesbians, was fascinated by them.' I went to bed in fear and trembling, absolutely petrified. I had never heard the word in our house—we had our mouths washed out for *hell* or *damn*. I went to the director and pleaded to get out of that room."

But Claire did want girls for friends. One told her, "I've been warned about you—you're loud and unladylike," and Claire tried to change. "I had an inferiority complex. I wasn't a bad person. A human being with faults, but good parts." Self-sufficiency, however, seemed natural to her. "If I wanted to do things, I'd do them myself."

After twenty years of city living, Claire dickered for land in Maine and bought ten acres for five hundred dollars; her nearest neighbors were a quarter of a mile in either direction. "My mother," Claire said, "didn't think I had a sane bone in my body, just because I wasn't married. But when she came and saw the land and the cabin I had had built, she said, 'You have to have a house.' They gave me my share of the inheritance, and I moved in here in 1972."

Today the house, with its time-silvered shingles and crisp white trim, and the acres of fir and birch would command a breathtaking price. Claire, clad in a paint-splattered yellow sweat-shirt and jeans that crowd her stocky body, finishes up her day's work. The shop, which adjoins the house, is open and smells of pine shavings, stain, and September sun. Claire has the look of Maine country folk: a pleasant, jowly face; short, live-and-let-live hair; brown eyes and glasses. Her manner is brusque until, vodka and cigarettes in hand, her body spreads to fill her chair by the fire and she says, "Life begins at forty."

Claire hadn't been in Maine long before she met Maggie—not her real name—a woman fifteen years older than herself. Maggie and her husband spent their winters in Florida and summers in Maine. "We began going places together, having fun. I had never had this kind of attention before in my life." Claire, however, made no secret of her disgust with Maggie's husband, Ian, a "wealthy miser." When it was revealed at a dinner party that he had disowned his daughter for marrying a Jew and wouldn't sleep in the same house with another daughter because she had been a bridesmaid at the wedding, Claire called him a "shit-ass," rose from the table, and stomped home.

All that winter letters flew between Florida and Maine. "I never wrote so much in my life. I suppose I was in love and didn't know it. When they came back in April, she came straight to my house, and her hands were all over mine. She stayed until two A.M." A couple months later the two women, caught in a bad rainstorm on their way back from Boston, booked into a motel room. "She patted the bed beside her. I got in. I didn't know if I was supposed to do anything and if so what. I was very uncomfortable. Finally I put my arm around her."

In July Ian came to Claire's house and said, " 'I don't want Maggie to see you anymore. I could understand it if she had fallen in love with another man, but . . . .' I went back to work. At five A.M. I sat bolt upright in bed. My God! that man thinks I'm a lesbian! I've never been so mad in all my life. I found him in his garden. 'I am not a lesbian!' Tears were streaming down my face. Maggie and I took a drive, and she said, 'I don't love him. I'm in love with you.' I said, 'I love you too. What are we going to do?' "

Maggie, in defiance of her husband, went off to see the daughter who had married a Jew, and Claire drove south to bring her home. To Claire the trip was a honeymoon, not sexual but filled with the breath-catching joy of being with someone she loved and who loved her. When they discovered that Ian had locked Maggie out of her house, they went to Claire's. For a week Maggie talked about divorce, then she announced, "I'm going back to Ian. He says you and I can be friends. There will be no divorce."

Although almost twenty years have elapsed since then, Claire's voice is husky as she says, "I helped her bring her things out of the house. I collapsed and cried until I had dry heaves."

Maggie and Ian remained in their summer house that winter, but Claire seldom saw Maggie except from her position in the choir loft of the community church. "She would leave little notes in my mailbox. I was becoming an absolute wreck. In February I decided it had to end. I asked her to take a walk in the snow. She said, 'Spring is coming. I'm leaving Ian.' She rented a room at the Y, but was mostly at my place. She dated Ian, however. Cooked him eggplant and cookies, played Hearts with him and the neighbors. She was a good Catholic and felt her body belonged to Ian even if he died. She was totally untouchable. It was frustrating, although I didn't know how to do anything anyway.

"One Sunday morning I was looking down from the choir loft.

The sun poured through the windows and over her. It hit me: 'Maggie and I have a lesbian relationship!' On the way home I said, 'I have something to tell you, but I can't find the words.' At last I got it out: 'We're in a lesbian relationship.' She smiled and said, 'Yes. I know.' " But after three months Maggie went back to Ian.

"I was getting sick of all this back-and-forth, her jerking the string, then dropping it. First she was going to leave him, then she was not. We were in the car when I confronted her. There were summer people all around, but I started screaming for her to make up her mind. 'You've got to do one thing or the other!' I was sobbing. 'In September,' she said, 'I'm moving into the Y.' 'Maggie, are you sure?' 'Yes. We'll be happy forever after.'

"The next morning an eighty-year-old neighbor came to tell me, 'Maggie won't get a divorce. Won't write. Won't see you.' Then she gave me a lecture on 'unnatural' relationships. She's been cold to me ever since.

"I hated Maggie for sending that old lady to tell me. I hated what she had done to me. I withdrew into a shell. Became a recluse." For seven years Maggie and Claire lived three miles apart and never spoke.

Claire was forty-eight when a young friend from town, home from college, visited her. "Every time I had ever asked Cathy about boyfriends, she'd just smile. Well, this time I told her about Maggie.

" 'I'm one, too, you know,' she said.

" 'I wish I knew what all this was about.'

" 'I'll loan you my library.' I read and read and read—thirty-five, forty books. Then my past began to fit. I went out and bought my own copy of Del Martin's *Lesbian/Woman*. Suddenly I felt at home, but I still didn't know how to go about meeting people."

Cathy had given Claire a copy of the *Lesbian Connection* newsletter, and from it she picked out the name of a correspondence dating service, the Wishing Well, and wrote for a sample. "I sent in my forty dollars for a six-month subscription and starting writing to the coded numbers." Claire chose women her own age, and the one who lived the nearest—in Albany, New York—she invited to visit. "She didn't have much education, so we did not have much to talk about. She thought I was inexperienced, so sex was out."

Spurred by that encounter Claire drove the thirty miles to town, walked into the bookstore, and bought *The Joy of Lesbian Sex*. "When I think what I must have looked like walking out of that store!" Claire had never been physically intimate with a man, so the book "gave me some idea of what it was all about."

In 1981 one of Claire's Wishing Well correspondents from the Midwest arrived for a ten-day visit. "In three days she cornered me on the sofa, burst into tears, said she loved me madly, and begged me not to send her away. She was ready to sell her house. I said, 'I don't love you.' It cooled me off, because I felt like I was being rushed off my feet. I didn't know how to handle it."

The woman returned home but bombarded Claire with phone calls and love letters, saying their relationship was "made in heaven."

"Like an ass I succumbed. I went out there and helped her move—bag and baggage. I knew the day the trip started that it wouldn't work, but I didn't know what to do. It's the one regret of my life.

"She was a complainer, ill educated, didn't get a job, was jealous of my correspondence with other women. One bitterly cold night in January we had a fight. I walked out of the house, went to the neighbor's to talk—not about her, but just to talk. When I came home, I tried to get this woman to have it out with me. She wouldn't, so I went back to the neighbor's and called a correspondent in Florida, who said, 'Tell her to get out. Don't make it easy.' I did. She cried. It was thirty below zero, but I walked to the other neighbor's for a drink and talk. I got home at two and said, 'We're not going to make it.' I offered to have her stay until warm weather." In the spring Claire drove her to the home of another Wishing Well correspondent in Georgia.

The next year Claire had another pen pal from the Midwest arrive for a visit; she, too, fell madly in love. "She was a sex maniac! I can take it or leave it. I've not had very much of it, and what I've had has not been very good, so it's immaterial to me." At first the woman had seemed "nice, interesting," but Claire was disappointed by her untidyness, her insistence on having things her way, her emphasis on play, not work. "Things got worse all summer. She thought she had latched onto a good thing. I moved up to the attic. She called me an alcoholic, threw my checkbook at me accusing me of having more money than I would admit to. In September I told her to go. 'Oh no, I love you so much!' Her three-toed sloth of a male friend came and got her, and I had the house to myself again."

In December another correspondent, preceded by a huge box of Christmas ornaments, arrived. Claire put her on the couch in the living room saying, "I'm just not interested in this bedroom business." The woman had an open-ended ticket, but Claire told her she'd better go back to California. "What she left me with was mono. She came back and nursed me for six weeks and was very kind, but I was not going to get married to her."

A physical-education teacher, who was also a preacher's daughter, was the next visitor, and the two women, although they got along very well, realized that schedules—summer is Claire's busiest season—and distance were against them. "I was celibate and alone and enjoyed every minute of it," but in January a series of accidents and illnesses left Claire less fond of being alone. "I'd like to be in a loving relationship, but a working one that has mutual agreement on both sides."

Claire's mother died ten years ago; her brother and her sister and husband and children support her choice of loving women. As one said, "She's still Claire, isn't she?" She has been invited to some lesbian parties but has found that "twenty- and thirty-year-old pot-smoking foot stompers are a crowd I don't fit with anymore—if I ever did. I'm not into cradle robbing. There are no lesbian bars within a hundred miles." She summarized her position: "A—I don't have time to hunt, and B—I'm not a hunter in the first place. So, basically I live alone and enjoy it." There are gay men with whom she corresponds, but she says of a large gay and lesbian New Year's Eve party that she attended; "I guess I'm woods-crazy—uncomfortable in crowds."

Her thoughts wander back to Maggie. "She was such an emotional experience—nonphysical except for hugging and kissing—that it took its toll. I would have laid down my life for that woman. Since she's decided we could become friends again, I've become very leery. I have a gut feeling that if anything happened to Ian, she'd lean on me. That's the last thing in the world I'd ever want to happen. She seems to have blocked out any time we spent 'together,' as though it had no meaning beyond two friends. It's very strange."

Maggie is now seventy-three; Claire, fifty-eight.

26. FREEDOM WITH AGE

SHELIA Scanlon is fifty, Boston born and bred: childhood in a wealthy suburb, devout Catholic, Harvard graduate, administrative assistant to high-level executives. "I got straight A's at Harvard—always pushing so hard for my mother's love. There hasn't been a lot of love in my life. You get in a routine—go to work, do a few things as a political activist and in the Church. I became sort of a workaholic; I read, listened to music. I was very rigid, compulsive. Everything had a place."

If Claire Wallis and Shelia had met in Boston in the late sixties, would they have sensed a common longing or merely seen each other as self-contained career women? Did others refer to them as spinsters or frustrated old maids and, observing their stocky frames and brusque, no-nonsense approach to life, add the appellation latent homosexual? Both women were painfully shy, both had strong ties to family and God, neither had ever twittered and fluttered for male attention.

In her forties Shelia was attacked by various physical ailments. "Actually I was suffering from lack of human contact. I was a lesbian and didn't know it. Couldn't get at it. Scared." As she wrote in a lesbian newsletter, "I was tormented and plagued about my sexual identity. The greatest obstacle I had to overcome was my own homophobia. I confess as well that although I was in no sense a 'party-line Catholic,' the Church's stance on homosexuality was somewhat numbing to me. I couldn't quite square being gay with being Catholic, even when I, in fact, was."

At forty-eight Shelia, then employed by the Farber Cancer Institute, arrived at work leaning on canes. At the front desk the receptionist, Dorothy Whitcomb, a married woman with six children, asked, "What happened to you?" Dorothy had seen Shelia often, but this was the first time she had done more than smile hello. The two women had lunch together, discussed Shelia's surgery, and Dorothy, an ex-Catholic turned spiritualist, offered to do a healing for her.

"What the hell is that?" Shelia had no intention of being physically touched by anyone.

Nevertheless, a friendship developed, and one night Dorothy, worried about Shelia's feet, drove her home. After a long talk in the car Dorothy, as a matter of course, hugged Shelia. "She probably," Dorothy says now, "almost had a stroke, but she liked it." The first time Dorothy was in Shelia's apartment, Shelia asked for another hug. "We had talked about her therapist trying to get at the little girl in her," Dorothy said, "so I sat on the couch and held her in a completely maternal way."

Dorothy is the Italian-mama type—broad-beamed, robust, dramatic, animated, and also very pretty and stylish with white hair in a fluff cut, silver dangling earrings, and bright clothes. As a high school senior she had become pregnant and married the father, who was five years older than she.

Dorothy would have had nine children by age twenty-six, but one died, and twins miscarried. She enjoyed raising the six that lived, yet adds, "My husband had little affection for them. I was the end-all and be-all for him. He was jealous of my family, friends, and sort of isolated me—I love people. He could be charming, but he wanted to stay home and rock on the porch and hold hands with me. He worked very hard—we had an Olds in the driveway, swimming pool, all that. I did volunteer work, always wanted to be helping people." Over the years she had grown apart from him.

Shelia began writing poems to Dorothy. "They were sweetly erotic, but we didn't know it. We were both very innocent," Dorothy says. "We had lunch together every day and twice a week did reparenting, where we sat on the couch and I'd hold her head on my chest. I'm psychic, so I could see her little girl. I went around saying to people, 'Isn't it a shame that people mistake spiritual love for sexual?'

"Shelia was beginning to figure it out, but I kept saying, 'A homosexual relationship is one thing I could never handle.' When I was reading one of her poems, I got sexually aroused, and it scared me. When she gave me flowers and later called saying, 'I think I'm falling in love with you,' I said, 'I think that only happens between men and women,' and slammed down the phone."

Shelia avoided her; Dorothy called; they talked; Shelia agreed to a platonic relationship; moments after leaving her, driving over the tracks on Beacon Street, Dorothy realized she was planning how to tell her son, who still lived at home, that she was moving in with Shelia. "I'm the queen of all denial," Dorothy admits. "I'd been stuffing all these feelings. But once I let down the barriers. . . ."

Their contacts that weekend, although continually interrupted by family, were emotionally—and sexually—charged. When, during a brief moment alone, Shelia hugged her and asked for a kiss, Dorothy replied, "But it wouldn't be only one."

On Monday while her husband was taking his morning shower, Dorothy packed her overnight bag: teddy shirt, bubble bath, toothbrush, and *The Joy of Sex*. Dorothy offered to drive Shelia home from work, and when they arrived, Dorothy took her bag out of the car trunk.

Shelia panicked and screamed, "You're not moving in yet!" She put her dog on a leash and "walked his legs off."

"By the time she came back," Dorothy says, "I had the bubble bath drawn. We figured out what to do, and everything turned out fine."

Two weeks later Dorothy asked her husband for a divorce, and two months later she and Shelia had found an apartment and moved in together. But, as Shelia wrote in the newsletter, "Given all the entanglements two fifty-year lives can produce (including being newly out lesbians) gave us enough ingredients for problems and soap operas for several lifetimes."

There was Shelia's mother, from whom she had never made a satisfactory break. There was Dorothy's mother, a victim of Alzheimer's disease, whom Dorothy brought with her when she moved in with Shelia and whom two of Dorothy's children later "kidnapped" so that she could have a "normal" life. There were Dorothy's six children, two still living with their father, and others in various states of independence who kept moving in with them.

Telling the children that she was in a sexual relationship with a woman was difficult for Dorothy. When, over dinner, her twenty-nine-year-old daughter asked, "Is there someone else?" Dorothy relates that she told her about Shelia, and they both cried. "It was very hard for her."

Her gay daughter of thirty-one and youngest son guessed. "But," Dorothy says, "that daughter came out for us all over the place in the wrong way." She is involved in drugs and alcohol and a bad relationship, problems that Dorothy believes are more the product of coming from a dysfunctional family than from her affectional preference.

The youngest daughter's comment on the situation was, "About time you're leaving him."

She told one son just before his wedding. "I thought he already knew, because he sent the invitation to me and a 'guest.' It came as a shock, but he hugged me and said, 'You're my mother and nothing has changed.' " At the reception, although invited to sit at the head table with her husband—her divorce was not final—Dorothy sat far back in the room with Shelia. "It was hard, very hard on Shelia."

"These last two years," Shelia admits, "have been both the hardest and the happiest of my life."

The women, with the help of a therapist, realized that as long as they were in the Boston area, Dorothy and her children would keep acting out a dependent relationship, thereby preventing the two women from making their commitment a priority. Shelia contacted the Concerned Catholic Lesbians and wrote to members in places where they thought they might like to live. Finally, after a year and a half "doing closure with all the significant people in our lives," as Shelia wrote, "we resolved with determination and finality to cut loose and strike out on our own to work out our special destiny together."

Dorothy's children and grandchildren gave them a going-away party in which each room was decorated as a holiday, including a fiftieth birthday cake in one. "Leaving children is a tough problem for a mother," Shelia says, "but now Dorothy has a new relationship with her kids, and it's much healthier."

Shelia and Dorothy's odyssey ended in Santa Fe, where they live as totally open lesbians. Shelia says, "In today's climate I would have been able to come out in my twenties. It's so much more wonderful to be out. When we really notice it is when we're with closeted people. It makes me proud to be visible. Young people need that kind of role model. There is an older couple here who try to tell us not to be out, who say bad things will happen to us. They pretend they're straight."

During her married years Dorothy had lived, as Shelia points out, "with a painted-on bright smile that swept reality under the rug." Now they both feel that they have truly "come home."

Women past forty who for the first time acknowledge that they are capable of same-sex love face a different situation than do teenagers or young women. For Shelia Scanlon the partnership meant loss of her solitude, loss of control of aspects of her life that she had nourished for forty-eight years. It meant someone else in her house, in her bed, and the instant acquisition of a huge family with all the attendant responsibilities and decisions. It meant a confrontation with forces that had loomed so large in her single life—the Church and her mother's approval.

For Dorothy Whitcomb falling in love with Shelia entailed a sharp break with forty-eight years of being a part of heterosexual society. It required her to take a step back from her children, appraise them with more realistic eyes, and demand that they accept her as a person, not a status-quo mom. It required her to leave a lifetime of connections with people and places, trusting her whole future to a new commitment—one labeled deviant by society.

Margaret Mead, who we now know had lovers of both sexes, wrote of women turning to women once their children were raised as a way of continuing nurturance and of subsidizing or replacing a distant, utilitarian husband/wife relationship with one of reciprocal friendship and intimacy. The poet Adrienne Rich, a wife and mother of the fifties generation, wrote in *Dreams of a Common Language* of the deep joys of coming to love a person of the same gender and also of broken rules, of a new life outside the law.

It is not valid to assume that these women consider their years of marriage and child raising as wasted ones; many view them as part of a continuum of a rich, full life. Those who had experiences with women in their youth may have the satisfied feeling of having come full circle; those for whom it is new may exult like a nineteen-year-old. Their years with women may be easier than those of life-long lesbians, because acquaintances may see them as having "paid their dues," as having been "normal" for forty or fifty years of their lives. Conversely, they may be more difficult because they are vulnerable to hurt from children and intimates who believe they are disgracing their children and former husbands. And there is the question of adapting to lesbian society.

Dorothy and Shelia's time of being isolated in a "special friendship," of, as Dorothy put it, "leaning on the fence and watching the weirdos in the gay-pride parade" was very short. As they shucked their respective states of heterosexual and spinster respectability, they quickly entered an exciting new world of urban lesbianism. They did not, like Claire Wallis deserted by her married woman and living in rural isolation, have to turn to the Wishing Well.

They could pick up copies of Boston's two major publications *Bay Window*, a gay male and lesbian publication, and *Sojourner*, a feminist/lesbian monthly, and find all the support they wanted. For lesbians *Bay Window* lists eleven neighborhood groups, fourteen political-action groups, ten religious groups, fourteen sports and entertainment groups, and under "Support Groups/Female" the twenty-one listings appear to cover every situation, for example: Former Nun Support Group, Lesbians Choosing Children, Lesbians over Thirty, Lesbians Inviting New Connections, North of Boston Committed Lesbian Couples, and a new one, Jewish Lesbian Daughters of Holocaust Survivors (JLDHS), as well as a partners group for those in relationships with JLDHS. The names of twenty-five more groups of both men and women and an equal number of student organizations are given.

Once Dorothy and Shelia accepted the word *lesbian*, they plunged into this culture that gave them validation, acceptance, and friends, that provided mirrors for both their ecstasy and their problems, and that encouraged them in their belief that they could form a lifelong partnership.

But isolated urban women, solitary or in "special friendships," still exist. A native of Boston, a suburban elementary school teacher in her late fifties who has had three very closeted relationships with women, had—in 1987—never heard of these newspapers. With her partner of twenty years gone, she doesn't know how to end her loneliness. She finds ingrained habits of secrecy and fear difficult to put aside and, like Claire Wallis, she is unskilled in "hunting," in putting herself forward as a sexual being. The situation is similar to a widow or divorcee who is unaware of or scornful of dating services. The heterosexual probably has co-workers, friends, and family eager to introduce her to eligible men, whereas the lesbian, unless she is part of the lesbian community, has no such support.

Women who acknowledged their attraction to women when they were in high school in the 1950s learned so well how to live double lives in order to deflect the hostility of society that they may never be comfortable outside the closet. Julie said, "It is very difficult for me to meet a straight person for the first time when he or she has already attached the word *lesbian* to me. I am very conscious of wanting to be liked by people, and if I step to the plate with two strikes against me—or at least perceive my affectional preference as two strikes—I am extremely ill at ease, inclined to just sit there like a lump on a log."

Shelia and Dorothy, who did not strive for thirty years to perfect the image of an invisible woman who loved women, did not have to overcome the legacy of being active lesbians while pretending to be nonsexual. Because they, at forty-eight, went directly from celibacy and heterosexual marriage into a lesbian community, they have been able to control, to a large extent, their relations with society. In that sense they have much more in common with a 1987 college student than a woman of their age who understood her "deviant" physical attractions in the 1940s.

* * *

Marty Alinor is such a woman. Extremely well known as an artist, extremely secretive as a lesbian, she is willing to tell her story only as long as her name is changed and her anonymity carefully guarded. "I don't want to be a bold-type lesbian. More is lost than gained through sensationalizing. And also I don't like people making prejudgments."

Standing in the garden that flanks her house, she speaks in the code of swift innuendo that her generation—she is sixty-five—raised to an art form. Once inside the house she says, "You didn't understand me because I didn't want to use any words that would let the neighbors over the wall know I was 'one of them.' There are a lot of very straight, politically conservative, badges-with-their-pictures-on-them people around here."

Marty thought she "was slow growing up—still having crushes on women. Very secretive. I wondered if someone could help me. I remember my sister saying, 'A girl made a pass at me! Ugh!' I was very mixed up. I was afraid to check *The Well of Loneliness* out of the library. It was about 'those kind of people.' Straights could check it out, I couldn't.

"It was all condemnation when I was young. All they said was, 'It's sick!' I was so sexually repressed that by the time I grew up, I thought sex was dirty. The family would come, my heart would be pounding, I'd tell those lies. I would have been more socially acceptable as a prostitute. Heterosexuality is the most important thing. Heterosexuals fit into society. My whole life I never fit into society.

"I married an airplane."

At twenty-one she stood tall, slender, broad-shouldered in a Women's Air Force Service uniform, a courageous, intense young flyer with confident blue eyes, blond hair, high cheekbones, and a long, narrow jaw. The love of adventure, of excitement, still emanates from her, although now the boundaries she breaks are artistic.

"It's embedded in my personality that I don't like to work for other people. Give me an airplane and it's mine. The same with my art."

As a child Marty saw Amelia Earhart, and flying became her passion. She towed targets for the military in World War II; she got her civilian instructor's license; she flew with an air show and, when the money ran out, became a crop duster. "The very first gal I had anything to do with . . ." Marty has trouble telling the story.

She and her friend, Louise, were trying to get their sail-plane rating. When Louise was ready to take off, there was a weight problem. "I threw out her parachute." Louise went up. "The wing came off. Terrible. . . . I didn't speak a word for two weeks. So terrible, unspeakable. Her brother had been killed in the war, and her mother came and shook me. 'Where's Louise?' "

From the end of World War II into the 1970s, women were forbidden to fly for the military, but Marty retained a reserve commission as a first lieutenant. After logging five thousand hours of flying time she grew sick of crop dusting and teaching and longed to see the world. "The air force didn't know what to do with me, so they made me an intercept controller." She was stationed in Montana and was responsible for scrambling fighter squadrons if there was any unauthorized penetration of American airspace. "I drank Maalox all the time. I didn't really enjoy it. Still wanted to go off to see the world." She describes her experience in Oklahoma with a WAF squad as "All kids. Drinking, slashing their wrists."

She got orders to report to Germany, but when they discovered she was a woman, they refused to send her. "I screamed that my furniture was shipped and I wanted to go. They sent me to Paris as a protocol officer." She had a marvelous time and also discovered art, but her lungs gave out with emphysema.

While in the service Marty was sexually "pure as a lily. No playing around in any way, shape, or form." She describes herself as feeling rather self-righteous when two women at flight school were asked to resign: "Marty, I'm so glad you're not one of those." During the Korean War the WAF were "getting lesbians out right and left. Two women were accused of necking in a car." Marty was called in to be the woman officer present at their interrogation. "The guys doing the questioning used such filthy language, I said, 'I'm not going to listen to it,' so they had to quit. I told the gals to call their parents and tell them the charges weren't true and to call their Congressmen.

"The military were out looking for gays and they could use any means to get a confession. I knew two who got out of the service and went into a nunnery. My God, those nuns must really be something! You have to escape from society some way."

A sergeant of Marty's had been investigated as a lesbian and was so paranoid that she saluted every time she saw an officer. The conversation Marty had with her illustrates how lesbians spoke to each other in a code each understood and yet could never be used as proof by anyone:

> "Tell me," Marty said.
> "Transferred here," the sergeant replied.
> "Cleared?"

"Yes."

"You're the first sergeant."

Marty did, however, feel the impact of being denied any intimate contact with people for years at a time. Her fellow officers were "dull and dating men. I never saw any officers who I thought were gay." But she admits that she was never good at picking out gay women and was always afraid of making a mistake and approaching a straight. She has been with three women in her life: a year with the young flyer before she was killed, another relationship of ten years, the last of thirteen.

Marty had pneumonia thirteen times while in the service, and by the time she got out at thirty-eight, she had to attend college under a rehabilitation program. Although for years she was never very far from the oxygen tanks, she was absorbed in learning her craft.

Her work, she believes, is "feminist, not political." She admires the women who are outspoken activists, who "are getting run over by men. But I don't want to be out sawing the limb off under me." For Marty her work is "the center, a wonderful way to express feeling about life and the world. I didn't have liberation when I was young, but I have a life now. There was a day you couldn't wear pants, but now we don't stick out like sore thumbs—the world is adaptable. Everything moves in a circle, and now we are coming into a more conservative time. But prejudice just hangs in there. Funny. Subdued. But it's always there."

When she talks about lesbians being accepted by society, she launches into role switching. "Not until they kill off all the straights. Those hets! Such a dirty way to have sex. It's okay to do it to have a baby. Any other time it's just plain disgusting."

Marty's last lover left six years ago. "For six to eight months I did nothing. Walked the floor and wept with the door locked. The dogs followed me with tragedy written on their faces. One day, I said, 'That's what I'm going to do—I'm going to work!'" She did —all day and half the night for months—and won a Guggenheim. Her middle has thickened with age, but she moves with the vital intensity of a woman just hitting her stride in her career.

She doubts if she will ever have another lover. "I have the wrong taste. All the women have been wrong, but I kept coming back. Why risk another? I've had all the experiences—alcoholism, infidelity—that I care to have." She pats the two dachshunds. "Dogs are the best bedfellows. I'm fully retired. I look around my house, and what would I be willing to give up? Probably nothing. I know women who just like to go to bed with somebody, but that's no relief for me.

"I am so private. My sister and I finally talked. I said, 'I guess I've always known.' She said, 'I didn't want to think about it. I never really thought what it must have been like for you.' " Sadness pulls at Marty's face, but she denies bitterness. "No. Never bitter. Only melancholy sometimes."

She walks to the sliding-glass doors and gazes out at the illuminated windsock that flies over her garden wall. "I had a real desire for freedom when I was young. Later flying became an escape from the problem of being something dirty and different. Because flying takes concentration, I didn't look left or right, so I didn't have any feelings about this bad thing."

Suppressing her identity has, she admits, "been harmful to me. I've had a hard time letting people in to know me. Now it's an abstraction. There is freedom with age.

"Now that the storm is over, I can say I made it through."

27. WE WERE OUT THERE

BETTY Deacon, tall and husky with brown eyes and a strong voice, lives with her partner, Geri Cox, in a partially renovated row house in a Polish working-class enclave of East Baltimore. Geri is a large woman, her pink skin and blue eyes shine. Bonnie Redmond, a neighbor and long-ago lover of Geri's, secures one end of the couch with her lean, big-boned body. They are all Polish, although Betty Deacon is half German, native daughters of blue-collar Baltimore—Senator Barbara Mikulski's natural constituency—Catholic and in their forties.

Geri graduated from high school in 1960. "Back then? It was horrible back then. There were no gay rights. There were no rights at all for women, much less lesbian women."

"They didn't call them gay people," Bonnie says. "We were queers when we came out. I was twenty-one. The police were always harassing the guys and the girls."

Geri's words are rolled in a soft Baltimore accent. "You could walk down the street just next to each other, and if you had short hair . . . I had friends who were beaten up. The kind of neighborhoods gay bars were in weren't the best, and the local drunks would just wait for you come out."

The first time Geri and Bonnie went to the bar, the bartender told them to get their hair cut short and put on pants. They did. Geri would leave her mother's house, go to a gas-station rest room, pull on black khaki pants, a T-shirt, and a man's white shirt, slick her hair back, and go down to the bar. "We did it," Bonnie says, "because we wanted to be accepted the way the rest of the crowd was."

Bonnie knew she was gay from the time she was thirteen. At fifteen Geri and a girlfriend were "taking off our knee socks and pleated skirts and getting into my bed at home."

Geri wanted to go into the service. "When I came home with all these brochures from the post office, my mother sat and told me, 'There's only two kinds of women in the service—whores and lesbians.' And I thought, I know that." The laughter is hearty, and Geri, cheeks red, continues. "Which is why I wanted to go in. I did not know where else the women were. I used to kiss girls in showers in high school, friends that I wanted to be close to. But they would run. Most of them were scared to death. I had a little friend I went to school with—she was straight as a pin—I just adored her. I sat with her every chance I got.

"So, at eighteen I started seeking 'em out. I wanted to know where women went. You can look in the telephone book now and find out where they are. What did you do back then? You could not talk to your parents. My mother would have had me on somebody's sofa somewhere or put away. And I couldn't go to the church—they would have said I would rot in hell."

Bonnie nods. "I was out with my mother one time. She made the remark to my aunt that if she thought one of her children were like that [gay], she would kill them."

"When we first started hanging out at the Capitol bar," Geri says, "there was a girl. I don't remember her name, but I remember what she looked like. She told me she was going to go home and tell her mother. I never saw her again. Her mother had her put away [in a mental institution]. I had lots of friends who disappeared like that. That was 1962.

"A lot of them ran away to get married. They couldn't take it. How do you take your lover home? Women didn't live in apartments then, or if you did, you weren't a very reputable woman. You only had your own apartment because you wanted to see men."

"When Geri and I went to get an apartment," Bonnie says, "landlords insisted we get a two-bedroom." They couldn't afford that, so lovemaking was conducted in "anybody's house that was empty, in the back of the car, the houses of faggots that we knew. What could you do?"

"The older I get," Geri says, "the angrier I get. Especially with men. I've gotten to a point where I hate men. The only men in my life I will tolerate are Betty's two sons. A guy could have had any apartment he wanted, walked in anywhere and bought a car for the first time, or gotten credit. I've spent half my life trying to fight for this shit."

She talks about Louise, the bartender who told her and Bonnie to get their hair cut. "That woman lived in a two-room shack that had no refrigerator—we had to go get her ice all the time. She was fifty-five years old when she died. Louise was exactly what I feared I would be when I got older. So, she was really a great motivator —the incentive for me to have five retirement plans in hand."

Anger about Louise crackles in Bonnie's voice too. "Her sons and daughter wouldn't have anything to do with her because she was a lesbian. She was a drunk. . . . I had a hard time dealing with it [my lesbianism] because I didn't want to hurt my mother and father. I drank a lot, and then I made up my mind this is the way I am. I'm going to have to live my life the way I want to, and if they can't accept it, tough."

Geri, who has been part of the bar scene all her life, says, "I drank some when I was young. Now I hardly ever drink."

Betty, who spent time in bars with her straight friends, adds, "I don't think that lesbians drink more than others. It's viewed that way because lesbians and gays were driven to bars because that's all they had."

"And what did you have to model yourself after?" Geri asks. "You certainly didn't want to model yourself after a woman. The lowest thing you could possibly be was a woman! You had to model yourself after a man! That's why women were so bulldyke."

Betty asks, "What were you, Ger?"

"A femme," Bonnie answers dryly.

"I was not!" Geri shouts over the laughter.

"One week you'd come into the bar in a skirt and blouse and the next week in jeans," Bonnie says from the safety of her couch corner.

"It took me six months to get *you* into pants!" Geri roars. Then she explains, "Femmes were looked down on and laughed at. And it's still like that, but not in the lesbian community. It's getting a whole lot better. It's really great to see women looking absolutely gorgeous in a dress and being as dykey as a dyke can be, and to me that's a real turn on!"

The two women discuss "bulldykes" who used to wear men's clothes day and night and never allowed themselves to be touched in lovemaking but used pressure against their lovers' thighs to produce orgasm. In a few couples the femme stayed home and the bulldyke went out to work. Children were not part of the picture.

"I never had the desire to raise children," Geri says. "There's nothing biological. It's societal pressure." Geri shoots a look at Betty. "I never even heard about kids until recently." Betty laughs and points out that Geri still has a collection of dolls.

Geri says that when young lesbians of the early 1960s looked into the future, they "didn't see anything. You lived day by day. You could never talk about anything when you got to work. I used to lie and refer to my lovers as my boyfriends. But you'd hide all the time. I was two people, and neither one of them was me. My older sister called me a bitch of a liar one time, but what are you supposed to say? I learned not to say anything. I'd say I stayed home Saturday night. I don't say anything anymore."

For twenty-two years Geri has worked for a large manufacturing firm, most recently as a technology assistant. Bonnie is employed in a small print shop at a college; her boss believes a woman's place is in the home. "It's sickening," she says.

Geri explains the stereotype of lesbians doing manual labor. "You know why they took jobs like that?" Geri asks. "Because they could dress the way they wanted to. They had more guts than I did. I went to work in my skirts back then. I was a keypunch operator. I got caught up in all that and didn't have the nerve to go apply for a dock job." She grins. "But I have done it the last couple years."

Betty's laugh is loud. "She calls me up and says, 'I'm out there on my forklift, and you ought to see me!' "

"I had fun! I controlled that whole dock."

Betty believes, "In a secretarial job, things like that, you're more subservient."

Betty grew up in a traditionally structured home. "On Monday you wash clothes, on Tuesday you iron, on Wednesday you dust upstairs." Her father, one of thirteen children, was an alcoholic; Betty herself was never abused, but there was continual verbal violence between her mother and father. "My mother held the power, but the only power she didn't have was enough over herself to get out of the situation. She chose to stay. She did it for me and my brother."

Betty attended a commercial Catholic high school, played softball and basketball, and was physically attracted to girls. She and her best friend would follow teachers they had crushes on to their homes and hide in the bushes. "But never at any point did we say to each other, 'Isn't it strange that we have these crushes on women?'

"The Church frowned on all sexuality. I used to go to CYO [Catholic Youth Organization] dances, where the priest would walk around and see if he could see light between the young boys and girls dancing. I seldom danced with boys, but I fast-danced, jitterbugged with the girls. My first date was to the senior prom—I was president of my class and had to find a boy to go with."

Two years out of high school Betty married, and in her early thirties she had her first affair—with her old friend from high school. "We were both very bombed, drunk enough so that we let ourselves go. The next morning she said, 'If I ever do anything like that again, kill me!' I said, 'Why? I want to do it as much as you do.' " When they talked, they found that they had had the same physical stirrings for each other in high school.

Betty stayed in the marriage "for the kids' sake. I did what I was supposed to do. But I was working out of it from the day I got into it. And I have a very slow process, so it took me eighteen years."

At forty Betty, although separated from her husband, thought she still had ten years to stay with her boys. "Then I met Geri. And she said, 'Ten years? What the f——are you talking about—ten years! Tomorrow!' Boy was that wild! Trying to run a home with two kids and this woman lying on me figuratively and physically. 'I always take my women home. When are you going to move in with me?' I say, 'Wait a minute! Eight years, six years, five years. . . .' 'One year,' she told me." Betty throws back her head in laughter.

"Here I am living at home with two kids, and she's living with a woman she was married to, literally, for ten years, so she can't take me home. So we have no place to go. We're sitting in a car making out until four or five o'clock in the morning. And she's saying, 'I can't do this anymore, I'm too old. This is embarrassing.' Forty-year-old women afraid we're going to get caught by a cop!

"Then she comes marching in the bar waving keys to a friend's house. And here are ten of my friends at the table saying, "Wooo, tonight's the night!' And I said, 'I have to finish this beer.' And she said, 'What the f——do you mean, you 'have to finish this beer?' I'll buy you six. Now go!' "

Geri explains why she felt so strongly about taking her women home. "What is it you grow up with? A family. And what else is there to model yourself after? You get furniture and you play house. That's what I grew up with. That's what I think life should be, and that's what I'm most comfortable with. I'm not comfortable out there seeing ten different women. I've met some good women. Now there's something else out there. But what was out there then?"

Her first live-in relationship lasted five years, the next eight, the third eleven. "I don't know why they haven't lasted forever. At first I thought there was something wrong with me. What I've learned is that people change, and if they don't change together . . . ."

"I'll tell you," Betty breaks in, "it's hard being number four. The look her mother gave me!" Again laughter envelopes the room.

"My mother's not an easy woman," Geri admits.

Betty and Geri have been together three years. "When we were first going together," Betty says, "she was trying to figure how we could get enough money to buy two houses so that we each could have one when we broke up."

"But things—houses, furniture—are burdens," Geri says. "They really are. We want to be here in this house until we're fifty-five and then we can sell it and buy a condo down on the waterfront. I'm retiring at fifty-five. I've got my five pensions."

Betty is employed by the city and feels very comfortable with people knowing her life-style, especially since the Gay Rights Ordinance passed. Geri works in an area where she needs security clearance. "To go down to a bar makes me nervous. I still get investigated. They go to your neighbors and ask what kind of people go in and out." She assumes she would be fired or transferred to another department if they named her a homosexual. "But if they ever did that to me, this would go on the front page. I would make their life absolutely miserable. If I lost my job, what else is there? I don't fear rejection from my family; they all know I've been with women for thirty years. My job is the only thing I keep quiet about. And when I retire, they can't take my pensions away from me!

"I believe the women will take over this world. I believe that with all my heart and soul, and it's just a matter of time. What men have we can freeze.

"We got Barbara Mikulski in there. We got Mary Pat Clark in there [as head of city council]. We almost had Geraldine Ferraro in there. Women have always dealt with life. Children have always been life. They have always dealt with the person, men deal with things."

Betty says, "There's a long way to go, but I'm optimistic." She has been involved in politics for many years and has shown Geri a different side of life.

"I stayed home with these women for eighteen years," Geri says from the depths of her armchair. "I didn't know you could go to Saint John's Church coffeehouse and be with lesbian women." Betty recently took her to a conference in Washington. "I'd never been to anything like that either. The *church* rented to *lesbian* women to have an *aging* conference! I expected to be bombed or something."

"The first year we were together," Betty adds, "we went to a campfest in Georgia."

"Fifteen hundred women! It blew my mind! I had never been among all women like that in all my life."

"And Bonnie went with us last summer and she loved it. She had a smile on her face all weekend."

Bonnie agrees. "I could relax, and they could hold hands. When we came back to Baltimore, I said, 'It really feels weird being back among the straight people, and I don't like it.' "

"The straights have told me all my life how I'm supposed to live." Geri's voice is loud. "What I'm supposed to look like, how I'm supposed to dress, where I'm supposed to work, what kind of job I'm supposed to work in."

"When Geri and I first got together," Betty says, "she used to put herself down. When she was around politically active women, she'd say, 'I haven't done that.' And I'd say, 'Ger, you paved the way for a lot of us.' "

Geri nods. "We were out there. We were living together."

"What she did in her life was as hard as what I did in my life staying in an oppressive situation. She may have been living with women, but it was also oppressive, because she couldn't be open. So, we came from different experiences. Physically I was in a marriage, but I was always surrounded by women in my political activism." Betty completed her B.A. several years ago; and Geri, with Betty's urging and support, has enrolled in a community college.

Geri observes, "A lot of my experiences are new—old as I am. Last Christmas this neighbor, a young couple next door, said, 'We're having a few couples in for a drink. Why don't you and Betty come over?' I thought that was pretty good. We're obviously 'a couple.' " She blushes with pride.

Betty explains that the neighbors are a young family with kids and are involved in the community. "I don't know what they say about us behind their door, but I think they appreciate us living here rather than the crummy person who was here before."

"We're clean," Geri interjects.

"I think they see our life-style being like theirs in a lot of ways. We're investing in the house; restoring it, which is the same thing they're doing; we go to work every day."

Geri's face is bright red as she admits that this was her first heterosexual party. "It was. Yeah! I sat there."

"It was okay," Betty says. "And the guy across the street took us over and showed us his house."

"That was another 'couple,' " Geri says, and laughs with pleasure.

"If our neighbor wants to invite us and never talk about our lesbianism, that's okay," Betty says. "But if he wants to challenge me, I'll stand up for that too."

253

"They have to accept us," Bonnie says dryly, "because we're not going away."

"There's more of us born every day," Betty adds.

Betty's sons were seventeen and twenty when she told them she was a lesbian. Both Betty and Geri agree that their reactions were positive, but Geri adds, "If Brian were sitting over at a friend's house and they were putting down queers, it would not be okay. That's why I told him, 'For your own good, don't tell the world.' If they were all high and drunk, they'd hop all over Brian. So it's not okay all the time.

"When the going gets rough, it's not okay."

PART 10
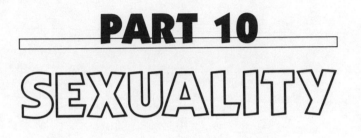
SEXUALITY

28. BETWEEN TWO WOMEN

WOMEN-LOVING women have been called by many names. In old Scotland the term was *dyke-loupers*. They had "louped" (jumped over) the "dyke" (the low wall that divided the fields) and gone over to the other side. That crossing over, perhaps the crossing over and back many times, results in experiences other women do not have. It gives them a perspective often expressed in their vocations as actors, writers, musicians, and perhaps more diffusively as professors, politicians, craftspeople. In the language of the Scots "dyke-loupers" were differentiated from "stugs," defined as hard, masculine women, and certainly the word was not used in the context "to lib," which meant to castrate a male animal. Without the hyphened *louper*, the word *dyke* represents the wall itself—hard, strong, rigid—and the concept of crossing over, of partaking of both the masculine and feminine worlds, is lost altogether.

Maybe this earthy, stony image of a dyke contributed to the idea of a lesbian as masculine. In Atlanta Marlene used the term *stone dyke*, which she defined as "rigidly butch," to describe Anita. It is also quite possible that the inflexible gender separations of the last hundred years mandated that anyone who erotically loved a female must have "male" feelings and the characteristics attributed to extra testosterone: a harder, hairier body; broader shoulders; stronger jaw; deeper voice; and a "natural lust" for seducing their prey—women.

The rejection of this male persona is possibly what led and still leads many women to call their relationship a "special friendship."

To conclude, as Kate in Spokane did, that they do not love a gender (women) but a person (Taylor). On the other hand, many heterosexual women will admit that men are not their favorite gender, yet they love "Tom."

Theories have been advanced that human sexual attraction is based on primitive instinct. For example, the strong jaw, which once meant greater biting and tearing ability, equates with a superior mate. But whether sexual cues are instinctual or learned, a woman attempting to attract a woman would obviously accentuate the physical characteristics, dress, and behavior that she believes will achieve her end. In the 1930s, when the words *homosexual* and *heterosexual* were coming into general use, masculine and feminine dress codes and behavior were so sharply contrasted that for the young lesbian it must have seemed imperative to mimic the male.

Of course, the masculine image of women-loving women presents the difficulty that if all lesbians look alike, then in fact, it is male attracting male. Thus the "natural division" stereotype was born: a "naturally heterosexual" woman or girl would be seduced by a lesbian who had male characteristics. The former "innocent" who *chose* her sexual *preference* was guilty of sin and should repent and be saved; the latter "invert" had a mental disease and should be cured by psychiatrists or, failing that, be removed from society. Given this scenerio, parents were watchful for inverts who might seduce their daughter, who was, of course, a healthy innocent.

The society that constructed the stereotype of the "true lesbian" as a masculine persona has more difficulty with an erotic scenario, because no matter how "masculine" a woman may appear, act, or think, she does not ultimately have a penis.

Erotic contacts, other than penetration of a person by a penis, have been relegated to foreplay and afterglow. If no penetration occurs, those involved were just "fooling around"; they explain to themselves and others that "nothing happened."

The central act is called *intercourse, copulation, consummation*, or *having sex*; penetration is the beginning and male orgasm the end, and—until recently, when pleasure, health, and communication made their appearance—procreation or the possibility of it the raison d'être. Hence the wonderment about "what lesbians *do*," the documentation by the Mormons of how many fingers were used to penetrate, and the assumption that lesbians must use dildos. Because two women together are incapable of that central act, their existence as lovers has been denied, downgraded to harmless play, or viewed as a perverted obsession.

That women could be sexually fulfilled by the foreplay of caresses, breast stimulation, and clitoral orgasm and by the tender cuddling of afterglow has been a concept considered laughable, or too threatening to contemplate, or reason for a clitoridectomy.

Judith Hill in Detroit commented that Dr. Ruth, in opening up the subject of sexuality, has done more for lesbians than anyone else. Certainly the clitoris, having been relegated to the position of a vestigial organ homologous with the penis of the male, has been so ignored or slightingly defined as a miniature penis that some grown women do not understand its existence or function. Lack of anatomical knowledge or absorption of phallocentric norms may account for some of the female, as well as male, bewilderment over lesbian lovemaking.

Del Martin and Phyllis Lyon wrote in *Lesbian/Woman*: "There is nothing mysterious or magical about lesbian love-making . . . . the mystery and the magic come from the person with whom you are making love." The occasions for and techniques of lovemaking between two women are as varied or as monotonous as they are between a male and female, and the results just as satisfying, exciting, or banal.

The difference is that a women-loving woman, like a women-loving man, experiences a sensual/erotic admiration for a female's carriage, her breasts, the flow of her hair; sometimes this attraction arouses desire. The lovemaking may be urgent. In *Flying* Kate Millet describes a passion so overwhelming that the women experience orgasm before they have had time to remove their clothes. Conversely it may be "a delicate adventure in incredible tenderness" as described by Laura, the narrator in Elizabeth Jolley's *Palomino*. "Yesterday the light and shade changed in the house and, in her presence, the empty corners were glowing mellow and soft and we sat and lay together on the couch most of the afternoon and evening. We seemed to love each other for hours into the night both putting off the climax exploring and touching with our hands fresh sensuality till the moments came and there could be no more putting off.

"I can look at my hands and at my body and see in them new purpose and meaning. 'Are you smiling, Laura, in the dark,' she asked me during the love we had in the night. 'Are you smiling, Laura, in the dark,' she asked, 'when I touch you and kiss you in these secret places.' "

Not only does the woman capture the ecstasy of loving the female body, but she also experiences the erotic sensations of the female.

Because the lesbian shares the eroticism of the male and because she partakes of both the lesbian and the heterosexual worlds, her culture might best be described, as Judy Grahm suggests, as a bridge, a transculture. Lesbians travel this bridge every day, but to adolescents or heterosexuals, that far end is shrouded in mystery and myth.

Some heterosexual women wonder, "Why do I keep going out with men when my experiences are so bad? I must be screwed up." For this woman to associate with lesbians who obviously enjoy their life may be a threatening experience. She may castigate herself with the thought, "If I were only strong enough, I'd go with women." But crossing that bridge is like learning a secret: it is not something that can be undone. The very knowledge transforms. Nor can the experience be forgotten.

Some rationalize, "I have enough trouble dealing with men on a sexual level, why add women too?" Others defend being with men by saying it is normal, natural. It was their parents' way, the way they were raised, the way their friends are. It leads to marriage, a recognized and honored state, and children. But if at the same time they believe, "All sexual expression is normal and natural," unresolved conflicts exist.

Becoming friends with women who love women presents a number of problems for heterosexual women. They fear a moment of closeness when they must either say, "I know what you want, but I can't give it to you," or be swept away across that bridge. The possibility of being casually rebuffed also exists: "Don't worry. You're not my type." Or as *Golden Girls'* sexually obsessed character Blanche said when she learned a visiting lesbian was attracted to Rose, "Rose? What's the matter with me!" Sometimes the straight woman becomes so preoccupied that a friendly smile or touch on the arm is reported to others as, "She made a pass at me." Women are raised to be continually wary of men's "uncontrollable lust," but sexually at ease with women—in rest rooms, dorm rooms, conference motel rooms, anywhere. Lesbians present a complication that many straight women would rather avoid.

When asked, some lesbians reply that they are highly sexual, others frankly say, no; Emily in Manhattan admitted she was only in her fantasies. Heterosexual women run the gamut from what has been termed nymphomania to "if he gets it once a month, he should consider himself lucky." Seldom, however, are sexual differences celebrated. Women are nervous, afraid that they are not doing it right, enjoy it too much, have the wrong partner, or aren't measuring up to what surveys or magazine articles deem to be satisfying and proper. In this sexually oriented century, *blame* and *change* are the bywords.

Society, however, is more likely to be flexible and tolerant in its view of heterosexual women's sexuality than it is of lesbians. Because they are perceived as deviant, it is often assumed that they are all alike in their deviancy, their "sexual appetites." One result of this lumping together is the assumption that lesbian relationships don't last. That women so afflicted are all doomed to flit from flower to flower in an endless, hopeless quest for mother.

George Bush, during his campaign for the presidency, stated that he did not believe homosexual couples should be allowed to care for foster children, because "I think a child should be placed in a home with a mother and father, and this is my view of the way it ought to be. Much more love in a situation like that, lasting love." In this statement Bush not only categorized all lesbians as unstable in their relationships but boxed them with gay men.

Looking at America today, it would be hard to decide in which homes there is "much more" lasting love. Now that the curtain of male/female marriage has been lifted to reveal wife battering, child abuse, affairs, incompatibilities so deep that divorce is common, and the explosion of people sleeping together, living together without benefit of clergy, "the way it ought to be" has an empty, even ominous ring.

How can love relationships be evaluated? How can a statement be made as to whether lesbians experience more love or more lasting love than heterosexual women?

In a sampling of fifty professional lesbian women whose average age is forty, almost half of them said they had had one committed relationship with another woman for an average of seven years. Another 25 percent reported two committed same-sex relationships, and the remainder were divided among those saying three, more than three, and none. Possibly heterosexual women would give the same replies couched in different words. "I was married for seven years," or "I have been married for seven years." Or "I'm on my second marriage," or "I'm going to stay single and have affairs," or "I'm celibate."

Use of the words *marriage, divorce, affair, virgin* are rare among lesbians. They will ask, "Are Betty and Geri together?" "Who's Randon with?" "Have Karen and Anne broken up?" Judith Hill said scornfully, "Marriage? That's what my mother did." And perhaps the less than legal vocabulary for their relationships makes them seem more fluid, more open-ended.

Statistics do not allow for variations and are often the perpetrators of stereotypes, but this sampling illustrates that what has been called the classic lesbian pattern of a series of two-year relationships is rare among these women. So was mention of one-night stands. Twenty percent of them had never had relations with a male, and 10 percent had been married to one. Half of them presently live with a woman lover, and three have children of their own. One has always had triangular relationships; one had a committed relation-

261

ship with a married woman for seven years. Like their straight contemporaries, some find variety exciting; some want a lifetime relationship; some are retired, not looking; some are lonely.

One aspect of lesbian sexual relationships that would baffle an outsider is the close friendships maintained with former lovers. Almost half the women reported that this was the case with them. Karen Strauss in San Francisco said that if she could ask for résumés from prospective lovers, friendships with former partners would be high on the list. These are not situations where ties are close because of mutual children or property; they are genuine continuations of adult friendships. A lesbian who has had an active sex life may find that her support group of half a dozen people is composed of ex-lovers and their present partners. The lack of genuine, knowledgeable relations with family and other heterosexuals; the small size of the lesbian community; and the disruption of that community by feuding ex-partners—all contribute to this situation. And as a Detroit woman noted, "When your friends and lovers are all the same sex, you'd go crazy being jealous of everyone."

But there is another factor at work that is less frequently found in the heterosexual world. Julie explains: "Sex is one of life's premier experiences, but a relationship should be multifaceted. If it is founded on the attributes of friendship, including similar basic values, that will remain after the passion diminishes. You have to get through that time of shedding attachments, jealousy over her seeing someone else. Get beyond that feeling of 'I've lost her for good' to 'All right, go for it'—and be happy about their transition as well as your own.

"You can't be a collector of people, getting them and keeping them, but the common bond of having shared bodies can enhance a continuing friendship with warmth and understanding. Lesbian relationships can be life-enhancing, instrumental in propelling life forward, not backward. Lesbians don't think in terms of 'I gave you the best years of my life.' I have never felt emotionally alienated from any of my ex-lovers. But when the passion goes, it's dead forever."

As with all men and women, there are bitter breakups, suicide attempts, feelings of total isolation, acts of dramatic anger, physical harm done, grudges nursed. But an annual birthday pool party among heterosexuals where openly accepted past sexual relationships abound is extremely rare. Among lesbians it's par for the course.

Sarah Pearlman, the Boston therapist, says, "How terrific it is to be a lesbian. I don't need to be cosmetically preoccupied and youth-obsessed in terms of attractiveness and, as an older woman,

I have much more potential for romantic relationships and community support than older straight women."

Sarah is fifty-three, and attractive, relaxed woman with soft, curly salt-and-pepper hair; her body is tan and fit. She came to her career as a clinical psychologist through nursing and has now almost completed her doctoral studies. In midlife she left her marriage and, riding the crest of revolutionary feminism, acknowledged her sexuality as lesbian.

Because she leads many workshops on lesbian sexuality, Sarah's clients are frequently women referred to her by other lesbians; one-third to one-half of her practice are lesbians, the majority in their twenties and thirties, occasionally in their forties.

She comments on a study portraying lesbians ranking below gay men and heterosexual couples in frequency of sexual relations: "Lesbians don't typically have a female partner who is insistent on having sex, and that leaves room for cycles of nonsexual behavior." Sometimes the women fear this may be permanent. "I try to help couples relax, let them see that there are cycles when they may be more sexual.

"Women are also very responsive to each other, and if they see their partner is not interested, they will back off. A heterosexual woman has to do it because she fears losing the man. Many men see intercourse as their right."

Sarah believes mechanical sex is more of a possibility with a male. "Usually with a woman there is some expectation of reciprocity. It's very hard to be totally passive.

"The other thing is, heterosexuals don't touch as much." Usually two women touch, hug, cuddle, and caress, reassuring the other in both erotic and affectional ways that she is loved. "A lot of the sexual edge gets taken away by that very natural response. If there is not distance, you don't have tension and you don't have that sense of other, of missing someone, which may be part of sexual excitement. Around the second or third year this becomes a very common couple struggle.

"Two women are much more attuned to emotional withdrawal and relational distance/closeness cues of a partner than a heterosexual couple, where the woman tunes in to the man. The good side is responsiveness, but there is a lot of guesswork, and women behave as though they know their partner's feelings and compulsively respond. They will, for example, sense distraction and translate it into emotional distance. You see this with women in heterosexual couples, but you don't see it with men. When a couple is too close, one way of making distance is sexually.

"In addition women work so hard for money. We don't have

men's income, we don't have their leisure. We work, we keep houses, we have children, and if you're an activist. . . . You fall into bed at night. It's not primary to feel sexual when you are just exhausted and want to pass out. Women have to plan sexual time, which is extremely hard. We are not a leisure class."

A lesbian couple will also have different emotional problems. "I think men are overwhelmed by too much emotion and too much closeness after the initial falling in love. What you see in heterosexual couples is, for the most part, that the men create a distance. They create it with their jobs, with their secretiveness, and—I'll be biased—with their obnoxious behavior. In the classic heterosexual couple, if there is such a thing, you see a woman dying for intimacy and communication and togetherness, and he doesn't know what she is talking about. She's got a 'made' distance there, which in some ways is also comfortable.

"With two women what seems to happen is that one woman takes on the distancing role. It would seem logical to assume that this is a person who needs more space, needs more distance, but shuffle the couple into a new relationship and lots of times the one who has distanced is the first to want closeness. It's as though someone has to distance, or both people will be crazy with too much intimacy.

"Women move in together fast. You know the joke: 'What do lesbians do on their second date?' 'Move in together.' I was surprised to see this dwindling of [sexual lovemaking] with couples who don't live together, because I had thought that living apart would establish enough psychological distance. So, there is more to it than just being together all the time." Oklahoma women noted that going to a party or bar where there are other lesbians sparks sexual excitement, which women in isolation do not have.

It is Sarah's belief that "as women, we just do not develop sexually. We have a fairly sick society, which is phobic about sexuality, very phobic about women, and very phobic about anybody who breaks certain rules of men's control over women and the patriarchal family.

"For lesbians to be free, female sexuality has to be free. Our total freedom is contradictory to male interests—though I would like not to believe that. The ultimate vision is to create a totally different social organization around people's relationships with each other. Up to that point we will have decades that are better, we'll have decades that are worse.

"A lot of the writings by people who look on the early years as formative note that our first relationship was with a woman. We caught a woman's smell, texture, everything. Freud went to great pains to describe how women became heterosexual when in a lot of ways it was much easier not to. My guess is that bisexuality is probably normal.

"I've done a lot of work in this field. Nothing holds. You can have all the descriptions in the world from Freud and the later Freudians, and nothing holds. There are lesbians, just as there are heterosexual men and women, who have not been able to break attachments to mothers or fathers. But there is no across-the-board dynamic.

"Probably if there is a genetic basis for homosexuality, it has something to do with our physiology. Some people are exclusive— they have absolutely no desire for anyone other than the same sex or the opposite sex. And then you see people who are in the bisexual middle, and I think it's experiences that tilt them."

In the classes she teaches, Sarah likes to stand theories on their head in order to shake the students loose from the stereotypes they have absorbed while growing up. "The theories, according to Freud, are that if you have an overwhelming mother, you don't really have a chance of establishing a relationship with your father; if you have an overwhelming father, you are intimidated because he is sexually intrusive, or violent or distanced. You are overwhelmed or under-whelmed." She laughs as she describes her students' startled reaction to her theory of "whelming." "If you are whelmed just right, you are lucky enough to be a lesbian. Underwhelmed or overwhelmed and you're heterosexual." She adds, "You can take a lot of this stuff with a grain of salt."

In regard to lesbians existing in the heterosexual world, she says, "A heterosexual falls in love, brings the person home, and every-body's dancing. Who dances for a lesbian? Where is the celebration for that relationship? Celebration for that identity? There are so many things that are spoiled and so many stolen from us.

"I get pretty angry when I see these women who are so smart and so decent and what they have had to deal with. But I'm not totally cynical. I think people can look at themselves and figure out playing fair—let's play fair.

"The other side of it is there are a lot of lesbians who really enjoy their lives. And when I look at heterosexual lives, I under-stand. My clients tell me it's not that they are not attracted to men, it's not that they can't picture a relationship with a man, or a sexual liaison or encounter with a man, but they can't picture going back into the straight life." And the straight life is, after all, what women grew up with.

"They like having a primarily women's world and like the kind of domesticity and closeness and companionship that two women have together. They feel good that they don't have to deal with men in the primary area in their lives. They have found themselves."

29. SEX IS WORLDS OF THINGS

MANHATTAN. The Village. The Women's Coffee House. Joan Nestle, a writer and teacher of writing at Queens University, has scheduled a reading. Seventy new plastic chairs are arranged to face a low stage; gray curtains cover the ugliness of old school windows. The admission is $4.00; a copy of Nestle's book costs $8.95. Joan is a big woman dressed in black boots, black tights, and black satin shirt. Flaming red nail polish and lipstick, big earrings, glasses on a turquoise string are her decorations.

She reads short sections from *A Restricted Country*: " 'As a woman, as a lesbian, as a Jew I know that much of what I call history others will not. Often one people's history to be glorified and celebrated is another people's hell. We choose the history that we save. . . .' "

Closing the book, she picks up a sheaf of typed pages, saying, "As most of you know, I come from the butch/femme tradition and am still of it and a celebrant of it, as I am of erotic writing. The story I am going to read is unpublished and is called 'My Woman Papa.'

"You work at a job that makes your back rock-hard strong. You work with men in a cavernous warehouse loading trucks while others sleep. . . . My woman Papa, who does not want to be a man but who does travel in unwomanly places, does unwomanly work. . . . She endures the bitter humor of her fellow workers who are men. They laugh at Jews, at women, and when the black workers are not present at blacks. . . . My woman grits her teeth and says when the rape jokes come, 'Don't talk that shit around me.'

"I like her sweat and her tattoos, I like her courtliness and her disdain of the boys. I mother her and wife her and slut her and together we are learning to be comrades."

The body of the story is a description of two women making love, one with a dildo strapped to her crotch. Like a love scene in a Harlequin romance, it is nonoffensive in its tenderness and arousing in its explicitness, but Joan does not avoid words like *cock* and *cunt*. The ending is a political plea.

"She is old and young, my woman Papa, strong and delicate, generous and frugal, she plays at women's festivals and hangs unicorns on her walls. Treasure these women among us. Do not let reactionary feminism drive them away. Do not let naive lesbianism exile them. They are rare and to be cherished. My woman Papa, my dusty sparrow, I know how special you are. In the fifties and before you were understood, now I have to explain so your mysteries will not be trampled in our battle against abusive power. So that your strength, both of loving and of need, is not mistaken for betrayal of your womanliness.' "

A discussion follows the reading. Joan explains, "To me sex is worlds of things. It's resistance, it's healing, it's gratitude, it's exploration, it's breaking boundaries. I don't know where my sexual writing will take me. And with AIDS, I feel it is important to keep the flame of sexual exploration alive—sometimes we may be able to do it only metaphorically. If literature is metaphoric of everything, that may be the way until the grass is green again."

After an exchange of views as to what constitutes pornography and erotica, Joan sums up: "I think sexuality—how it is expressed—is such a precious thing, such a fragile thing. Everyone should find a territory they feel at home in so that they can explore sexuality. The thing I have no truck with is violence.

"To write erotic stories from your lives is a way of saying thank you to someone who has made you feel beautiful and warm. You never see your own back until you are given a photograph of it, and similarly people may never know how beautiful they are when they are making love unless you tell them."

Joan Nestle, as she records so frankly in her book, is also the child of a mother "who liked to fuck." She writes of her youth: "And then my deepest joy, when the hot weekends came, sometimes as early as May but surely by June. I would leave East Ninth Street early on Saturday morning, wearing my bathing suit under my shorts, and head for the BMT, the start of a two-hour subway and bus trip that would take me to Riis Park—my Riviera, my Fire

Island, my gay beach—where I could spread my blanket and watch strong butches challenge each other by weightlifting garbage cans, where I could see tattoos bulge with womanly effort and hear the shouts of the softball game come floating over the fence.

". . . as we moved down Flatbush Avenue, teenagers loud with their own lust poured into the bus. There were hostile encounters, the usual stares at the freaks, whispered taunts of faggot, lezzie, is that a man or a woman, but we did not care. We were heading to the sun, to our piece of the beach where we could kiss and hug and enjoy looking at each other."

Joan believes that to "advocate androgyny as the safest road to heterosexual acceptance" can become "the basis for a truly destructive kind of role playing, a self-denial of natural style."

But what is the natural style of a lesbian?

Connie, a lesbian in her sixties, shakes her head with its cap of pure-white short hair. "This butch/femme bar scene was not all there was then. Some of us knew, and married to have children. Some didn't know and married. Some stayed with their woman. Some never knew. Some acted as though they never knew. There were all kinds of us.

"There were circles of gay women who never set foot inside a bar. I always had gay friends, but that wasn't the only thing in our lives. Political consciousness, our work were the important things. I was very active in the peace movement, the women's movement."

Connie is small, slightly hunched and she holds her purse with both hands. She is dressed in black, soft jeans and jacket. Her words, like Marty Alinor's, imply rather than state, and she flatly refuses to reveal, even anonymously, any details of her life. "Oh, no," she says wide-eyed, "I couldn't possibly do that."

Julie, born in 1940, the same year as Joan Nestle, was nurtured in an upper-middle-class family and never went near a bar, but her special friendships were nonetheless passionately sexual affairs. Her lovers—although she never used the word then—were women she knew through college or professional ties. Her mother had taught her that the key to success was associating with the "right people," and her criteria for gay friends was how well they blended into the system with appropriate dress and social skills. Julie's choice of lovers was probably no different, except for gender, from the ones she would have chosen as a heterosexual.

In the 1940s a woman from a working-class background in Washington, D.C., had friends who bound their breasts, wore men's boxer shorts, and shaved. She herself drank, used drugs, and "carried my mattress on my back for years. My lover was a street prostitute. That's how we made our living."

A woman born in 1959, call her Carley, was left with her grand-mother at birth by a mother whose five children all had different fathers. Carley had undergone an abortion at fifteen and shortly thereafter begun such varied sexual activities as ménage à trois with married couples; at nineteen, as she sat in a lesbian bar, she was recruited as a prostitute. She formed a love relationship with another prostitute, and they bought a house in a middle-class Connecticut neighborhood. Her partner became pregnant by a client, and Carley helped to deliver the baby. Clad in denim with keys on her belt, Carley played the role of father. The relationship deteriorated, and Carley moved out of state; at twenty-nine she married, and quit The Business.

After two years of monogamous marriage, she says of relations with men and with women, "I couldn't choose. It wouldn't be fair to choose. The important thing is balancing the male and female within yourself."

Mabel Hampton is a small eighty-five-year-old black woman with frizzled gray hair. Boston's *Sojourner* magazine interviewed her. "There was none of this one woman this week another next week." But Mabel was not isolated. Clubs, as the women of that day called them, were another way of gaining private space. Women with extra rooms would invite women, couples and singles, for the weekend. They would eat, meet new people, party, and make love to their partners. Mabel Hampton had one partner for forty-two years.

In *A Restricted Country* Joan Nestle writes about the Sea Colony bar, where "we were surrounded by the nets of the society that hated us and yet wanted our money. Mafia nets, clean-up New York nets, vice squad nets. The physical nets were visible. . . . It was the other nets, the nets of the righteous people, the ones that reached into our minds that most threatened our breathing. These nets carried twisted in their invisible windings the words *hate your-self because you are a freak . . . hate yourself because you are sexual.*"

All lesbians were and are affected by the invisible nets, and even those like Julie who did not frequent the gay bars or beaches felt the effects of the physical nets. By dissociating themselves from the women who shielded their faces from the vice-squad flashlight and dissociating themselves from the word *lesbian*, they restricted the sexual side of themselves to home or apartment or a room within their parents' house. And even in those sanctuaries, as Julie says, "I never expressed affection for my partner in front of others, even if I knew that they were gay too. I was afraid to get too comfortable with it. Afraid that, if I did, I would someday make that mistake in front of straights."

Marty Alinor said, "I grew up so repressed, I thought sex was dirty."

This extreme restriction of physical and psychological territory restricts the expression of sexuality. How can one *choose* a sexual partner if only one is available? Even if a lesbian community exists, the need to express sexuality and the need for gay friends often results in "an army of ex-lovers."

In some communities bars are still the only place to socialize and find sexual excitement. Two women in the bar of the very upscale Philadelphia gay men's restaurant Equus say they prefer it to the lesbian bar, Sneakers, which is in a bad neighborhood. They are older married women from South Philly and come on Mondays and Tuesdays, when the hot dogs are twenty-five cents and the beer fifty. They say South Philly is no longer filled with solid Italian families. "You know what happened? All those Italians had gay kids. So did the Polish and the Irish." A waiter, Jim, says that during the week 90 percent of his customers in the restaurant are gay women—in couples or groups. "They come here," he says, "because our gay waiters are not hostile to women. In other gay bars they are."

Karen Lewis of Oklahoma City noted that a lesbian bar affords the isolated couple the opportunity to dance and hold hands across the table, but also the opportunity for one of the partners to attract or be attracted to another woman. The problem is similar to a heterosexual couple moving to a new city and attempting to find mutual friends in the bar atmosphere of drink, music, sex—and jealousy.

A lesbian in her fifties said that in her youth butch/femme was a way of protecting the relationship. "No femme would ever go into a bar alone. If she did, she was loose, a bad woman. Butches did, but they had to be careful who they asked to dance. If a single butch neglected to ask another butch's permission to dance with her woman, there would be a fight. But the femmes would flirt, and the butches would take a chance." She laughed. "To us then it was exciting."

In the mid-1980s Mercie, one of the owners of a women's club/bar in New Hampshire, said proudly, "There are no fights here. Women feel free to ask other women to dance."

271

A woman who owned a restaurant added a lounge, and a local newspaper reported that it was a "real woman's bar." The owner, a lesbian herself, was horrified at the numbers of women-loving women who came that Saturday night. Public space where lesbians can be as overtly sexual as the straight men and women who share it is rare indeed.

The sexuality and territory of the heterosexual woman was, and is, also restricted by visible and invisible nets. In the fifties her prescribed script was to marry young, immediately bear three children, stay home, and concede adultery and bars to males and bad women. The economic ties to her husband meant food and shelter for her and her children, and his earning power defined where and how she lived. The lesbian had the freedom and responsibility of the male in making her own way in the workplace. If she belonged to the working class, she, like her male contemporary, headed not home to a dingy apartment after work, but to the bar, which was a more satisfying home. A teacher like Julie went camping or to concerts with her "special friend."

But the heterosexual woman at home with her children was idolized by society while the lesbian's invisible nets, "the ones that reached into our minds," confined the women who came of age before gay liberation into a ghetto of silence, half-truths, and lies. The 1972 dedication in *Sappho Was a Right-On Woman* tells of the toll: "To those who have suffered for their sexual preference, most especially to Sandy, who committed suicide, to Cam, who died of alcoholism, and to Lydia, who was murdered . . ."

Stereotypes allow the general public to solidify partial truth into conviction. Just as the stereotype of the lesbian as a butch bar dyke made generations horrified of "them," so the present notion that lesbians are liberated, that the bad old days are gone, can sweep present realities under the rug. The dangers of simplification as opposed to the complex language of human life being lived is apparent when young people speak. A young woman sits on a stool in Equus, the Philadelphia gay men's bar. She lives in New Jersey, but attended a teacher's college in Chicago. "Nothing has changed," she says. "It's just as hard to come out now. It took me seven years. Some neighbors finally brought me here and laid out the scene."

Sometimes Julie's anger breaks through. "What's the big flap about? Just because I don't want to go to bed with a man!" She pauses. "No, they would probably accept that. What they won't accept is that I do want to go to bed with a woman."

PART 11

VARIATIONS ON A THEME

30. LABELS FALL SHORT

THERE are women who refuse the
label of lesbian or heterosexual, who consider themselves simply
sexual beings. Some lesbians do not believe such a creature exists;
they describe them as either straights who play around with women
or lesbians who have not yet admitted their true orientation. Straight
women may consider bisexuals as simply confused, going through
a difficult time after a divorce, or too strange even to think about.
Maybe someone like Margaret Mead could keep a picture of an ex-
husband on the mantle and a woman lover's beside her bed but not
an "ordinary" woman. But these women who reject classification
believe that they are in fact ordinary, that "everyone is bisexual."

Pam—not her real name—grew up in a secure family in a small
town. Although her sexual education was as brief as most girls' in
the early fifties—a hasty talk by her mother before she left for school
to see the sixth-grade movie on menstruation—she did not feel
uncomfortable about her body. She enjoyed the sensations she felt
while reading romantic books and she loved kissing boys. At fifteen
she bought Tampax and spent a long time in the bathroom with a
mirror figuring out how her parts matched those in the diagram.

She and her best girlfriend frequently slept at each other's houses.
"We never touched, but I took pleasure in watching her undress,
lying in bed with her. She was two years older and introduced me
to Shakespeare." When Pam graduated from high school in 1964,
she had never heard the word *lesbian*, but with boys she had barely
stopped short of "going all the way."

At forty-one Pam is a quick, intense, slender woman with a small, oval face and fly-away hair. "I was very idealistic about marriage. I was in love with Keats and I wanted the greatest love affair of all time." She went off to the university, where she expected to find someone to marry. "It was great to be free, and I was hot to trot."

In her freshman year she had "some terrible sex" and came close to being raped on a blind date. During her sophomore year she went with one man. "I wanted to be in love. It was he who felt the Catholic guilt for us sleeping together." She once went to a gay bar in D.C. "Really a costume party. Bizarre."

In her junior year Pam attended a fraternity party with a premed student. "I liked how he talked, the fact he was tall. While we were dancing, I thought, 'I wonder what it would be like to be married to a doctor.' " They were engaged a month before graduation and married in August 1968.

"It was a lovely wedding. The reception was at the Holiday Inn, and we set out for Niagara Falls." Two things happened that night. First, as she snuggled close to him in the car, dreaming of the love affair of the century, of this being forever, he suggested she move over and put on her seat belt. Second, when she wanted to cuddle after lovemaking, he told her he couldn't sleep with anyone touching him.

"He wanted to screw a lot. He thought five times a day was normal. He was into quantity, I was into quality. I got sore a lot and would suggest 'Let's do everything but.' " Alan refused. Once Pam angrily suggested they drill a hole in the mattress and she could go do something else. He became furious. "It was our first fight. I was scared it might mean divorce. I guess I was more cooperative after that."

Pam enjoyed being pregnant, loved seeing her two children born, and adored breast-feeding. "My son is the apple of my eye—always will be. My daughter is absolutely everything you would want a daughter to be." But when her little girl was ten months old, she knew she was breast-feeding for the last time. "I regained my body. I was alone. It was exciting."

After seven years of marriage, when the children were one and two, a friend told her Alan was having affairs. "I knew she was right. There I was, my tears falling in the Brunswick stew. I felt very sad, very insecure.

"It took a year, then I made love to a male friend of mine and I cried. Giving up virginity is much different than when you give up the notion of fidelity." Alan and Pam agreed not to talk about their affairs to each other and vowed that their marriage would always come first. Pam did not see many men, but at thirty-two she did become pregnant. "I had been using a diaphragm. I wasn't sure who the father was. No way was I going to have another kid."

She had an abortion and had her tubes tied. "It was a major turning point. Now I was in charge."

One night, out with with a woman friend, she stopped back at the house between dinner and a movie. "Alan was screwing a nude woman in front of the fireplace. I came back home at one-thirty, crawled into bed with him, and said, 'It's okay. I can take it.' "

A few months later he told her he was in love with someone else. "I said, 'Break it off.' He said, 'I can't.' He was crying. It was a terrible, terrible time. We had gone through all the poverty together and now . . . We went to a counselor, and his recommendation was that with therapy we could hold the marriage together. Alan refused. I raged at him. 'How can you say that?' He was sobbing. We stayed up all night. I sat in the closet and took off my wedding ring.

"He left on Labor Day. The kids were four and a half and six. They needed me. I was a rock. But it hurt for a long, long time."

Pam went through times of being alone with her vibrator, of "screwing everybody I could," and finally on a weekend with co-workers from NOW she and a woman friend experienced an erotic attraction. "It was not a spark, but a forest fire. It was the biggest turn-on of my life."

For months Pam vacillated between feelings of "wanting to close my eyes and lose myself in this woman," of fearing "the intense caring," and of "not wanting to be a lesbian." She was scared of losing the children if Alan found out and scared of homophobia in straight people.

Pam went on to share her body with other women, but kept both male and female lovers at arm's length. "I love having freedom to be with myself or whoever I want to be with. I've taken chances, done wild things. If it came my way and it was appealing, I went for it. Not abusing, not using. I've always told the whole truth. Occasionally I have a ménage, mostly one other woman and a man, once with two women who were ex-lovers of mine. It's nothing you would want a steady diet of, but it is nice every once in a while as a special treat."

Four years ago she had a love affair with a woman who was married with two children. "She was a wonderful lover, but liked to break up and make up. Many women's relationships are just as fucked up as men's are."

Then Pam met a woman, call her Alison. "She's fourteen years younger, but wise beyond her years."

Alison, a handsome blonde, had a minimal home life as a child; at nineteen she quit college to start her own highly successful computer business. She, like Pam, is a sexual person and has enjoyed both men and women since age fifteen. She lived with a man for four years, but has always known that she would never be dependent or married in a traditional sense.

Pam says of her and Alison's relationship, "We've been lovers and friends for over two years. It is my finest, happiest, most sexually satisfying relationship. But it is not practical to live together. I'm holding on to my family, my space. I don't want to be coupled. I have the best of all possible worlds. I love with my arms wide open. And I am loved.

"For five years I've had a male lover who is married to a friend of mine. She and I have lunch together and talk about him. Sometimes we get together as families. He and I are best friends, we talk about everything, analyze everything, and occasionally are lovers. He enhances my life.

"And so does Alison. I choose to be a practicing bisexual. But I am not monogamous with these primary relationships. I love feeling free to say, 'Yes.' Mostly women. An occasional man. I tell my male lover and Alison everything. You have to tell the whole truth when you have multiple lovers.

"It doesn't suit my life to be a lesbian. My kids are twelve and thirteen, and there could be ugly complications from their father. And as they become sexual, it's hard for them to cope with a parent's sexuality. We talk about everything, but not my lovers.

"I have no interest in marrying again—ever. I don't see living with a man.

"I have been asked to run for political office, but the fact that my nonconventional life-style could be exposed keeps me from it. What a bitch. What a terrible offense—I love.

"At seventy I think I'll still be real happy I didn't say no to things that came my way. I'll think back on all the luscious experiences and what terrific fun they were."

In the fall of 1988 Alison moved in with Pam and her children —in a monogamous, committed relationship.

At a Unitarian conference a theologian spoke of a vision of many genders. Sarah Pearlman, the therapist, thinks one of society's problems is the division of genders, making people one of two. "And there is such discomfort when characteristics or attributes don't fit the one or the other, when women have hair or men are slight. We can't even think in terms of degrees. Until that is totally broken down we can't have a utopia."

278

Penis or no penis, everything seems to rest on that basic difference. Boy/girl changes to man/woman with all the attendant trappings of masculine/feminine, manhood/womanhood, but because gender is so tied to the genitals, erotic behavior is the most rigidly categorized.

Lives that contradict these categories are concealed, and others who by chance discover them dismiss the behavior as weird, not as a possible, viable variation. For example, when Winnie, Rose Mary Denman's partner, reveals that she and her husband did not have intercourse for twelve years, our sexually oriented society brands this as rare and abnormal. Similarly, a married women having female lovers is acknowledged as possible, but a husband who ignores or accepts or encourages this behavior is beyond belief. Married women-loving women are perhaps the most invisible of all.

A New Hampshire woman in her fifties says, "I have had three long-term relationships—all with married women."

Another woman does not "rock the boat" of economic ties and grown children's expectations by leaving her husband. Her lover of seven years, with whom she spends most of her time, is content with the arrangement.

Diane, a heavyset, pleasant woman, lived most of her life in Moorhead, Minnesota. Twelve years into her marriage she fell in love with her friend. "One day I believed homosexuality was deviant, the next day I was there and it was wonderful." That relationship lasted six years; her marriage thirteen more for a total of twenty-five. She has two daughters, and when one was eighteen, "we came out to each other together."

Joan lives in a town of sixteen thousand in Pennsylvania. When, at thirty-one, she fell in love with a woman, her husband invited the other woman, Linda, to come live with them. For a long time Joan's sexual relations with her husband had been limited to several times a year. Linda became part of their socioeconomic unit, helping out at the law office where Joan and her husband are partners, taking care of the two boys, and later Joan's daughter whom her husband very reluctantly sired as a love child for her and Linda.

Linda's life had been one of primitive poverty in North Carolina. Daughter of an alcoholic father, sister of a suicidal gay brother, Linda had worked in a textile factory, fished, and drunk heavily. Eventually she came to resent her role as housekeeper for Joan and her husband and sons, but she loved the baby, which she had helped to deliver.

"We were not one big happy family, but we tolerated each other," Joan said. "We were discussing who would leave, when

Linda was killed in a car accident. She was thirty-six, we had lived together a little over three years. I was in the accident too."

Joan, a tall, feminine blonde, feels the community knows she is gay and accepts her. But she is unhappy in her new relationship— "my basic needs are not being met because of her homophobia, and I drink more than I want to." Joan, whom her husband believes "always gets what she wants," complains, "I want to live with her. I don't see what her problem is."

Some lesbians live in friendship with gay men; some marry them and have children. Some lesbians, tired of "looking," retire in a nonsexual relationship with an ex-lover. Others, exhausted by the burdens of independence, marry a older man.

A midwestern woman believes that everyone has their own unique tapestry. Dee—not her real name—was born in 1938. She worked for an established international service organization in both Korea and wartime Vietnam, in the Peace Corps in Latin America, and for fifteen years as a social worker in Detroit's Black Bottom and the Hispanic community. In her early forties she journeyed to West Bengal to work with Mother Theresa among the "poorest of the poor." "I am blessed," Dee says, "with the nature to see a glass not as half empty, but as half full. And to want to fill it completely.

"The first identity I struggled with was my ethnic identity. Being Asian-American, I was neither white nor black. On an application form I always had to check 'Other.' My mother was a farm girl, a Caucasian. My father was brought to this country from the Philippines by a Tennessee farm boy and finished high school in Eagle Rock, Tennessee. Eventually he attended Cumberland University and received a law degree. Filipinos at that time were allowed no rights whatsoever; they were wards of the nation-state. When he graduated, there was no way except by a special dispensation from Congress that he could practice law. So he went to Detroit, where there is a Filipino community, and became a domestic. A 1934 newspaper article that pitted Detroit domestics against New York's to see who had the best butlers cited my father because of his degrees.

"It wasn't until the Second World War, when they took aliens and women into the factories, that he got a good job. My parents' marriage only lasted ten, twelve years." Dee's father told her later that his wife had been "considered nothing but a slut and a whore for having married him." "My mother couldn't withstand the assault on her own self-esteem.

"I was headed for the factory where my mother worked, but the assistant principal of my high school dragged me out into the hallway and argued with me about filling out this application for a scholarship. The Urban League gave me the scholarship, which was wonderful. That is essentially where some of my own commitment to struggling people comes from.

"I never sat still long enough to let my sexuality catch up with me," Dee says. She had two loving relationships with men with whom marriage was not an option, then in her thirties she became involved with a woman. For five years she called herself lesbian, but ultimately found she could not deny her very positive experiences with men. "It parallels my ethnic development in the sense that when I could no longer deny my Asian heritage and my father, I went through a time of being very Asian and not white. I'm Asian! And then coming back to claim my mother's heritage so that I had both totally.

"When I fell in love and experienced my first lesbian relationship, it was all. I took on all the trappings that were around it. Didn't socialize with male friends. My energy was all toward women for about five years. Ultimately I had to leave the relationship because I needed something else. That then gave me the opportunity to see that I could be attracted to many women," as well as men.

Dee feels that having sexual experiences with both men and women enhances her life, even though on occasion "both gay and straight friends write me off.

"We are all sexual beings. How that gets realized is open. With me labels fall short."

281

31. BEING GAY IS MINOR

"I'VE been brought up with such shit that being gay is minor."

Fran is forty-seven. Her five-foot-five body is quick and trim, and her face is pure Irish—very white skin, high cheekbones, green eyes, and a reddish tint to her hair.

Fran has lived in the Park Slope section of Brooklyn since her return from California. Posters and pictures of Fran's children fill the walls of her first-floor apartment. "I figure," she says, waving an arm at the bay windows that face the street, "this was once the dining room." It is now kitchen, bathroom, closet, and living/bedroom, a helter-skelter home where the focus is on people, not things. The phone rings frequently. A friend wanting to go out, then another friend, her lover Linda, and three times it is her twenty-five-year-old middle daughter—the last call "because I didn't hear you say, 'I love you.' "

"She," Fran says, "knows I have a woman lover and doesn't know how to approach it. It's accepted, but she doesn't want to say it."

Yet another call is from her mother in Queens, mourning the death of her daughter, Fran's sister. Fran reassures her. "I'm coming on Saturday, Mom. We'll hang out. We both can cry together. If you don't cry, don't get it out, you'll get sick." She hangs up and calls her twenty-one-year-old daughter, who lives in the apartment below her grandmother. "Go up and make Grandma giggle. Get her a chocolate bar."

Fran grew up in the streets of Spanish Harlem. At eighteen she became pregnant by a black/Puerto Rican. Abortion in 1958 was for Irish Catholic Fran out of the question. She wanted the best care for her baby, but the Salvation Army turned her away; hospitals wouldn't take her without insurance. When her labor pains started, she walked to the finest hospital in the city and sat down on a park bench. She gritted her teeth until she knew the baby was almost there, then she crossed the street into the emergency room.

"The arrogance of survival," she says. That theme has run through her life.

Fran's Irish mother, who has no idea who Fran's biological father is, was married to a Puerto Rican, a "mean drunk." She herself was a "nice drunk." During the late 1940s, when neighborhoods were being demolished for public housing, the family of eight slept on the floors of abandoned buildings. At twelve Fran was sent to Long Island to live with "a nice, middle-class Jewish lady." There she became acquainted with meat and vegetables and kids who took pride in good report cards, had bikes, and went to proms. But the woman was abusive, "evil" Fran calls her. At fourteen she returned to 125th Street and became a gang leader, a war lord who played the role of liaison with the other gangs and wore razor blades in her rolled hair, her "rats." "We had to live in the streets, so we had to make them comfortable, make our territory *safe*."

At sixteen the disruptive Fran, who stole from lockers and set classes in turmoil, was told by teachers, principal, and guidance counselor to quit school. She did and got a job at Bell Telephone "with all the other delinquents." Married to the father of her first child, she was, from eighteen on, pregnant and taking care of other women's children. After the last of her four children was born, she took a job as a teletype operator on Wall Street. Every morning she fed and dressed the children, traveled an hour or more by subway from Washington Heights to her mother's in Brooklyn, dropped off the children, returned by subway to her job in Manhattan, and after work reversed the commute. "Winter would make me die. Getting four kids ready. . . . But there was the rule that kids were left with family, otherwise there was more guilt." When she became a "runner" she was on her feet all day. "But I was good at it. It was my first interaction with the three-piece suit, the man who opened the door for me. I didn't grow up in that environment, seeing adults treat each other like that."

When she and her husband moved to Co-op City, with its forty-nine thousand apartments, people said, "Fran and Julio moving on up." Because "the place was geared to the middle class—bus drivers, et cetera," Fran felt her children would get a better education there than in Harlem. She became active at her children's school as a "PTA mom."

"Between thirty-five and forty I started thinking—before that I had been too overwhelmed to think. Questioning—why am I an extension of Julio, of kids? My priorities changed. At forty I acted on it." Her children ranged in age from sixteen to twenty-four.

"It was scary to leave. Women hide behind marriage. You don't know who you are. I went to California and went into mourning for a year. It was the death of a marriage. I felt black—my insides were dark. I had to block thinking of my kids.

"My husband had had total control. I thought that was the way it was supposed to be. My generation comes from tough women who just took it. I feared him. That wasn't right. I should act out of respect. We were hardworking—both of us." Julio now runs several dry-cleaning and laundromat establishments. "Before, I kept quiet and got beaten. I speak softer than I used to, but I like honesty and openness.

"I became unattracted to some behaviors of men, but I still look at them." Flirting with men always seemed natural to her, and she had to learn a new system of expressing attraction for women. During her first visit to a San Francisco lesbian bar, a woman stared at her. "I didn't know this was the mating call in the women's world. It was very strange to me."

Fran has been separated from her husband for six years and has been with Linda, a forty-year-old professor of physical education, for four years. "I'm most comfortable with women at this time because of their gifts of being open to sense and feeling." In a group of gay women where each in turn was stating her sexual identity, Fran said, "I'm involved with a woman right now. Nothing else is important. This is the present." It was, she adds, "an offensive answer."

She and Linda have never lived together. "Being married for twenty-five years and with four kids, I've been so many extensions. Living with someone gives you a responsibility. You have to interact, be responsible for your own presence and responsible for theirs. That's part of being a mate. You also have a responsibility not to hurt the person you live with; you need to learn to be together and separate."

It is a forty-five-minute drive between their homes, and Fran admits that Linda resents that travel time. They see each other from Saturday morning to Monday morning and talk every day on the phone.

"I'm not wrong in not wanting to live together, I'm different. What you take from your mate is so powerful—and Linda and I use this in our lives now. Some who live together are miserable. Living apart allows freedom. You don't have to worry about getting home 'on time,' there's a balance."

Two weeks before, Fran's sister, who still lived in Harlem, died of cancer. "Nobody should have to die in conditions like that. Such poverty. The Dominicans are outside selling crack and playing boxes—they're really crazy." Her voice is heavy. She adds, "Her husband was a good man."

"Because I am a survivor, I don't go to Linda with pain. She has never seen insecurity in me before. Being with a woman, I want to be mothered. But having been a mother, I am more intuitive and I know when there is a need for extra reassurance. I am an old soul. Because of my bad childhood I know what is going on with others. I can feel the sadness that others feel. I want someone who *knows* the pain is there, just gives me distraction from it. I'm learning that not only can I take pain, take abuse, but I can take something I like."

Fran read her first book when she was thirty. "I couldn't sit still to read. I got restless because I always had to do so much, always moving. I want to read books about strong women who don't just think—who do." With Linda's help—Fran had, for example, never learned fractions—she passed her high school equivalency exam. She works as a teacher's helper in a local high school and is taking her first two courses at a community college. "I just got introduced to James Baldwin and he dies! I was so pissed! He grew up on the same streets and died in France, where I want to go."

Fran's youngest daughter, a full-time student at Fashion Institute of Technology, is a dark-skinned, fine-featured woman who has competed for the Miss USA title. She and her brother—the two youngest children—don't know the sexual side of their mother's relationship with Linda. "They are," Fran says with a flick of her hand, "too middle-class."

The twenty-five-year-old is struggling to assimilate the knowledge, but her oldest daughter knows and has been with women herself. This daughter is separated from her husband and raising two children alone. Fran says with pride, "I delivered my first grandchild. I was the coach. Who can do it better than the mother? A Dominican/Arab is the father—he's into drugs and crazy. She lives in Harlem. The Chinese and Koreans stand out there in the middle of all that and sell flowers!"

Fran says this daughter needs therapy. "I was doing drugs, poor nutrition when I was pregnant with her. And she was my first. I treated her like my doll, my toy. I did it all for her. Anger at her father was part of it."

Her twenty-two-year-old son is in a "don't-worry-Mom-I'm-here-stage. My culture dictated comfort from a man—it is comforting, I can accept it. He is bright, in college, has saved twenty thousand dollars working for his father."

Her husband, Julio, "knows about Linda, but he doesn't want to deal with it. I still love him and he still loves me. But it is not healthy."

Fran and Linda have many lesbian friends. They love fun—have dressed in tuxes and been hosts for women giving get-acquainted teas for gay women. They love parties—they put their arms around each other, their heads together, and lustily sing the theme song of *La Cage aux Folles*, "I Am What I Am."

But Fran's definition of "I am what I am" is not easy for society to understand. She is a mother, a daughter, a woman's lover, a separated wife, a human discovering James Baldwin. No glib category explains her, and she refuses them all. "I'm involved with a woman right now."

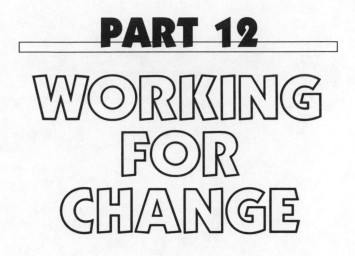

PART 12

WORKING FOR CHANGE

32. FEMINIST LESBIANS

"I'M not convinced that there is a tremendous difference between gay women and straight women," Kathleen says. "The difference is between women who have some awareness of what the world is all about and women who don't. It doesn't matter so much how they define their sexuality, but how they—"

Her partner, Barbara, interjects, "—define their womanhood."

Kathleen finishes, "And how they define the world."

Both these women, high school graduates of the class of 1969, came of age simultaneously with feminism. During the 1970s organizations that primarily served women—feminist health centers, rape crisis centers, battered-women's shelters, women's resource centers, women's bookstores—sprang into being across the country. NOW, the National Abortion Rights League, and other advocacy groups were formed; Planned Parenthood clinics and the YWCA were revitalized. Those involved took the name of *feminist*, a term long associated with women who publicly claimed for themselves the masculine attribute of leadership for political change.

The additional label of *lesbian* was often attached to them because, as Jan Harrow said of the Women's Center at the University of New Hampshire, "Anytime there is a collection of women without men, they are seen as man-haters or dykes 'talking about those women's things.' The way you deflate issues is to ascribe to them a label."

At first lesbians held their tongues in order not to further damage the reputation of these fledgling organizations. But a growing consciousness of gay liberation brought about bitter struggles.

Between 1968 and 1971 the National Organization for Women was rocked with controversy. The book *Sappho Was a Right-on Woman* by Sidney Abbott and Barbara Love, tells the story this way: in 1971 Rita Mae Brown resigned from the New York City NOW chapter, accusing the members of being "middle class club women not ready to think about the issues of race, sexual preference or their own class privilege." "Lesbianism," she said, according to Abbott and Love, "is the one word which gives the New York NOW Executive Committee a collective heart attack." A year later the president of New York NOW, who had been harshly criticized for supporting Rita Mae Brown and Kate Millett, was defeated in a questionable election for chairwoman of the board. Of the election Abbott and Love wrote, "Just as she was purged so were her supporters, and friends of her supporters were under suspicion."

A few months later the national organization voted to legally and morally support lesbianism. In many organizations problems took years to resolve.

In the early 1980s a woman who has been administrator for two highly successful women's centers sits in her office, her eyes blurry with tears. She is a woman past fifty who is married with children; call her Margaret. She confides she is leaving the organization, that she cannot work in a collective environment. A collective as opposed to the traditional hierarchical chain of command requires a dilution of authority to a greater or lesser extent. Radical lesbians, she believes, have forced her into an untenable position.

She rises, shoves the door almost shut, then whispers in anguish, "I put on the lavender armband!" At a national conference she attended, all women, gay or straight, were urged to wear them as a symbol of solidarity. "I've marched with lesbians. I've worked with them for years. They are my friends. I don't criticize their sexual life.

"But," she says raising her chin, "I will not concede that their life-style, their politics, are superior to mine."

Barbara, Kathleen, and their friend Carole, lesbians in their mid-thirties, have all been involved in feminist activities since the early 1970s. Barbara, a fair, auburn-haired woman from a working-class background, is a YWCA director and occasionally works with political campaigns. Kathleen, who holds several degrees and is an attorney with a large law firm, was active in Jane (the early-abortion service in Chicago), NOW, and for ten years a member of the board of directors of a shelter for battered women. Carole, previously an administrator for Child Welfare Services, has for the last four years directed the shelter.

In the early 1980s the shelter was split between women who wanted a collective and those who perceived an organizational hierarchy as more efficient. Kathleen explains that the director who preceded Carole came from a job where she could not be out as a lesbian. Tired of that dual life, she saw the shelter as a way of merging her work and personal beliefs. Once on the job, however, conflicts emerged between what she felt were sound business decisions and the wishes of her gay friends with whom she worked. The collective process of rotating responsibilities eventually resulted in such confusion that no one was sure who could sign checks that month.

Barbara describes Carole's predecessor as "a part of that politically correct community" who judged every act in terms of rebellion against patriarchy. Those who saw loving women as an extension of their feminism sometimes, to the distress of women like Margaret, made a package of their politics and their sexuality.

"I used to get really frustrated with the politically correct," Barbara says. "They sat around for days making decisions. They never got anything done."

Kathleen believes that "at the same time those women from the gay community were advocating participatory democracy, they were incredibly manipulative—expert at getting their own way. Our radical women's community, which I believe is predominantly gay, rejected anything that looked like establishment, but in reality misused political power."

"When I came to the shelter four years ago," Carole says, "there were a lot of people who were into processing the issues and their lives to death. In my naiveté I have hired people who were gay and felt it was a safe place to play out a whole gay agenda around collectives, radical women's stuff, but our organization is much more sophisticated at this point. Maybe it wasn't at the outset, or even five years ago, but it is now. We have a staff of thirty-three people. The budget is almost a million dollars."

Kathleen says, "When the shelter opened its doors in 1977, we had thirteen thousand dollars in the bank. There was the feeling of a collective. I don't think hierarchy is a uniquely gay issue, because there are many women who are uncomfortable with traditional modes of organization and decision making."

Neither does she believe that being gay has much to do with working for service organizations. "I think it has more to do with being female." She uses the example that at her law firm it is women who are drawn to *pro bono* work for the less fortunate. She believes that the newly hired young men would be if it were presented to them as an obligation for which they were going to be rewarded. "But the women feel an obligation to do it despite the obstacles. Basically women have better instincts. Not all of them—there are some real piggy women—but basically they care more about what is good for the world and the group."

Barbara says, "Going back to the days of the first feminist networks, there were a lot of gay women involved in quote/unquote women's issues. If you were going to be gay, it was politically correct to be involved in these things. A lot of the leadership was gay. I don't know why that happened. I swear half the national Y staff is gay. On the state level everybody knows I'm gay, and nobody cares."

She explains the Y's attitude. "One, we're a women's organization and we're tolerant of women. Two, we're tolerant of differences. That's what the Y is built upon—being tolerant of the downtrodden and the oppressed. Saving the world. There were a lot of women in the 'old Y' who never married. They were little old ladies, and I don't know if they fooled around or not."

But it was not lesbians who founded the shelter. According to Kathleen, "There was one gay women—me, although at twenty-six I wasn't quite sure. There was a widow, the Catholic Daughters of America . . ."

"I don't think it matters," Carole says. "There are straight women who are as radicalized as gay women. Maybe in the seventies gay women provided the leadership for them. I don't know. One thing in the lesbian life-style that might contribute to their leadership is energy and availability of time to invest. No children, lack of other commitments and responsibilities, an enormous amount of flexible time that they can choose to commit in a very different way."

"So often in a male/female relationship," Barbara comments, "you're talking about the woman having to come home and make dinner and be there for the husband. In Kathleen's and my relationship there is not the expectation that one of us is going to be home for the other one."

Kathleen adds, "And even men who are very involved with their children don't make the same kind of commitment to them as women do." She gives the example of a male lawyer saying he could not work the following Sunday because of his daughter's birthday party. But she feels he will renege on his family commitment and work because his job is his priority, whereas his wife, who is also an attorney, would not make that kind of compromise.

However, none of the three believe that gay women without children transfer their nurturing capabilities to service-oriented organizations. Barbara says, "I happen to want to make the world a better place for women. The kids I enjoy, but they come with the mother. It has nothing to do with my being gay—I think I'm just crazy."

"If I look at my staff in terms of gay and straight," Carole says, "the similarities are remarkable." The six leadership positions at the shelter are sometimes filled by a majority of gay women, sometimes straight. "Similarities of personality, of life-style, of dedication, of interest, of commitment. Some gay women are more radical, more willing to take risks, but we [the shelter women] are about as socially correct as we can be. I spent last night at a restaurant running into some very rich and famous people. Board members introduced me around. The gay woman I was with was wondering, 'Where does this drill end? Is everything you do a photo opportunity?' "

Carole believes it would matter a great deal to some of the board members if they knew she was a lesbian, and Barbara adds, "If B—— knew, he wouldn't give any money, and that's the bottom line."

"I think," Carole says, "organizations like the shelter and the Y, with some rare exceptions, are not into dyke-baiting because it is not in their self-interest. They know that gay people work at the shelter, for all the world I might be one of them. You don't talk to me about that, I don't talk to you about that. It's just not relevant to the problems we're struggling with. It's not a political issue.

"This man Barbara was talking about—I have been with him in some of the major corporation offices in the city, trotting right along in my little high heels and my little outfits, and it's all just swell. I'm comfortable, he's comfortable. I couldn't play out some gay agenda. I don't ask my board members who they fuck and I don't expect them to ask me. I have a political agenda around domestic violence, not around my life-style.

"To be effective, I think you have to buy in—most feminists would argue with this—and figure out a solution to making your way in both worlds. It's very noble and very righteous to say, 'I'm gay and I'm politically correct, and I understand these issues.' The truth is that none of us fully understand these matters. They are very complex and intricate and always in a state of evolution. I don't mean that you have to tolerate bullshit, but I don't think you attain your ends by taking such strident stands that people will not even hear you."

Carole is, however, very concerned about the patriarchy, the control of institutions by men. She sees oppression of women in the family, the judicial system, education, the business world. "Every institutionalized system in this country oppresses women, not gay women, not straight women—women." She believes this system weighs most heavily on the poor and on women with children and that if the government continues to introduce or reintroduce reactionary policies, they will suffer the most.

In a truly repressive society, she believes, "Gay women would probably fare better because they are tougher as a people, they're stronger, they're more insightful, they're more emotionally there for themselves, and they don't have children. They may, in some instances, have more emotional problems, but I think they are better able to cope with the problems they have. I am far more concerned about how women and children may fare in our society than I am about the issue of lesbianism."

Because Carole herself was, as a child, abused by men, she can empathize with the survival needs of battered women. "But I don't have any extraordinary animosity toward men. I don't have any interest in developing a relationship with one of them, but I do have a couple of close friendships."

Nor does she see the workers in the shelter as antimale. "We don't hate all men. We'd like to kill violent men, that's all. Pummel them to death with plastic guns. The battered-women's movement has taken a very clear position that our issue is protection of women from death.

"I'm outraged that there have to be shelters in this country for women, that women must flee their homes, where they should be the safest. I don't think it has anything to do with hating men. I don't personalize it at all, except in cases like Mrs.——, where there is an immediate threat [of his finding and killing her]. It is much more a societal problem, and I view it as the patriarchy, not individual men. Individual men are problematic because they kill individual women. How our institutions react and respond is the issue. Men have an unfortunate and unschooled grasp on our society."

Although the shelter serves a widely varied population, the women actually in residence are those with the least education and least resources. Occasionally victims of lesbian battering are admitted, and the other women are nervous if they know. "All the homophobic stuff," Carole says. "The one who really blew them apart was the transsexual. A he who was becoming a she, who was not presenting herself as still having a he part. The humor was lost on some of my staff." Males who have been battered by either women or their gay partners are not sheltered there, but services are provided.

Carole believes that sometimes shelters get the reputation for lesbianism because for many battered women this is the first time in their lives they have ever been treated with tenderness and therefore may grow very dependent on the nurturing women at the shelter.

Carole's friends are gay and straight, male and female, and last summer she spent ten to twelve hours a day working in a political campaign in addition to directing the shelter. "Although I do discount my lesbianism on one level, it is not something that ever leaves me. I've made these choices about my life-style, and it permeates everything I do and say. Not on a political level and not on a public/personal level, but on a very personal level."

Carole believes, "The more visible lesbians become, the more tightly men are going to hang on to their power, and there is going to be an enormous backlash, enormous oppression or efforts at oppression. I think it's going to be fought out and won by who's shrewder, who's more skillful at using the tools of the trade, whether those be legal challenges, education, or enlightenment."

The fact that lesbians will not allow themselves to be objectified by men is what Carole feels "may save our society. We don't have an emotional investment in what men have to give in the same kind of way that straight women do. The advantage that we have is that we don't care." She illustrates this philosophy by saying that if her wealthy board member got out of line politically, she could step on him, "squish him just like that." Not that she is insensitive to his humanity, but to his allure as a male.

A Minneapolis lesbian views women and feminism from a different perspective. Caroljean Pint, thirty-one, went through law school but never took the bar exam. Believing that "it's not good for the spirit to work a forty-hour week," she serves, a few days out of every week, as a legal aid for a woman who does family law. The rest of her time goes to lesbian-community building activities like the Womyn Braille Press, an organization that tapes radical feminist and Third World material and distributes it internationally. She gives free legal advice and educates women about legal matters.

She calls herself a separatist, although she believes a new word is needed. "In order for women to bond with each other, they have to separate themselves from men. They must see the violence men have perpetrated. In order to have the same sense of separation as lesbians do, straight women have to have some compelling experience on an emotional or physical level.

"My primary commitment is to lesbians. In spending I will buy from lesbians even if it costs more. I'm careful about time spent with nonlesbians so that my time and energy are not drained off. I look at every situation to see how it will affect the lesbian community. Blood family is not central to me, and I do not have longtime relationships, so my sustenance comes from lesbian friends."

She believes that change will come through spiritual means. "If we do our own stuff, all kinds of positive change will happen. I follow my deepest path to honesty, integrity, hope, goodness. If more people do that, then the world will automatically change."

Judith Hill, born in 1942 the child of a doctor in a small Nebraska town, is president of the board of the Michigan Organization for Human Rights (MOHR), which is heavily involved in legislation and litigation around gay and lesbian issues.

"At one time I wouldn't even have *belonged* to MOHR. Now I'm ready to do that. I had a problem identifying with questions as a lesbian; most issues are feminist."

She has been active all her life with groups concerned with human values and basic rights because it is her belief that "one of the reasons you are here is to perform services for humankind, improve the lot of people."

MOHR is an organization of fifteen hundred men and women; its budget has gone from $30,000 to $250,000 in a year and a half. "What AIDS has done is to bring about coalition building, but also, in this time of fundamentalist fervor, it has brought 'This is God's will.'

"I am really disturbed by mass mentality. Good or bad, I don't like it. It reminds me of Nazism. I work with rational straights, but homophobia is not a rational issue."

Karen Strauss, the twenty-nine-year-old resident of San Francisco, says, "I've got the best of it all. I'm a professional lesbian, live in a wonderful city, have financial freedom." She grew up in a comfortable middle-class family in Queens, New York. "A very Jewish world. My parents gave me a sense of history, of their own experience with oppression."

During her early twenties in Boston she followed a politically correct lesbian/feminist line. "I believed in the myth of the collective process, where every voice had equal weight, where everybody's needs were to be met, where there were no leaders in place. That was me then. But it was absolutely chaotic. Lesbians are abandoning their 'political correctness,' and the women's movement is moving into a new phase as well."

Karen is development director for the Lesbian Rights Project, a public-interest law organization that provides legal information and direct representation to lesbians and gay men who have been discriminated against because of sexual preference. "Our underlying commitment is to lesbians, but if men's cases have relevance to lesbians, we take them."

The ten-year-old organization handles military, employment,

and housing cases and has become expert on family issues. "Our organization has done a lot of work setting precedents that sexual preference in itself is not grounds for refusing custody in California. We have a wide network—attorneys from all parts of the country will call us for guidance and trial strategy. We are the best equipped in the United States to deal with gay and lesbian family issues, although there are many other groups, such as the Lesbian Mothers National Defense Fund, that are doing great work."

Karen, a dance major in college, moves with firm grace; her short hair is dark and curly, her eyes clear blue. "I don't think there are many people who choose to be gay. It's so much easier to be part of the dominant culture. I wouldn't choose not to be white. I'm a lesbian and I'm not doing it to be fashionable. It's not in style and it's not going to be in style for a long time."

Karen says she did not like being a child, she was impatient to get on to doing important things. Now she says in her soft, deliberate manner, "There is meaning in what I do. This is the first time lesbianism has been my vocation. Living and breathing it every day has made me more radical.

"I would like to think that the lessons lesbians have learned in caring about people will get passed on. We need a gay presence in the lives of people in all decision-making positions. We should not waste our resources fighting against people who hate us but in giving to people who need the necessities of life. What I get out of being lesbian is being able to do that, to share the power."

33. A PASSION FOR JUSTICE

"MY daughter was twenty when she told us she was gay. My husband was very fearful he might lose his job if it were known—he was in a new position. We cried a lot. We went in the closet. We told no one.

"We are WASPs. Our kids had everything going for them, college, everything. To see one's child in a victimized, marginal society . . . No parent expects it. We were very fearful for her, and at first I thought she would be ghettoized. All the myths and jokes were real to me and they stayed with me for a very long time. I wouldn't have chosen for my daughter to be lesbian. She's twenty-seven now.

"For five years we were by ourselves. We did not get angry, which is not typical. We were very supportive of her, but behind the scenes we were very sad. My husband kept saying it would pass, and I didn't want to carve anything in stone, so I waited to join Parents-FLAG until she was twenty-five."

Parents and Friends of Lesbians and Gays is a national organization, the outgrowth of various support groups for parents, one of which had been in existence in New York since 1973.

Elaine Mumford, who had originally joined the Washington, D.C., group, founded the Annapolis, Maryland, chapter. Her open and intense manner and casual, stylish attire is reminiscent of another Parents-FLAG woman, Nora Tuthill of Exeter, New Hampshire. Nora's gay son, after attending Parents-FLAG meetings in Washington, D.C., had, by leaving gay magazines on the coffee table, "nudged" Nora into saying, "What's it like to have a gay roommate?" which gave him the opportunity to reply, "Fine. I'm gay too."

In the fall of 1987, three hundred members attended the sixth international convention in Washington, D.C., the theme of which was "Equality for Our Gay Children—Let's Make It Happen." The workshop topics ranged from AIDS to coupling to suicide. The following Monday the participants lobbied their legislators. Nora Tuthill reiterated the reasoning behind this: "People [legislators] may say your children are deviants, disgusting, et cetera, but they'll have a harder time saying it directly to you."

Vic Basile, executive director of the Human Rights Campaign Fund, spoke to the Washington conference and told the parents, "You are the ultimate bridges between 'us' and 'them,' between understanding and ignorance."

In a column entitled "My Daughter Is a Lesbian," which appeared in *The New York Times* of February 24, 1988, Robert Bernstein, a lawyer in the Justice Department tax division, wrote, "It is estimated that there are upward of 25 million gay people, who by definition started out with some fifty million parents. Sooner or later, a large portion of those parents will want to enlist in the crusade for their children's dignity."

Bernstein and his ex-wife had participated in the October 1987 Washington March for Gay and Lesbian Rights under the Parents-FLAG banner: "a grizzled crew of a few hundred parents in a sea of mostly youthful people variously estimated at from 200,000 to 600,000 people. Dramatically, however, this token symbolic presence touched off a stirring in the crowd that soon grew to a thunderous roar of cheers and applause that followed us all the way down Pennsylvania Avenue—a measure, surely, of the yearning of the young people for the support and understanding of their own parents."

The Alexandria (Virginia) Gay Community Association ran a thirteen-week ad campaign. One of the ads read, "Are you abusing your child without knowing it? 1 in 10 teenagers is gay. If you are teaching your children to hate gays, you might be teaching one of them to hate himself. That's a form of emotional child abuse."

According to Ann Muller's 1987 book *Parents Matter*, whatever the reaction—hostile, sad, tolerating, or accepting—an overwhelming number of parents don't tell anyone else. They don't even tell other family members whom they know also have a gay child. Parents may never discuss it with each other. Muller writes, "One family in four has a gay member, but because the history of this reality is never passed from generation to generation there is no healthy cumulative data." She found that most gays over forty have not and will never tell their parents.

Muller gathered her information from one hundred young gays

and lesbians who have come out to their parents. She was able to interview only ten sets of parents. She discovered no patterns of what type of parents are more accepting or rejecting—with the exception that those with a prejudicial mind-set usually extend that prejudice to include their children. Over the long run, however, she found that gay sons were more accepted than lesbian daughters, and she reasoned that this is because the sons often still achieve their primary sex role of being "successful" in business, while the lesbian does not achieve hers of becoming a wife and mother.

She found that mothers sent double messages to their daughters, but that underneath they really wanted her to be what they had been—a wife and mother—and that fathers' attitudes toward their lesbian daughters actually deteriorated over a five-year period. Other contributing factors Muller found were the mother's jealousy over replacement by another woman and the fact that because the daughter was more likely than a gay son to have dated, the family could hope "this was just a phase."

Muller's conclusions, since they come overwhelmingly from children, not parents, may be flawed. Young people are as prone to be defensive as parents are, and because they have not yet experienced life as an adult, their judgments of their parents are often incomplete. Nancy in Ann Arbor now admits that much of her parents' original hostility was not to her sexual orientation but to the "very dykey" woman she first brought home. "They just love Sherry," she said.

At a university a young woman reported in a self-righteous tone, "My mother was okay with my lesbianism until she had to confront the reality of me with another woman. That made her uncomfortable." Was the girl, in fact, witnessing a quite normal parental reaction to a child's sexuality that had nothing to do with lesbianism per se? Or was this other woman a person who would make any parent uncomfortable? Or did the mother perceive that this would not be a healthy relationship for her daughter irrespective of sex? Or was it as the daughter perceived—a mother recoiling from the reality of her lesbianism?

Parents-FLAG is one way for young people and adults to communicate with people who are not their own parents or offspring, to separate the whole intimate history of the parent-child relationship from the question of sexual orientation and listen to the other side.

For probably the majority of its members, Parents-FLAG is not a crusade but a personal healing. Elaine Mumford said that it gave her and her husband "the feeling we were not alone. The most important thing is to see gay young people—doctors, lawyers. It dawns on parents that the group is not composed of monsters. The kids who attend are those troubled about how to tell parents, or they have had bad experiences in telling them. They can talk to other parents and see that they, too, were furious at first. Kids can see how it is from the other side. See the stages of denial, grief, and the bargaining 'don'ts'—'Don't talk about it,' 'Don't bring your lover home'—to finally helping them with a celebration of the life-style."

Parents-FLAG can also be a way through the personal pain of being forbidden by a spouse to speak the name of their gay child, the embarrassment of a lesbian daughter who "dresses like a slob," the guilt of "Where did I go wrong?"

Nora Tuthill said, "At first I felt terribly sorry for myself, then I put it on the back burner. I didn't start to read for two or three months. It was hard to go into the bookstore, where I was known, to order the books William had suggested. The more I read, the more I understood. Now I want to bridge the gap between what we have learned and what the heterosexual world knows. The wonderful thing is you can't believe now [three years later] that you hurt at first. You feel so damn sorry for all the years the kid went through this crap alone. It gets easier and easier, but it shouldn't have to be hard in the first place."

Parents slowly learn what their children have. Nora has. She's watched her family smile and change the subject. She's heard her mother say she won't give William an antique sideboard "because he won't have anyone to leave it to." She went to her Episcopalian minister, and he said, "I have difficulty affirming homosexuality." She gave him her phone number so that other parents of gays who came to him could call her. A year and a half later she asked, "Do you ever hear from any?" "None," he replied. She gave him books to loan out; she never saw them on his shelves. The silence and isolation baffled her. She sent announcements of Parents-FLAG meetings to newspapers all over the state, but every month the same people showed up—all ten of them.

But the local papers spotted her ads and ran feature stories on the Tuthills. AIDS has made gay newsworthy.

On a bright December morning in 1987 gay and lesbian rights activists met in a community center in a working-class area of Baltimore, Maryland. Many of the hundred men and women present represented groups: Gay Democratic Club, 33rd Street Bookstore, Women's Law Center, Democratic Socialists of America, Government Task Force on AIDS, Gay and Lesbian Community Center, Parents and Friends of Lesbians and Gays, NOW, Metropolitan Community Church, Presbyterians for Gay and Lesbian Rights. . . .

Their spirits were high. Gays and lesbians in Baltimore have, for the first time, voted as a block, and their choices—Kurt Schmoke for mayor and Mary Pat Clark for head of city council—have been elected.

A man and a woman acted as facilitators of a brainstorming session: "What do we want from the Schmoke administration?" People stand and state their concerns. Since city councils had twice since 1980 refused to pass an ordinance making discrimination against gays and lesbians illegal, that is a primary issue. A man adds, "Make sure that teachers are not excluded from the gay rights bill —no exceptions." Another says, "We must educate straights out of their belief that a gay rights bill is going to give gays *special* rights."

Others propose actions the new city government could take. "Have the mayor appoint gays and lesbians, who are open, to all kinds of commissions. We should, for example, submit résumés to the Historical Preservation Commission." Another suggests having "an openly gay paid staff member so that government people can see a gay or lesbian walking around the halls and observe that they don't have three heads and attack children. Or have someone already up there come out. Have people who know gays and lesbians tell them they have support and urge them to come out publicly." Having the mayor appoint a commission for gay and lesbian concerns similar to the existing Women's Commission is another suggestion. One man would like to work toward the establishment of a place for gay youth similar to New York City's Harvey Milk Center.

Some of those present would direct actions toward the public to create pressure on the administration and also to educate them through forums. One person said, "We should prepare a history of our attempts to improve everyone's living conditions, because people have lost respect for us and need to see that we work for many good causes."

One speaker reminded the audience, "Few people are against us, but they are much better organized."

Although many suggestions pertained to the AIDS crisis, men and male issues did not dominate the meeting. After lunch small groups worked on the suggestions made and organized for action.

In late spring of 1988 the Baltimore city council—in a surprisingly strong vote—made it illegal for anyone to discriminate against another person because of his or her sexual orientation.

"A Passion for Justice" was the theme of the 1988 Annual Unitarian/Universalist Lesbian and Gay Conference held in Portland,

Maine. A hundred people—ministers, church office holders, members—braved a snowstorm to attend.

Ellie Haney, who holds a doctorate in theology and ethics from Yale and is a leader in the Portland feminist spiritualist community, addressed the group. "Sexual preference is not the issue—heterosexism is!" She believes asking for rights implies they may be either granted or denied, whereas attacking a prejudiced attitude is placing the responsibility where it belongs. For example, a challenge to the assumption that male/female marriage is the central pattern of living would be "public ceremonies for any relationship which provides refuge and support" so that "varied and valued patterns" may be established.

She does not define her ethic as one of personal freedom or choice, but a personal/political one of living toward a vision where childhood, adulthood, and elderhood are all respected and humans are not divided by race or class or gender.

The enunciation of this philosophical vision was followed by inspirational stories of goals achieved. When Kim Harvie became pastor of a Provincetown, Massachusetts, church two years ago, "32 members were on the books—some of them dead." Now membership tops 450. She attributes her success to three factors: celebrating the holidays for the large Jewish population, the beauty of the church itself, and the curiosity of the huge number of Provincetown lesbians and gays. Kim's personal attractiveness and radiant belief in herself as a person and a lesbian are undoubtedly the reasons the curious stayed. "When people say, 'But you don't look like a lesbian!' I say, 'I *am* a lesbian, so I *look* like a lesbian.' "

Other churches ask her to do workshops on erasing homophobic attitudes. Occasionally she encounters hostility. "Sometimes I feel like crying," she said, adding, "They are not evil people, they are ignorant." Her faith in people's educability was bolstered when, after a very traumatic session at one church, the search committee contacted Kim and invited her to be their pastor.

Reality followed inspiration as the ministers and members of this most liberal of all Protestant churches randomly rose and briefly stated their concerns.

One told of his congregation's responses to the questionnaire, "Do we have a problem with homophobia?" "The gays and lesbians said yes! Some heterosexuals said, 'No, we have no gays. It is not an issue here.' Others asked, 'What's all this about? We don't ask anyone's sexual preference.' For them it's the old idea of 'just keep it quiet.' "

A man attending a singles group—all heterosexuals—said he

finds the sessions meaningful and doesn't want to quit, yet he wonders what will happen if he reveals he is gay.

A person from Chicago believes gays and lesbians in his church "don't connect with each other, don't know who the others are."

A Boston woman, serving as an interim minister, says she is not politically out. "But more and more lesbians are coming to church. I feel there is tension between them and the regulars, even though the regulars like the warm bodies. The church is in a working-class, family-oriented neighborhood and is fearful of survival, afraid it won't attract community people with the lesbians there. I don't know what to do."

As one person finished speaking, another would rise.

"We need to help ministers by coming out to them, letting them know we are there. Then if they say, 'I don't know any gays and lesbians, that's their problem.' "

"Ministers should give sermons that include lesbian and gay words. Say in announcements: 'Thirty-two weddings of which eight were same-sex.' To be included like that sends chills up my back."

"We gays and lesbians need to come out as religious people to our friends, so that they can see there is more to us than our genitals."

Kim Harvie: "On paper we have the entire UU church with us. We need to call them to accountability. We are a SWAT team."

Worcester, Massachusetts: "Since I came out, the congregation has turned one hundred and eighty degrees. When one of the Scoutmasters made a homophobic remark, people sought me out to apologize." Another person challenged him: "When they also tell the Scoutmaster to shut up, that's when you'll know they've changed."

Houston: "There is tension between our straight women's group and the lesbians. The hundred lesbians are upstairs doing something more interesting, so they don't come down to the regular service. Don't set yourselves up in opposition to what the general church wants."

Boston: "We have had a reputation for being very accepting, but the minute you turn your back, it all slips away. Not one person on our seven-member search committee for a new minister even identifies with gays. You need a structure to keep it accepting."

"How about talking about an 'in-reach' ministry? Of all the targets for UU conversion, gays and lesbians seem to be a natural."

"I'm in a church but not out. I've had experience with straight people who mean well but can't keep their mouths shut. Some men can afford to be out, but people like teachers can't. The congregation needs education on how to keep things confidential."

"If the minister is not an activist, nothing will happen in the long term. When he/she preaches about those issues, people will come to understand."

Three Rivers Church in Pittsburgh, Pennsylvania: "Let's not wait for the ministers. We're ready to constitute services on Sunday evenings where gays and lesbians can sit with their arms around each other like straight people do. We run *big* ads publicizing them."

"What we need are new congregations for gays and lesbians like Provincetown."

West Coast: "There is a deafening silence on homosexuality in our congregation. We call ourselves a 'welcoming' congregation, but lesbians and gays are only actually welcomed when they find the others who are like them. People are frightened. They would say no to a homosexual in the pulpit."

"How much of us can we share? I'll tell you. Tolerance and silence and nothing more."

A New York City group watches over the media. Gay and Lesbian Alliance Against Defamation (GLAAD), believes, "Defamation is not just Jerry Falwell screeching. Defamation is the inclusion of homosexuality on a laundry list of social ills ('crime, drug abuse, homosexuality . . .') Defamation is mentioning a gay or lesbian angle only when the story is negative. A criminal who claims to be gay is a 'gay criminal.' A gay humanitarian is just a 'humanitarian.' Defamation is the use of the archaic label *avowed homosexual* to describe those who have chosen to live their lives honestly and openly as gay people. Defamation is the absence of gay and lesbian history. Defamation is gay and lesbian invisibility."

GLAAD opposes defamation in a number of ways: by meeting personally with editors of newspapers, by alerting members to defamatory remarks in the media by a PhoneTree or the *GLAAD Bulletin*. The latter, for example, called attention to ABC's *Heartbeat*, which portrayed a nurse practitioner "who happens to be a lesbian" as "supportive and wise . . . an achiever," and whose relationship with her lover "is treated warmly and respectfully." The newsletter urged readers to write in support of retaining the show.

GLAAD, Parents-FLAG, the Unitarian Universalist church, were a few of the many organizations represented at the First National Conference on Homophobia held in Washington, D.C., in May 1988.

The conference, which attracted over one hundred leaders in homophobia education from the fields of formal education, religion, health, and the media, was cosponsored by such diverse groups as the Methodist Federation for Social Action, the Lesbian Rights Committee of NOW, the American Psychological Association, the World Congress of Gay and Lesbian Jewish Organizations, and the Vermont Coalition for Equality. The group was mainstream, middle-aged, divided equally between male and female, and sexual preferences, unless openly stated, were impossible to ascertain.

Some of those attending represented large organizations such as the Fund for Human Dignity and the National Gay and Lesbian Task Force. A few, a staff member of the American Association of University Women for example, were looking for information to take back to their group. Others were simply individuals working on their own or with a small group to ease the fears of the heterosexual world. Some were new in the field; others had been out there for years.

The diversity of their personalities and approaches was illuminating. A white-haired woman with the Lazarus Project in California conducts programs in local churches. A Ph.D. candidate does research on the homophobic attitudes of mental health service workers. A lesbian, "wife of a lesbian minister" in a Seattle church, leads Scripture study and consciousness raising. An Ithaca, New York, woman conducts sexuality workshops for teens, parents, and professionals. A man provides staff training in the Philadelphia school district. A woman from Denver gives homophobia workshops for business organizations like AT&T. The director of the Equity Institute in Amherst, Massachusetts, has worked with over three thousand educators and students. Brian McNaught, who speaks to ten thousand persons a year in colleges and businesses, also conducts workshops for such diverse groups as the police and athletic coaches. Other attendees have created training models and slide shows, written books and plays.

The proposed projects that emerged from the workshops were directed toward creating positive attitudes and a safe environment in K–12 public schools and institutions of higher education, in churches, the military, counseling, and the media. Concurrent with the goal of dispelling fears about gays and lesbians was the theme of openness, such as the announcement of National Coming Out Day on October 10th, the anniversary of the 1987 Washington March.

The atmosphere of empowerment engendered by numbers, dedication, and expertise was tempered by the reality of present conditions. Lee Chiaramonte of CBS referred to homophobia as "cultural malpractice, a reflex behavior. Some very valuable people," she said, "are homophobic." Greg Herek, a professor of social psychology, added that "homophobia is not seen as dysfunctional in the United States today, and it is encouraged to remain."

There are, however, courageous people with a passion for justice who are encouraging it to disappear.

PART 13

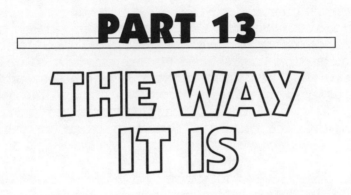

THE WAY IT IS

34. INTENSIVE CARE

KATHLEEN and her partner, Barbara, the feminist lesbians, live in an early 1940s brick row house just inside the metropolitan boundary of an mideastern city. The lawns are neat, cars remain unlocked; families and singles, blacks and whites, mix in a quiet suburban life-style. Kathleen, a girl who left her private school commencement loaded with academic prizes, is a newly minted lawyer with a prestigious law firm. Barbara, a native of the city, is an executive with the YWCA. Their combined incomes of seventy thousand dollars allow them the luxury of a mountain cottage that they own with another couple.

Kathleen, after having had relationships with both men and women, made a firm decision in her late twenties that she did wish to live as a lesbian. Shortly thereafter she met Barbara at a feminist function and invited her out to dinner. "I'd spotted her in the spring and had my eye out for her," Kathleen says. Barbara was her age but without sexual experience with either men or women.

Barbara jokes, "I'd heard she was involved with two other women, so when I suggested an affair, I thought I was safe." Their partnership is now seven years old. It has not been, however, an easy path. Barbara may quip that Kathleen's three years as a law school student placed the most stress upon their relationship, but there has been a far graver involuntary problem.

The two women met in 1980, and a year later, when they were both thirty, they moved in together. Shortly thereafter, while having dinner out with friends, Kathleen, noting Barbara's small, funny smile, thought that she was upset about something. Barbara insisted nothing was wrong. In the following weeks Barbara began having trouble with her eyes: double vision, difficulty keeping her eyelids open. An opthalmologist said she should see a neurologist. Terrified of the possibility of a brain tumor, they sought out the best doctor they could find and made an appointment.

"Today," Kathleen says, "I would naturally go into the examining room with her. But then we had only known each other a year and a half. It had been a big step for Barbara even to say, 'I want you to come to the neurologist with me.' "

"There is," Barbara says, "a different perception when you take your friend with you than when you take your husband with you. I think he's automatically included by most doctors. When you take a friend, she has to physically walk into the examining room with you. You have to say, 'This is Kathleen, my friend,' and sometimes they say, 'Fine,' and sometimes they ignore her."

So Barbara was alone when she learned the diagnosis: myasthenia gravis.

This unusual, but not rare, muscular disease is similar to multiple sclerosis, but not degenerative. All the diagnosis meant to Kathleen then was that Barbara would have to take some pills for the rest of her life. "Normal amount of denial," Barbara says now. But she also remembers that the night before she was to enter the hospital for her week of tests, Kathleen asked her to come to bed without turning on the lights. "And here's little tears coming down from her eyes."

Barbara's parents—call them Martha and Edward—accompanied her to the hospital. They must have had the trauma of déjà vu, because Barbara, a child polio victim, had been there for a year when she was two. "The visiting hours were from two to four on Wednesdays and Sundays," Barbara recalls. "My mother talks now about standing in the parking lot listening to me cry because they had left." "Imagine," Kathleen says, "living from age two to three seeing your parents for two hours twice a week."

Martha raised three children and worked as an administrative assistant for a large insurance company but masked her strengths with acquiescence and a protective hovering that Barbara's illness exacerbated. Edward, a quiet sensitive man who has difficulty expressing emotion, "comes into a hospital room ready to leave," according to Barbara.

The difference between multiple sclerosis and myasthenia is, in Barbara's words, "Death. You die with MS." Doctors understand myasthenia better, and it is a more easily treated disease. Occurring most frequently in women in their twenties and thirties and in older men—Aristotle Onassis was a victim—myasthenia affects the automatic muscles, those responsible for essential functions such as breathing, smiling, talking, holding the head erect. Apparently the virus can be triggered by something as simple as a bad cold. Although Barbara recognizes that major life events can cause stress resulting in disease, she views her commitment to Kathleen as a happy, positive step more likely to relieve stress than cause it.

While in the hospital Barbara began taking Mestinon, a drug with potentially dangerous side effects. She tried to resume her normal life, but grew progressively weaker; the Mestinon was not effective. The next step was an operation to remove the thymus gland. This gland, which is responsible for setting up a person's immune system, has usually disappeared by adulthood, but in myasthenics, like Barbara, it has sometimes grown even larger. The antibodies the thymus produces prohibit the muscle receptor cells from receiving the proper chemicals, and muscular disability results.

During the month's wait for the surgeon to be free to do the operation, Barbara fell down a lot. She got stranded in the ladies' room of a restaurant because she could not get up from the toilet seat. Her friends finally rescued her and then drove to a lesbian bar to dance and listen to a friend sing. Barbara walked in the door and fell flat on her face. The music stopped; everyone stared. A nurse who works with myasthenics rushed to help. "It was nice," Barbara says, "having someone there who understood, because she spread the word that I was not drunk." When tired, Barbara slurs her words, further evidence to strangers that she is inebriated.

The thymus operation took place in May; Barbara had health insurance, so money was no problem. During her first visit Barbara had been assigned a primary nurse, call her Candy, who told Kathleen all the right things to do in order to see Barbara before and after the operation. "Obviously," Barbara says, "she knew we were a couple and that was fine with her."

Barbara remembers the night before the operation, when two volunteers from the Y came to visit. "They just wouldn't leave. If Kathleen and I had been married, they never would have done that. They would have understood that we wanted to spend that time together." Kathleen adds, "As far as they were concerned, I had no more status than they did." "The friends that knew," Barbara says, "had already come and gone."

Kathleen stayed until eleven and was back the next morning at six. She went up to surgery with Barbara, then went home to sleep. When she called to see if she was in intensive care yet, the hospital didn't know where she was. "They'd lost her!

"Her parents are in the waiting room. They are so passive. No one would tell us where Barbara is. The receptionist in the surgical

waiting room says Barbara's going to be in the recovery room overnight and I want to know why, but I'm not supposed to be asking
questions. If it had been her mother or her husband asking questions,
it would have been different. Her attitude was, who is this woman
who wants to know? She tries to tell me the doctor wants Barbara
there. No doctor *wants* his patient to be in the recovery room
overnight!

"The problem was that the hospital was very full, but Barbara
was lucky. Because she had a private doctor, they got her into
intensive care. Her parents were allowed to see her, but they
wouldn't take me back. Later a nurse came into the intensive care
waiting room to take Martha and Edward in again, and for a change
Edward spoke up. 'Well, what about her sister? She's been waiting
here too.' So the three of us trooped back."

"My parents," Barbara says, "had gotten used to my strong
friendship with P——[an older straight woman] and seen that she
could be as close as a sister was."

"Her mother," Kathleen says, "has always had more trouble
with our relationship than her father."

"She feels displaced."

If the family had been hostile, they could have kept Kathleen
from seeing Barbara. "And," Barbara adds, "they could have made
it very stressful for me. If Kathleen had said, 'I'm her sister,' and
they had said, 'No, you're not,' it could have been ugly." As it
was, visiting times were divided, and no one was uncomfortable.

Later Barbara heard two stories from her nurse, Candy. When
there was a discussion about Barbara's positive syphilis test, her
neurologist said dryly, "Well, given her life-style, I don't think she
has syphilis." Another time Barbara's roommate's nurse flounced
up to Candy and asked, "What are you going to do about your
patient?" When Candy looked at her blankly, she said, "She's gay!"

Barbara laughs, noting that the nurse might have thought it was
contagious and that her patient would catch it. The roommate had
been very friendly and had enjoyed Barbara's and Kathleen's
company—Kathleen was there from noon until night for four
days—so it was definitely the nurse and not the patient who was
disturbed.

The operation had taken longer than anticipated—three hours
instead of two—because the CAT scan had not picked up on the
fact that the thymus was cancerous. "Now," Barbara says, "we
don't like to use that word. There were abnormal growth cells,
which do not metastasize." The gland had grown all over Barbara's
chest cavity. "Everything they could see they got," Kathleen says.
"He worked real hard at it," Barbara adds.

"The surgeon came in to the waiting room and told Martha and Edward and me," Kathleen says. "I was upset."

"Hysterical," Barbara interjects.

"I was terrified I was going to lose her." Kathleen's voice roughens. "That she was going to die."

"I was heavily into denial," Barbara says. "Medical science could cure this. The little pills didn't work, so, okay, we tried the next step. I'm a professional optimist. The operation was a piece of cake. I was back to work in ten days."

Kathleen adds, "We treated it all as an acute illness. You treat the illness, then you go back to the way you were—other than popping the pills and writing the checks for the medicine, of which, thank God, Blue Cross/Blue Shield covers eighty percent." Barbara's work insurance covers major medical expenses. If it did not, it would be impossible for her to be covered under Kathleen's policy unless her employer negotiated a different contract with their insurer. "My law firm would never do it—that takes a certain level of consciousness. In my policy *dependent* is defined as 'spouse' and 'child under a specific age.' Very limited."

"Now the Y," Barbara says, "might try to change their contract with Blue Cross/Blue Shield if the situation were reversed. So that Kathleen could be covered. At the law firm Kathleen would be laughed out of the building."

"I'm not sure I would ask." Kathleen admits that revealing her relationship would bother her. "Maybe if I were a partner. . . . It's all right as long as I don't make waves. I'm not announcing that I live with a woman I love. It's none of their business, and because of that, why create reasons for them to look at anything other than my performance? I would not expect my male partner to participate in social functions, adopt those obligations. But yes, it is more difficult because you have to pretend you don't *have* a private life."

For a year after the operation everything was fine; they both returned to their normal intense involvement in work and politics. Then Barbara began getting a little bit weaker, a little bit worse. "I couldn't drive. I couldn't move my foot from the gas to the brake. Important point there. I couldn't eat because I couldn't chew. Got down to one hundred and ten pounds. Some problems breathing when I'd be in bed at night." Barbara explains that difficulty with breathing makes her feel as though she is angry.

Kathleen used to lie awake watching Barbara breathe. "Many times I would wake up in the night and put my hand on her stomach. Is she breathing?"

Kathleen points out, "You have to laugh because if you don't laugh, there is nothing left." Before Barbara had her thymectomy

she fell often, and Kathleen and another housemate joked about
having Barbara wash the kitchen floor because she was down there
all the time anyway. A visitor thought them terribly insensitive.
Barbara defends making light of things. "That's why I like the
bathroom story. You can laugh."

"It's getting harder," Kathleen says.

It was time for the next step: the drug prednisone. Although the
neurologist had assured Barbara the drug would make her "strong
as a horse," she explains why she had been putting it off. "Prednisone is not a nice drug. You can retain water. A friend of ours
on only fifteen milligrams a day looks as though you could stick a
pin in her and pop her. It can give you cataracts, diabetes, high
blood pressure, glaucoma, mood swings—it tends to heighten whatever emotional state you are in."

"We have some of those," Kathleen says with a laugh. Barbara
has developed cataracts, but nothing else.

"Barbara tends to be a little manic anyway," Kathleen says. "So
this prednisone . . ."

"I would start crying over nothing. Things overwhelmed me."

In the first year and a half "we moved quite rapidly through the
steps," Barbara affirms.

Kathleen amplifies. "We both knew it would be a lasting condition, but there was never a sense that Barbara and I would be able
to do any less than we wanted to do."

Barbara had bought a new shift car, and Kathleen was saving
money for law school; they never foresaw moving into a one-story
house, Barbara having to quit work, any major adjustments. As
long as they did what the doctor told them to, life would go on as
usual. Barbara speculates that if she had had a male partner, his
attitude would more likely have been, "I want you to stay home
and watch your health." "I can't imagine doing that because I'd go
crazy, but I can imagine a conversation along those lines. A man
to take care of me while I did a little volunteer work on the side."

"If we had been male and female, married and in our early
thirties," Kathleen says, "we most likely would have had children,
and that would have changed the whole dynamics." They also note
that if Barbara had been in the traditional role of breadwinner, the
changes would have been more drastic.

"We came into our relationship as two independent people and
have worked very hard to keep that," Barbara says. "Yes, we are
committed to each other, but our lives and what we choose to do
with them in terms of our work are our choices." They agree that
success in that area might be more difficult in a male/female relationship, and Kathleen laughs as she adds, "I think that's one of

the reasons that neither Barbara nor I are in one. The men that I know, even the younger men, want a woman to take care of them and put them first. And I *never* wanted to put anyone first. I'll be equal, but . . . Also, I'm smarter than most men I know, and men don't like that in an intimate relationship."

When Kathleen entered law school in 1983, she quit her $22,000-a-year service-oriented job, and they lived on the $14,000 Barbara made at the Y; grants, loans, and savings covered school costs. "This was one time," Barbara says, "when being a gay couple was an advantage. My salary didn't count at all on her financial-aid statements."

"Married people I know who had a lot less money than we had couldn't get financial aid," Kathleen explains. "The last year of law school they paid me money because I was a major editor on the law review. I came out only six thousand dollars in debt."

The prednisone enabled Barbara to work her usual forty-five- to fifty-hour week. She received a promotion to coordinator of the Y for three counties, a raise to $20,000, and enjoyed feeling strong again. Then, in the fall of 1985, symptoms reappeared. Barbara explains that it is difficult to differentiate between stress, a bad day, and the disease getting out of control. Around Christmastime they knew they could no longer rationalize away what was happening. Barbara could not drive. The prednisone levels were adjusted upward again.

In February Barbara got a bad cold. Because of her weak chest muscles she could not cough to clear her lungs, and her breathing was affected. "We have one night of panic in bed. Oh, I loved Kathleen that night. I'm up and down, I can't sleep. I come back to bed and I'm upset. We agree I should call the doctor. 'What do I do if he says he can't do anything?' 'That's what he's going to say.' "

"I was asleep,' Kathleen interjects.

"The next day I made her stay home from law school. It got worse throughout the day, and at night it was horrible. I couldn't breathe." They called the doctor, and Barbara had so little breath, she couldn't speak. The doctor notified the hospital that a patient was coming in "near arrest." By the time they arrived, Barbara had calmed down enough to breathe, leaving the nurses baffled by the call of "near arrest." "I sent Kathleen home in the wonderful belief that they would do something. The next morning it was so bad I had them call her to come back and hold my hand."

Kathleen raced to the hospital. "They had put her in this room and were ignoring her. She was having a lot more trouble breathing. I was getting ready to raise hell. And the doctor arrives. He had people hopping! Here we are racing three blocks horizontally and seven floors up to intensive care. Barbara's on a gurney, incoherent. There are the doctor and three or four residents. And they are racing because she is having increasing difficulty breathing, and it's clear to them she is in big trouble!" Barbara had developed pneumonia.

"Intensive care had the respirator ready, so they put me in the waiting room and said, 'We'll come tell you what is going on.' The head resident was a woman, and she came out to tell me Barbara was okay. I told her it was nice to see a woman as head, and she said, 'You should have seen us last month. I had an all-woman team—medical student, junior resident, and me, and we'd walk into a room and the patient would say, 'Oh, here come the nurses,' and we would say, 'Oh, no, here come the docs.' It was wonderful."

"I made it very clear to the people in intensive care," Barbara says, "that Kathleen was the person I wanted around."

Kathleen continues. "I was exhausted as well as incredibly upset. I had slept for maybe four hours and not much the night before that." She called Barbara's boss, who is a friend of both theirs and Martha's, to have her call Barbara's family. "I could not have held it together."

Because Barbara had made it so plain that Kathleen was to be the contact person, an insensitive nurse told her parents they could not visit. "I," Kathleen says, "had to deal with them in a very different way than ever before. It brought it home to them that I was an extremely important person in Barbara's life. As I recall the conversations, I went out of my way to make it clear to them that it was not a number-one and number-two situation, but rather a whole bunch of people that really care about Barbara."

"I think it would have been much more difficult with your parents," Barbara says.

"Oh, with my mother! Not with my father."

"I would have had to fight all the time."

"My father hardly ever says anything, but now on the phone he always asks, 'How's Barbara?' Never my mother."

"I was thinking," Barbara says, "that your mother might still want to take care of your brother, even though he's married. But she wouldn't do it because they *are* married. Maybe the symbolic marriage ceremony makes those people be a couple, which doesn't happen in gay relationships. Your mother would fight tooth and nail with his wife if he were in a hospital, but she would have to watch herself."

Kathleen agrees that her mother would respect the relationship even if she did not like his wife. If Kathleen were in a car accident, the possibility exists that Barbara might never see her again.

Kathleen's voice is grim. "We're going to make it damn hard for that to happen. The principal thing is durable power of attorney. Most powers of attorney are written to terminate when someone becomes incapacitated; those written to kick in at that point require a medical determination that the person is incapacitated. A durable power of attorney lasts forever. It says that this person can make decisions for me. It continues despite any incapacity." She is going to explain to her parents that it is not being done to exclude them, but to include Barbara. "Then if my parents wanted to exclude her, they would have to go to court and get that thrown out. Not that they might not be able to do that, but they would have to do something more than say, 'I have more rights than you do because I am her parent.' " Her parents would also have to contend with a wide circle of respected, articulate friends who support Barbara and Kathleen's relationship.

Both women have written living wills precluding extraordinary medical measures. They are buying their house as joint tenants with right of survivorship, which is similar to having bought it as a married couple. From the beginning they have had a joint checking account; they have planned their wills and have named each other as beneficiaries of their life insurance policies.

"For lesbians," Kathleen says, "wills are very important, because the laws are such that if you don't leave a will, your estate goes to your family. How many of us necessarily want our parents or siblings to get what we have? Obviously, I don't want that to happen to the exclusion of Barbara."

"If we hadn't had a joint checking account," Barbara says, "there are some points at which I could not have paid my bills. It meant someone didn't have to go into 'my' money. It was 'our' money."

"I think," Kathleen says, "that a joint checking account is a statement that many people aren't willing to make. Those checks have got both our full names and one address. There ain't much escaping that there's something there."

In February 1986, a year after her bout of pneumonia, Barbara began going downhill again. There were few options left on the doctor's list. Barbara pushed for plasmathesis, cleansing the blood of antibodies by removing it, putting it through a centrifuge, and replacing it. One day a week she lay on a table for three hours with a needle in one arm and a needle in the other. "Going through it was no big deal," she says, but after a couple months she decided to stop because she came to believe it was simply a very expensive holding action. Blue Cross/Blue Shield has balked at paying the bills.

"The major problem this past year," Kathleen says, "has been trying to deal with Barbara's illness while on the job. Making myself available to take her to the doctor's, be at home with her when she needed me. I was real spoiled by three years of law school, and before that I was the boss where I worked and had a lot of leeway. But now how many times can I go in late because I'm taking Barbara to the doctor?"

All spring Barbara was driven by her mother to the Y, where she managed to put in about thirty hours a week. At home she had to go upstairs to bed—usually at seven—before she became too weak to climb the stairs. They slept in the back bedroom because Barbara was not able to get out of the waterbed without help. "That," Kathleen says, "was a major sacrifice. I've had that bed twelve years." "True love," Barbara adds.

Because she was having a great deal of trouble holding up her head, the doctor thought it might be a neck problem, perhaps a ruptured disk. When that was ruled out, he sought a second opinion from another neurologist, because, as Barbara says, "He didn't know what in the hell to do with me."

June 13th was Barbara's last day at work. She had fallen while visiting a pool. "I was out of my gourd. The whole week had been disastrous. I stayed home—upstairs."

The doctor they were referred to was in research, and Barbara had to wait two weeks for an appointment. "Kathleen came with me. My mother's nose was a little out of joint, but she held her own." A resident asked Kathleen to leave while he did a physical exam and promised to call her back, but never did.

"I wasn't important to him," Kathleen says. "I wasn't anyone he had to relate to. When we went back to see the neurologist the next week, I wasn't moving. He was fine. He would turn and look at me as he was talking. It was a three-way conversation."

They had had a very bad night before that visit. Again Barbara couldn't breathe. Kathleen says, "I was so close to calling A—— and saying, 'Get your fanny over here and help me take Barbara to the emergency room. I could not have gotten her downstairs at ten o'clock at night by myself.'"

The new doctor raised the prednisone level another 10 milligrams a day and started a new drug called Imuran. Barbara got worse for another month before the drug took effect. "She was like a rag doll, except much heavier than Raggedy Anne to lift."

"We would have these wonderful yelling and screaming matches coming back from the bathroom," Barbara adds. "I was terrified of falling, or walking that far. I could make it before five, but after that . . ."

Kathleen says, "She reduced her intake of liquids incredibly because she couldn't lift a glass." The difficulty in swallowing forced Barbara to live on pudding pops, macaroni salad, and microwaved pasta meals. "It wasn't worth buying and cooking anything because who knew if she could eat it or not."

"The fear that it was never going away was the worst part," Barbara says, and Kathleen got several panic calls during the day at work. Because she was unable to concentrate, Barbara could not read or even watch VCR movies.

It took two strong people to get Barbara out once a week for her blood test. The test was necessary because, in Barbara's words, "This new drug can do wonderful things to your liver." Imuran also suppresses the immune system, which makes Barbara vulnerable to disease. She now takes nineteen pills a day.

By the end of August, however, she was operating at 60 percent of normal. "Physically I'm probably not that much removed from where I was when I stopped working two and a half months ago. But my emotional reserves are gone. There's nothing left." She tells stories of the difficulties of coping with so-called handicapped facilities. "I'm turning into much more of a disabled person's advocate than a gay advocate."

"It's been stressful," Kathleen says, "but it hasn't been stressful on the relationship. I don't think there has ever been a thought in either of our heads about the relationship being affected. If anything, it gets stronger. It makes it very clear to me how important Barbara is. Here we are planning how to intertwine our lives for the rest of our lives."

Barbara says, "I still have the dream of us being in the first gay nursing home sitting on the front steps."

They glance at each other and smile.

35. SOMEBODY'S LYING

IN Frederick, Maryland, Christmas wreaths shudder in the gusty wind, shoppers hustle and bustle. To the south of Main Street development houses squat lifeless, save one where a lavender balloon bounces against the white siding and cars line the driveway and curbside. Pleiades is meeting today.

The kitchen, the dining area, the living room of the small ranch house are filled with women. Fourteen more of those enchanted women remarkable for their vitality, their solid eye contact, their handshakes, their smiles. Ages range from sixty to twenty-four, their dress from suits and heels to jeans, their occupations from college administrator to supervisor for a construction company to counselor of mentally ill adults. A microcosm of all invisible women-loving women. They gather, some cross-legged on the floor, four together on the couch next to their partners, one stiffly on a piano bench, and their voices—some soft, some strong, some hesitant—tell the stories of what it is like to be a lesbian in America today.

Pleiades began the year before when two of the women decided the Frederick area needed a lesbian-support social group. They gave the three or four lesbians they knew a date and place; sixteen women showed up. "Yeah, by golly, even in Frederick." Stephanie Pettey, one of the founders, is blond, bright, and vivacious, a special education teacher in a public school. The name Pleiades was taken from the constellation that represents the Seven Sisters, who were, according to myth, transformed into stars by Jupiter to enable them to escape the attention of Orion. The name is also apt for a lesbian group because one of the Sisters and two hundred of the other stars are invisible to the casual observer.

"We've been going hell-bent ever since," another of the women says. The accents are country southern; all live within an hour's drive of Frederick. Pleiades, which meets the first and third Sundays of every month, is a loose organization with small committees to make arrangements, give directions, and put out a newsletter, which now reaches one hundred and sixty women.

Their activities have included potlucks, hikes, cross-country skiing, a reading group, a crab fest, videos—"*Desert Hearts*, is there anything else?"—dances in people's homes and at the Unitarian Church in Hagerstown. Once they rode inner tubes down the Shenandoah River from Harpers Ferry, West Virginia—two of those present are from that countryside of precipitous hills and shaded gullies. Kass Newman, a forty-four-year-old, tall, blond postal worker, adds, "Everybody came down the river, and I sat on a rock and waved. It was one hundred and ten degrees that day."

They have experienced no hassles when they have been together as a group. "But sometimes in Frederick itself we are less willing to call attention to ourselves," Lynn, a forty-two-year-old accountant, a large woman with a strong pleasant face, says. Last Saturday night, however, there were sixteen of them in a restaurant in Hagerstown, a town reputed to be even more conservative than Frederick.

"We decided," Stephanie says, "to be low key in the beginning and not bang the city and county of Frederick over the head with the fact that there's this community here. We're going with their rate of comfort and at the rate with which we are comfortable. As we grow, we're making our presence known."

Kass says, "Even when Gloria and I didn't know that there was a large women's community, I was never paranoid. I knew that people knew about us, people at work, people in the community. In fact, everybody in the town knew before we did. People in the post office were making remarks to me about us being 'an item,' and I said, 'What in the hell are you talking about?' I was married."

"And I was *happily* married!" Gloria adds.

"It must be you're so dykey looking," Stephanie says, and everyone laughs. Kass has short white blond hair and in the right clothes could pass for a society matron, and the round face and big smile of Gloria Eby, who also works for the postal service, portrays a gentle mother of two.

"When my husband died," Gloria says, "everyone was patting me on the back saying how brave I was. I wasn't brave, I had her." They moved in together when their four children were teenagers. "The children didn't mesh, and we disagreed on discipline," Gloria says. "She thinks I'm too easy, and she's a screamer."

"My kids are real active," Kass says. "They fall out of trees."

"Mine sit and read books. It got to the point where we weren't speaking and I said, 'Kass, we have to separate. If we don't, we're not even going to be friends.' "

Gloria began looking at houses, and Kass thought she was choosing her children over her. "Oh, I hated her. That was a real hard time for us. Besides separating, there was no one to talk to about it. We had no network, no friends." They knew only one lesbian and had not talked openly about their relationship to parents, co-workers, or their children. For the last three years the women have lived two miles apart. Gloria feels that when her children are out of college, then they will live together again.

"After the October March in Washington," Kass says, "I went off the deep end. I told three women in the post office right on Monday when I walked in. 'What did ya do this weekend?' 'I went to Washington.' 'Oh, to see the museums?' 'No, to march.' " The announcement didn't even cause a ripple.

Fifteen Pleiades marched as a group under their own banner, which as one woman pointed out "did not say Frederick, Maryland." Stephanie had hoped to be on TV, but when a camerawoman approached them, Gloria refused, out of deference to two women in education who were concerned about being identified.

Ann Murray, a tall, lean handsome woman of forty-two from Harpers Ferry, says, "That's one thing I did before the march. I called my family and said, 'Hey, I'm going to march.' " Her family has known her life-style for seven years.

Gloria called her son and said, " 'Listen, I'm going out of town this weekend. I'm going to Washington.' He said, 'What for?' 'I'm going to march,' and he said, 'Please, Mom, don't get arrested.' " He's twenty-three. "It's so much nicer now that both the kids know—we can joke about it. And my mother knows."

Sue, an attractive black-haired woman with a trim, athletic body, rents this house with Stephanie. Her voice is very soft. "I had real mixed feelings about marching. I didn't feel strongly enough about it to want to go. Later I regretted it." Her voice drops to a whisper. "I remember the next morning being so disappointed I hadn't gone and I wanted to do something. So I drove to Pennsylvania and came out to my folks." There is a hush, as though goose bumps run down every women's arms.

"It was very difficult. They used words like 'We're concerned about you, but we still love you.' " She pauses, clearing the lump from her throat. "That was my little march. I couldn't go back and redo the march that I had missed, so I did that."

"Marching gave me the feeling of not being hated," Stasia Ruskie, the youngest of the group, says. "I had never done anything like this, and to go down there and see all these other people who love you for who you are, what you are. And all these people lining the march route and giving the I-love-you symbol [in sign language]. Everywhere in the world we're hated and despised, and to have so many people accept us and affirm us. . . ." As a technician working in AIDS research, she had heard a lot of denigrating remarks about gays. After the march she came out to her co-workers.

The group recalls various instances of walking down the street with a woman and having young men yell, "Les-be friends!" or "Dykes!"

Wanda, a retired professional woman who has come still attired in her church clothes—stockings, heels, skirt, and jacket—points out that any group that is different is harassed. Gloria remarks that she hears the term *queer* ten times a day at work, but "I'm not sure they know what the word *lesbian* means." Another adds, "Women's sexuality is so devalued that two women together are not really having quote/unquote 'real sex' anyway."

A couple of the women note that lesbians have suffered a lot of trauma at the hands of men, but they don't know if it is more than straight women have. Another woman named Sue, the partner of Meg, who is a counselor for mentally ill adults, says "We're willing to talk about it more."

They laugh over the fact that at work it is the straight women who gripe about men—"after all, they have to live with them, we don't."

Wanda remarks that she was the only gay one in her family of seven girls and one boy. "I think you're born gay. I was dating a fellow and he said, 'Hey, you're gay.' We were in a canoe on the river when he told me. I almost fell out." Meg dated a boy in high school who later turned out to be gay.

Gloria tells of a friend whose three sisters are gay. "They have such a wonderful Christmas—all women." Of the fourteen women present, one has a bisexual sister, one a gay sister.

When Carol Bird, a petite and endearing twenty-six-year-old, told her father, he threatened her by saying, " 'Well, your grandparents will have to know this.' Like I would say, 'Oh, I was only joking. No, I'm not gay.' " Four years later she discovered that he had never told her grandparents or her brothers. "No one knew. So I had to do it all over again."

Another woman says, "I told my mother, but she won't tell my father. She won't tell anyone else. We don't talk about it."

Some of the women agree that they would not tell their fathers, but Lori, a tall dark-eyed cartographer, made sure to tell both parents "so they won't be all alone in this."

Lori found support from Parents-FLAG when she lived in Washington. "Everybody told their stories, and I went through a box of tissues. It's wonderful to have the support of older heterosexual people. They had a hot line for parents who had just found out their children were gay and were going through the 'where did I go wrong?' phase. It made it a lot easier for us in the area to come out to parents because we knew there was someplace we could refer them to. We had pamphlets, everything. We could say, 'I'm gay. Here, read this,' and run."

The women discuss the media: "I think it's nice to see gay relationships on TV. They are beginning to touch upon them. They've made some movies that are not just seen in small theaters that show foreign films. I like to see that. I think it's showing a level of acceptance. On the other hand, I don't like the way the media treat women in general."

Personal Best, Lianna, Desert Hearts, particularly the latter, rate high among the women. Stasia says, "It was nice to go and see *Desert Hearts*. I didn't like *Personal Best*—where they always go back to a guy. Well, that's not the way it is. It's nice to see a movie with women who live happily ever after. Why do heterosexuals watch love movies? It makes them feel good. Gives them hope."

"It would be nice to see that we are allowed to have the same damn feelings," another adds.

The women haven't found a reflection of their feelings in books either. Wanda says, "The problem is accessibility. I don't feel like driving to Baltimore or Washington to go to the bookstores."

"About the only mainstream books are Rita Mae's [Brown] and Lisa Alther's."

"I find that the fifties' butch/dyke stereotypes remain in books. It's not like the way it really is now when you can be yourself."

"The straight world doesn't want to hear that. The publishers have to cater to the general public. They don't want to hear we're ordinary people."

A woman who is taking graduate courses in human development said that one of her texts was apologetic that they could not talk about lesbians because the studies had all been done on male homosexuals. "There was one small paragraph on lesbians and two pages on gayness."

"Everything that Gloria and I found in the library," Kass says, "pertained to gay men's relationships. There was nothing for us."

There is no lesbian bar or bookstore in the area, and the women have talked about finding some sort of facility of their own. Bobbie, a forty-six-year-old manager of an aerial-photography business in West Virginia, believes that a restaurant or a bookstore would be preferable to a bar. She talks about her own alcoholism. "I think when you are outside of a relationship, you tend to go to the bars because there are no other places to go. For me it was a crutch, a release. All my inhibitions disappeared when I had a drink—usually with a bunch of women in a gay men's bar. They were heavy drinkers—I believe like attracts like—then we took our drinking problems right along to the private parties." Bobbie has been sober now for five years.

Gloria says, "We know some young friends who are into softball, and that's the thing to do after the game—go out drinking. Heavy drinking. Baseball was the excuse—who cared about the game?"

One woman sums up the discussion by saying, "It's socially acceptable to drink whether you're gay or straight. It would be real hard to do a study to find out specifically about the lesbian community."

Pleiades' meetings seldom involve even wine or beer. "I think it has a lot to do with our attitudes about ourselves," Stephanie says. "Because we feel good about ourselves, we don't have to hide behind alcohol."

"In this group," Bobbie says, "people won't let you get down. They care."

Some of the women have been involved in personally distressing situations because of federal government policies or legal conflicts. Bobbie was almost discharged from the Navy through guilt by association. "They do an incredible head trip on you. They go through your personal belongings in front of everyone. You just get so angry, you blurt things out. The woman who was representing me was a lesbian who was hiding, so she was no help at all." Wanda, who was in the air force for nine years, advises, "You just have to keep your mouth shut. Deny everything."

A young woman tells of a friend who went through a very painful security job clearance check by the FBI. After receiving a tip that she was a lesbian, agents went to all her former employees asking if she had ever attempted to fondle them.

Meg was named in a court case as being involved with a woman who was filing for divorce and trying to keep custody of her two children. The connection was made by the woman's husband, who found a portion of a letter written to Meg in a trash barrel outside his mother-in-law's house, where his wife was staying. Meg had no right to claim her privacy was invaded, whereas the husband was merely "reprimanded for trespassing." Meg was subpoenaed.

Urged by friends, she went to a lawyer, who advised her, "I'm not a criminal attorney." She replied, "I'm not a criminal." "You are," he said. "Under the sodomy laws of Maryland, you are." A month earlier the Supreme Court had upheld Georgia's sodomy law. Fortunately the hearing was held in front of a woman, who thought the whole issue was irrelevant to the case.

"It is the only experience I've had of being discriminated against or hated as a lesbian," Meg says. "But I got a real good look at the system, and it has made me more cautious. In some ways, however, I'm less cautious because I don't apologize for who I am. I'm surrounded, for the most part, by both gay and straight women who accept me. I had a straight attorney who was sensitive to what was going on, to what I was feeling. When it was over, he said, 'Now you can go back to living your life the way you have a right to.' Knowing that he is in Frederick has made my relocating here much easier. I think a large portion of Frederick is ready to accept the fact that they have a gay and lesbian community."

"I see Frederick changing," says Lynn, who has lived here nineteen years. "A lot of the people are moving here from the cities. Certainly a very large gay male community. Politics are changing. Gradually we're getting more liberal people in offices that used to be filled basically by retired county farmers. I see change, but it's not going to be overnight. I've finally decided to speak up about the gay jokes. If it weren't for my children—they don't know—I don't think I'd have any problem being out in the community.

"I came out all over town to ministers when I was looking for a place for us to have meetings. People who had known me when I was married. They just didn't seem to have any problem with it."

The women agree that sometimes lesbians spend a lot of time and energy hiding when everyone knows anyway. Wanda says, "You can have your private life. Some people may suspect, but they are perfectly happy unless they are told. Then they have to deal with it."

Other women speak up against protecting the straight world, and Kass adds, "There are an awfully lot of nice people out there who are gay, and how are the young people going to have role models unless they come out?"

Bobbie admits that while she was drinking, she believed the stereotype of the sadness, the loneliness, the bars. "Up until I got sober, I wouldn't wish this life on anyone. Now I'm having second thoughts, because it is a good life. I look at the heterosexual side, and it's no better. I can see that now."

"When I was married," Kass says, "my mother used to say to me at least a hundred times, 'Why are you so sad all the time?' And I didn't know why. I was miserable. When this thing clicked between Gloria and me, I knew why. I've never been happier. I think it's important that men know that there is nothing they can do sexually to make us change our minds." The group loudly agrees with her, Stephanie echoing, "Nothing!"

"I'd hate to have to interact with a man all the time," Lynn, who was married for nineteen years, says. "It's so frustrating. They don't want to communicate. They want to be powerful, they want to dominate. With women you can negotiate, you can communicate. I think it's a much better life."

Ann leans forward from where she sits in front of the couch, her short salt-and-pepper hair in striking contrast to the blonds and browns around her; her voice is deep and strong. "My socialization is strictly with my friends. I don't socialize with people at work." She works as a rehabilitation therapist at a VA hospital. "I don't socialize with people in my neighborhood. These folks are my family."

Ann has lived for twenty years in West Virginia; she never wanted to marry, have children. "When we played house, I was the daddy." She and a former partner belonged to a straight social group, but they never let them know they were gay. The two of them were alone in that knowledge. "For how long?" Stasia asks. "Twelve years," Ann replies. A murmur of sympathy and anger rises from the younger women.

Meg's partner, Sue, who is sitting on the couch with her, says, "I joined Pleiades because I realized, finally, that there is no one I could go to or call up to talk with about my particular problems. There are some gay people at the college, but it is a very conservative campus. I think because we are dealing with a women's community, there are a lot of parents who don't want to know that there are lesbians influencing their children at a very malleable age. Parents don't want their daughters having close contact with 'queers.' So I feel I have to be very quiet. I'm not sure what our college president would do if I went out marching in Frederick carrying a banner.

"The administration is paranoid about the fact that we are a women's college. They don't want a lot of those girls coming out as lesbians and having the parents criticize the college as an organization. Because they would."

She believes that there are a lot of lesbian students on campus;

they are just not politically active anymore. "Today they are almost more afraid to come out."

The women explain that Pleiades is not an organization for out-of-town students, or those going through confusions about sexual preference, or those excessively concerned about confidentiality.

But heterosexism does impose restrictions on them. At work on Monday Pleiades must, for all of its members, become an unnamed, unfocused "bunch of women."

"It bothers me," Stephanie says, "to not be able to say I was with a group of lesbian women. It just bothers the hell out of me, it really does. Because I think everyone here is so neat and I just can't say anything." Others nod in agreement. Stephanie doesn't know what would happen if the people at school knew, "And I'm almost to the point where I don't care. The march touched me so deeply. Really touched my soul and told me that I'm okay. I'm tired of hiding, I'm tired of lying. By keeping the old attitudes, I'm actually telling myself I'm not okay."

"I'm like Steph," Lynn says. "I just want to scream at work sometimes."

Gloria says that after the march she and Kass decided that if anyone asks, they are going to lay it on the line by saying, "Yes, we are." Kass adds, "And damn proud. I've never been ashamed of loving Gloria."

"I can understand that," Gloria interjects.

"Sometimes I get real ashamed of all the hell I put my husband through for twenty years. I didn't marry him to hide or anything, but it was a horrible marriage. I can remember thinking, 'God, maybe I'm a lesbian.' "

Gloria describes her marriage as good, "But sexually I wasn't real happy. After the wedding night I wondered, 'Is that all there is? Maybe there's something sexually wrong with me.' But I did love the fella. More like a brother/sister relationship as far as I was concerned."

Kass's face is bright with anger when she says, "One morning a visiting minister burst forth in the middle of his sermon with 'thieves, murderers, and homosexuals.' Well, I was so full of rage I could have gotten up and said, 'How dare you!' That's what you feel like doing. You're just full of rage."

The women sit silent, staring and nodding at their own memories. Lori says softly, "When I told my mother, the first thing she said was, 'Promise me you'll never molest a child.' "

Gloria summed up. "Somebody's lying. There are so many nice women here."

A lot of nice women everywhere. Invisible women who happen to love women.

EPILOGUE

"The worst sin towards our fellow creatures is not to hate them, but to be indifferent to them: that's the essence of inhumanity."

—George Bernard Shaw

INDIFFERENCE has been the least understood and perhaps most devastating factor with which lesbians have had to contend. Indifference is unawareness, ignorance, an apathy that reduces women-loving women to insignificance. It is the plastic wall that shields the majority from being disturbed. It creates an "us," toward whom we express kindness and caring, and a "them," whom we choose not to fully see or hear.

The existence of this wall, even if not openly named, is embedded in every woman's story told here. Tolerance and silence and nothing more. Who dances for the lesbian? You might as well be dead. Parents may murmur, "You are our daughter. We'll always love you," even as they withdraw into denial or self-pity or incomprehension. Friends may say, "Hey, that's fine with me," then proceed to discuss men and love as though the lesbian had no comparable experience. Acquaintances drift away.

The pain is akin to a young girl handing her father a poem she wrote that expresses her deepest feelings and having him turn on the television before he sits down to read it. Or playing for a friend a cherished piece of music and having them talk over and through it. However subtle or blatant, indifference is a denial of worth.

The absence of empathy, the unwillingness or inability or lack of opportunity of the majority to stand in the lesbian's shoes, has deprived the women-loving woman of intimacy outside her circle of lesbian friends. Her own invisibility has abetted this condition, but how much hurt can she risk? Pretending, playing out a part on the other side of the wall, refraining from beating against it, is the choice of many. This, however, creates a shadow of sadness—not because she is unhappy loving women but because she is shut off from the richness of a fully integrated life.

As "one of them" on the other side of the wall of indifference, she is also vulnerable to prejudice. Unlike the helplessness she feels at averted eyes and changed subjects of conversation, the sharp clarity of hatred arouses in her either fear or a combative spirit. She may, like Cyrano de Bergerac, brandish her sword and cry, "Here comes, thank God, another enemy!" and allies from the majority may rush to stand with her.

But the wounds of rape by men, or personal debasement by those in authority, or abandonment by parents, are deep and lasting. The scars remain invalidated, certainly unhonored, because the perpetrators of these cruel and brutal acts are not viewed, not named, as dangerous and inhumane people.

Of what are the women in this book guilty? Who have they harmed? What is their crime? Ten million, more or less, is an enormous number of people to place behind a wall of indifference where bigots of every stripe are free to roam and rant.

To acknowledge that this inhumanity exists within families, within businesses, between loved ones, and with the encouragement of some churches and a government pledged to protect the rights of all its citizens is to acknowledge an enormous failure in our culture.

An admission of the failure can be, however, the first step toward redemptive change.

SOURCES

Topics and ideas mentioned in *Invisible Lives* are treated in more detail in other works. Most of the titles listed below were suggested by the women who were interviewed. They are books that helped them or their parents and friends understand specific areas, or books that simply added richness to their lives as women-loving women.

Lesbian Voices

Valentine Ackland. *For Sylvia.* New York: W. W. Norton, 1986.

Marcy Adelman, editor. *Long Time Passing: Lives of Older Lesbians.* Boston: Alyson Publications, 1986.

Ruth Baetz. *Lesbian Crossroads: Personal Stories.* (William Morrow, 1980) Tallahassee, FL: Naiad, 1988.

Jeanne Jullion. *Long Way Home: The Odyssey of a Lesbian Mother and Her Children.* San Francisco: Cleis Press, 1985.

Audre Lorde. *Zami: A New Spelling of My Name.* Trumansburg, N.Y.: Crossing Press, 1984.

Moraga, Gomez and Romo-Carmona, editors. *Cuentos: Stories by Latinas.* New York: Kitchen Table Press. 1983.

Joan Nestle. *A Restricted Country.* Ithaca, NY: Firebrand Books, 1987.

Adrienne Rich. *Dream of a Common Language*. New York: W. W. Norton, 1978.

May Sarton. *Recovering: A Journal*. New York: W. W. Norton, 1980.

Barbara Zanotti, editor. *A Faith of One's Own: Explorations by Catholic Lesbians*. Trumansburg, NY: Crossing Press, 1986.

Rosemary Curb and Nancy Manahan, editors. *Lesbian Nuns: Breaking Silence*. (Naiad, 1985) New York: Warner, 1986.

Youth and Parents

Harriet Alpert, editor. *We Are Everywhere: Writings by and About Lesbian Parents*. Trumansburg, NY: Crossing Press, 1988.

Sasha Alyson, editor. *Young, Gay and Proud*. Boston: Alyson, 1985.

Don Clark. *Loving Someone Gay, Revised Edition*. Berkeley, CA: Celestial Arts, 1988.

Betty Fairchild and Nancy Hayward. *Now That You Know: What Every Parent Should Know About Homosexuality*. New York: Harcourt Brace Jovanovitch, 1981.

Ann Heron, editor. *One Teenager in Ten: Writings by Gay and Lesbian Youth*. New York: Warner, 1983.

Nancy Garden. *Annie on My Mind*. New York: Farrar, Straus & Giroux, 1982.

Brian McNaught. *On Being Gay*. New York: St. Martin's Press, 1988.

Isabel Miller. *Patience and Sarah*. New York: Fawcett.

Ann Muller. *Parents Matter*. Tallahassee, FL: Naiad Press, 1987.

About Lesbians

Sidney Abbott and Barbara Love. *Sappho Was a Right-on Woman*. New York: Stein and Day, 1972.

Carol Becker. *Unbroken Ties: Lesbian Ex-Lovers*. Boston: Alyson Publications, 1988.

Alan Bell and Martin Winberg (Kinsey Institute). *Homosexualities: A Study of Diversities Among Men and Women*. New York: Simon & Schuster, 1978.

Boston Lesbian Psychological Collective. *Lesbian Psychologies.* Urbana, IL: University of Illinois Press, 1987.

Boston Women's Health Book Collective. *The New Our Bodies Ourselves.* (Resources Listed) New York: Touchstone/Simon & Schuster, 1984.

Merilee Clunis and Dorsey Green. *Lesbian Couples.* Seattle: Seal Press, 1988.

Judy Grahm. *Another Mother Tongue: Gay Words, Gay Worlds.* Boston: Beacon Press, 1984.

Lillian Faderman. *Surpassing the Love of Men: Romantic Friendship and Love Between Woman from the Renaissance to the Present.* New York: William Morrow/Quill, 1981.

Nym Hughes, Yvonne Johnson and Yvette Perreault. *Stepping Out of Line: A Workbook on Lesbianism and Feminism.* Vancouver: Press Gang Publishers, 1984.

Jonathan Ned Katz. *Gay/Lesbian Almanac.* (A documentary history) New York: Harper & Row, 1983.

Barbara MacDonald with Cynthia Rich. *Look Me in the Eye: Old Women, Aging and Ageism.* San Francisco: Spinsters/Aunt Lute, 1983. $6.50.

Del Martin and Phyllis Lyon. *Lesbian/Woman.* (Volcano, 1972) New York: Bantam, 1977.

Karen Thompson and Julie Andrzejewski. *Why Can't Sharon Kowalski Come Home?* Spinsters/Aunt Lute, 1988.

George Weinberg. *Society and the Healthy Homosexual.* New York: St. Martin's Press. 1972.

Fiction

Lisa Alther. *Other Women.* New York: Knopf, 1984. (Includes all the entanglements of life as a lesbian)

Madelyn Arnold. *Bird-Eyes.* Seattle: Seal Press, 1988. (Young girl committed to mental institution for loving a woman)

Becky Birtha. *Lovers Choice.* Seattle: Seal Press, 1987. (Short stories by black author).

Rita Mae Brown. *Rubyfruit Jungle.* (Daughters, 1973) New York: Bantam, 1977. (Witty and Southern)

Margaret Erhart. *Unusual Company.* New York: E. P. Dutton, 1987. (Love story)

Doris Grumbach. *The Ladies*. New York: Fawcett Crest, 1984. (Fictional/historical account of two Irish women of the eighteenth century who eloped as a married couple)

Gail Pass. *Zoe's Book*. (Houghton Mifflin, 1976) Tallahassee, FL: Naiad, 1987. (Literary look into the English Bloomsbury group)

Elizabeth Jolley. *Palomino*. New York: Persea Books, 1980. (Older woman's love story)

Jane Rule. *Desert of the Heart*. Tallahassee, FL: Naiad Press, 1964. (1987 movie *Desert Hearts*.)

May Sarton. *Mrs. Stevens Hears the Mermaids Singing*. New York: W. W. Norton, 1965. (Of love and poetry)

Sarah Schulman. *After Delores*. New York: E. P. Dutton, 1988. (Witty and contemporary)

Jeanette Winterson. *Oranges Aren't the Only Fruit*. New York: Atlantic Monthly Press, 1987. (Fundamentalists and an English lesbian)

Meg Wolitzer. *Hidden Pictures*. Boston: Houghton Mifflin, 1986. (Married woman falls in love with a lesbian)

Small Press Addresses

Alyson Publications, 40 Plympton Street, Boston, MA 02118

Celestial Arts, P.O. Box 7327, Berkeley, CA 94707.

Cleis Press, P.O. Box 14684, San Francisco, CA 94114.

Crossing Press, Trumansburg, NY 14886.

Firebrand Books, 141 The Commons, Ithaca, NY 14850.

Kitchen Table Press, P.O. Box 2753, New York, NY 10185.

Naiad Press, P.O. Box 10543, Tallahassee, FL 32302.

Press Gang Publishers, 603 Powell Street, Vancouver, British Columbia, Canada.

Seal Press, 3131 Western Avenue, Seattle, WA 98121.

INDEX

Southern Baptist church, 158
Spinsters. *See* Solitary women
Spokane, Washington, 25–31, 82
Springfield, Massachusetts, 36
Stein, Gertrude, 90, 182
Steinem, Gloria, 83
Stereotypes of lesbians, 15–16,
116–117, 125, 127–134, 192,
250, 272
Straight, use of term, 19
Stricker, Jackie, 83
Subculture, lesbian, 190–193
Suicide, 117–118, 137, 142, 272
Sununu, John, 114
Support groups, 241–242
Supreme Court, and sodomy
laws, 328
Sweet Honey in the Rock, 186
"Sweet Woman" (song), 183, 184,
186

T

Teachers, gay and lesbian, 106,
114, 214, 302
Teenage gays and lesbians. *See*
Gay and lesbian youth
Therapy, 138, 139, 164
Third Sex, The, 189
Toklas, Alice B., 90
Toronto, 51, 52, 83
Treadway, Leo, 113, 115–118
Tuscaloosa, Alabama, 158–159

U

Unitarian Universalist Church,
94, 303–305
United Methodist Church, ban on
homosexual ministers, 93–96
United Parcel Service, witch hunt
at, 163
University of New Hampshire,
120–126

Unusual Company (Erhart), 188
USA Today, 85

V

Vacations, 26, 83, 185
Village Voice, The, 164
Violence, against homosexuals, 90

W

WAF, 244–245
Waiting for the Moon (film), 90,
189
Wedell, Tom, 76
Well of Loneliness, The (Hall), 33,
113, 182, 243
Wicca, 151–152
Widows, 323–324
Williamson, Cris, 182, 183, 184,
186
Wisconsin, gay rights legislation
in, 88–89
Wishing Well, 234–236
Witchcraft, 151–153
Women's bookstores, 76, 138,
150, 161, 174, 187–188
Women's clubs, 16
Women's Coffee House (New
York), 175, 267
Women's music festival: Boston,
1987, 186
Women's sports, changes in, 131–
132. *See also* Athletes, female
Women's studies classes, 124–
126, 190. *See also* Education
Womyn Braille Press, 295
Woolf, Virginia, 188
Worcester, Massachusetts, 304

Y

Youth. *See* Gay and lesbian youth